STOLEN LIVES

STOLEN LIVES

Twenty Years in a Desert Jail

MALIKA OUFKIR and MICHÈLE FITOUSSI

Translated by Ros Schwartz

talk miramax books

HYPERION

NEW YORK

Originally published in French as *La Prisonnière*

Printed in the United States of America. For information address: Hyperion, 77 W. 66th Street, New York, New York 10023-6298.

Map by Neil Gower. Unless otherwise credited all photos are

Library of Congress Cataloging-in-Publication Data

Oufkir, Malika, 1953–
[Prisonnière. English]
Stolen lives : twenty years in a desert jail / Malika Oufkir and Michèle Fitoussi ; translated by Ros Schwartz.
p. cm.
ISBN 0-7868-6732-9
1. Oufkir, Malika, 1953– 2. Women political prisoners—Morocco—Biography. I. Fitoussi, Michèle. II. Title.

HV9841.O8413 2001
365'.45'092—dc21
[B] 00-053220

FIRST EDITION

10 9 8 7 6 5 4 3 2 1

I dedicate this book to the Beavers.

To 'Scrooge', my beloved Mother, the most wonderful woman. I owe my survival to her.

To 'Petit Pôle', Myriam, my adored sister, whose courage I salute.

To 'Mounch', Raouf, my brother and my friend, my support, my example of dignity.

To 'the Negus', my sister Maria, who gave me the opportunity to begin my life over again in the country of democracy. Thank you.

To 'Charlie', my very talented sister Soukaina, in whom I have faith.

To 'Géo Trouvetout', Abdellatif, my young brother, who inspired me with the strength to fight and hope.

To 'Barnaby', Achoura, and 'Dingo', Halima, for their loyalty through every ordeal.

To 'Big, Bad Wolf', my beloved father, who I hope is proud of us.

To Azzedine, my uncle, and Hamza, my cousin, who died too young.

To the children of the Beavers, Michaël, Tania and Nawel, my nephew and nieces. May this account not prevent them from loving their country, Morocco.

M.O.

To my daughter Léa, who was constantly in my thoughts as I listened to this story.

M.F.

CONTENTS

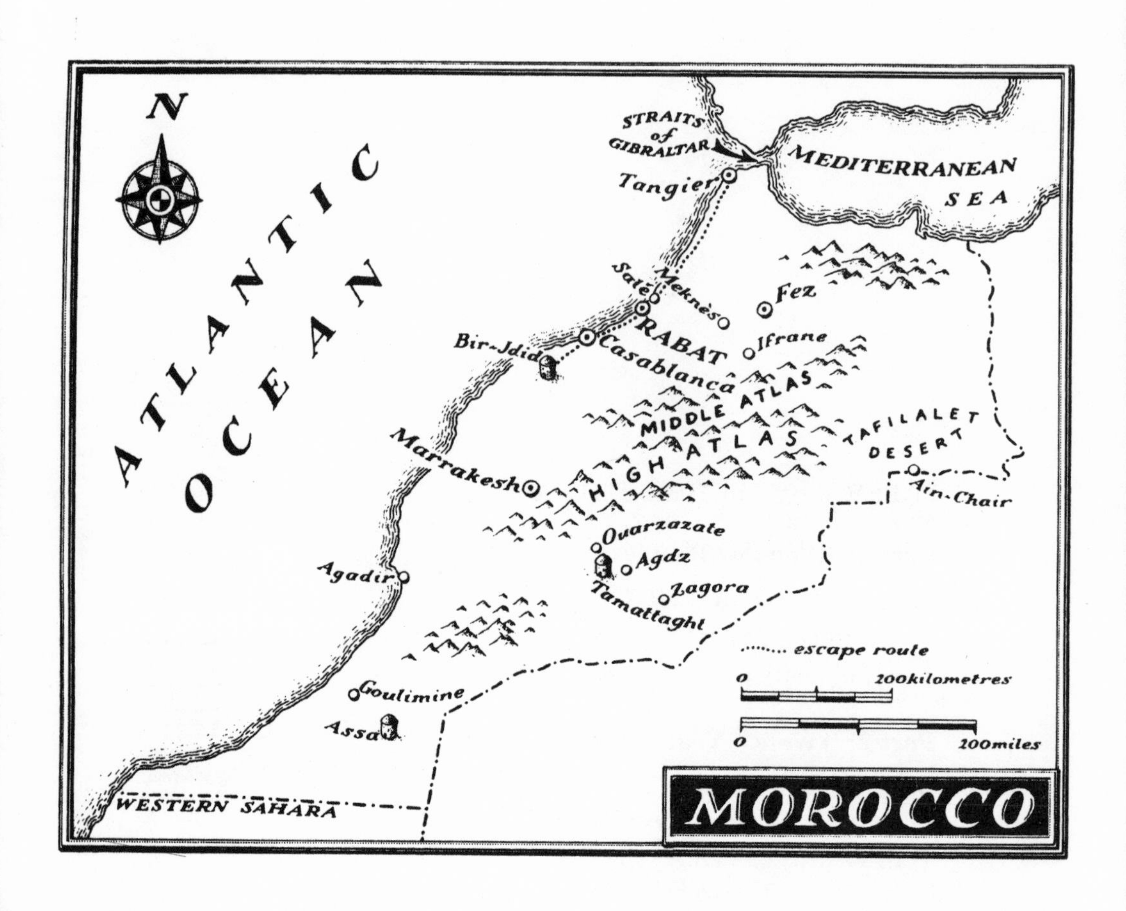
N
ATLANTIC
OCEAN
STRAITS of GIBRALTAR
MEDITERRANEAN
SEA
Tangier
Meknès
Salé
RABAT
Fez
Bir-Jdid
Casablanca
Ifrane
MIDDLE ATLAS
HIGH ATLAS
TAFILALET
DESERT
Marrakesh
Ain-Chair
Ouarzazate
Agdz
Zagora
Tamattaght
Agadir
Goulimine
Assa
escape route
0
200kilometres
0
200miles
WESTERN SAHARA
MOROCCO

PREFACE

Why this book? It is clear that even if we hadn't met by chance, Malika Oufkir would have written this account one day. Since her escape from prison, she has always wanted to tell her story and exorcize the painful past that continues to torment her. The idea was slowly forming in her mind, but there was no hurry. She wasn't ready yet.

Why write it together? That is also clear—we had a helping hand from fate. We met by chance and immediately became friends, which gave her the courage finally to unburden herself, and prompted me to shelve all my other plans to listen to her and transcribe her account.

We met for the first time in March 1997, at a party to celebrate the Iranian new year. A mutual friend pointed out a slim, pretty young woman lost in the crowd of guests.

'That's Malika, General Oufkir's eldest daughter.'

The name gave me a start. It evoked injustice, horror, the unutterable.

The Oufkir children. Six youngsters and their mother, incarcerated for twenty years in appalling Moroccan gaols. I recalled snatches of newspaper stories. I was overwhelmed.

How can anyone appear normal after such suffering? How can they live, laugh or love, how can they go on when they have lost the best years of their life as a result of injustice?

I watched her. She hadn't seen me yet. Her behaviour was that of someone used to socializing, but her eyes revealed a barely disguised grief. She was in the room with us, yet strangely elsewhere.

I carried on staring at her with an intensity that would have seemed rude, had she only noticed me. But she had eyes only for her companion, clinging to him as if her life depended on it. At last we were introduced. We exchanged a few cautious platitudes about our respective countries, she being from Morocco and I from Tunisia. We were both trying to size each other up.

I observed her covertly all evening. I watched her dance, noticing the grace of her movements, the way she held herself erect, her solitude in the midst of all those people having fun, or pretending to. From time to time our eyes met and we smiled at each other. I was perturbed by this woman. At the same time, she intimidated me. I didn't know what to say to her. Everything sounded trite, pathetic. Questioning her would be intrusive. And yet I was already burning to know.

At the end of the party, we exchanged telephone numbers. At that time I was finishing off a collection of short stories due to be published the following May. I still had a few weeks' work ahead of me. I suggested meeting as soon as I had finished. Malika agreed, without abandoning her reserve.

Over the next few days I thought about her continuously. I kept seeing her beautiful, sad face. I tried to picture myself in her situation. Or at least to imagine the unimaginable. I was besieged with questions. What had she been through? What did she feel now? How do you return from the grave?

I was deeply moved by her extraordinary destiny, the suffering she had endured, and by her miraculous survival. There is only a year's difference in our ages. She was imprisoned in December 1972, at the age of nineteen and a half, the year when I, with my baccalaureate under my belt, was starting my preparatory year at the Ecole des Sciences Politiques. I obtained my diploma and have since fulfilled my childhood dream of becoming a journalist, and then a writer. I have worked, travelled, loved and suffered, like everyone else. I have two wonderful children. I've lived a full, rich life and had my share of experiences, sorrows and joys.

Throughout that entire time, she had been incarcerated with her family, away from the world, in horrendous conditions, her horizons limited to the four walls of her cell.

The more I thought about her, the more driven I was by a single desire, a mixture of journalistic curiosity, the excitement of the writer and pure human interest in this woman's extraordinary destiny. I wanted Malika to tell me her story, and I wanted to write it with her. I was gripped by this idea. To be honest, I was obsessed.

That week, I sent her my books as a friendly gesture, in the hope that they would convey my ardent wish. After I had finally delivered the manuscript of my short stories, I called to invite her to lunch.

On the phone, her voice was faint. She was finding it hard to settle in Paris. She had been living with Eric, her companion, for barely eight months. In 1996, nine years after her breakout from prison, the Oufkir family had finally been granted permission to leave Morocco, thanks to the escape of Maria, one of the younger daughters, who had sought political asylum in France.

The affair had made a big splash. Maria's strained little face had appeared on TV, and shortly afterwards, again on the small screen, the French public had witnessed the arrival of some of the family on French soil: Malika, her sister Soukaina and her brother Raouf. Myriam, their other sister, joined them shortly afterwards. Abdellatif, the youngest, and Fatima Oufkir, their mother, still lived in Morocco at that time, Malika told me over a lunch that went on long into the afternoon.

I listened to her, fascinated. Malika is a remarkable storyteller. A Scheherazade. She has a thoroughly oriental narrative style, speaking slowly in an even tone, building suspense, and gesticulating with her tapering hands for added effect. Her eyes are incredibly expressive; she swings from melancholy to laughter. At the same moment she is a child, a teenage girl and a mature woman. She is all ages rolled into one, but has not really lived through any of them.

I knew little about the history of Morocco, or the reasons for her imprisonment. I only knew that she was incarcerated with her five brothers and sisters and her mother for two decades, in retaliation for her father's attempted coup d'état. General Muhammad Oufkir, the second most important man in the kingdom, tried to assassinate King Hassan II on 16 August 1972. The plot failed and General Oufkir was executed; he died with five bullets in his body. The king sent the family to live in exile in the most frightful conditions, in a penal colony from which, generally, nobody ever returned. Abdellatif, the youngest, was only three.

But Malika's own childhood was even more unusual. She was adopted at the age of five by King Muhammad V, to be brought up with his daughter, little Princess Amina, who was the same age. On the death of the monarch, his son, Hassan II, personally took charge of the upbringing of the two little girls, as well as that of his own children. Malika spent eleven years living at the court, in the seclusion of the harem, virtually never leaving its confines. She was already a prisoner, inside the splendid palace. When she finally escaped, it was to enjoy a golden adolescence for two years while living with her parents.

After the coup d'état, the young girl lost both her beloved fathers. Malika Oufkir's tragedy is in this double bereavement that she has secretly borne for years. Whom do you love, whom do you hate, when your own father attempts to assassinate your adoptive father? And when the latter suddenly becomes your tormentor, and that of your family? It is agonizing, heartbreaking. The stuff of a novel.

Gradually, I began to realize that the same idea had occurred to both of us. Malika wanted to tell me the story she had not yet disclosed to anyone. At that Iranian party, we had instinctively been drawn to each other.

Even though there were so many differences between us, of background, social circles, education, children, profession, character and even religion—she's a Muslim and I'm a Jew—we belong to the same generation, we have a similar sensibility, the same love for our native Orient, the same sense of humour, the same way of seeing people. We already felt a sense of kinship, and our friendship continued to blossom, confirming our initial gut feeling.

We would write this book together. But it took a while for

Malika's wish to crystallize. We signed the contract with Grasset in May 1997, but it was not until January 1998, after numerous ups and downs, that we were at last able to start work, in the utmost secrecy. For Malika was afraid of being spied on and having her phone tapped. During the five years the Oufkir family had spent in Morocco, just after their release, they were daily victims of police harassment, and so were the few friends they saw regularly. Malika had retained the habit of never talking about important things over the telephone and of glancing over her shoulder when walking in the street. In Paris, she was still unable to shake off the terror that had haunted her for twenty-five years. She didn't want 'them' to find out that she was writing her story until the very last minute.

I also had to be discreet. Only a few of my close friends knew about our work. For the best part of a year, I led a double life. I didn't talk to anybody about Malika. And yet we worked together up to three times a week and we spoke on the phone every day.

The rest is the story of a friendship that developed and was consolidated day by day, as the book advanced. From January to June, we met either at my place or hers. We had our little rituals, the two tape recorders to ensure we had a copy of the tapes in case 'they' stole them, the tea, the little cakes, my children bursting in to chat, and Eric's phone calls full of tender concern. Then I began writing, and Malika revising, which wasn't always easy. Telling her story was already distressing enough. She had to start over again several times when talking to me about the painful episodes. Seeing her nightmare in print was often too much for her. I sometimes worried that she would give up, that her fears or her ghosts would get the better of her. But she went through with it to the end.

Gripping from start to finish, Malika's story was agonizing, shocking, horrifying. I trembled, shivered and empathized, experiencing hunger, cold and fear along with her. But we also had countless fits of giggles, for Malika is a wizard at the humour that enabled the Oufkir family to survive. She made fun of everything, and laughed at herself too. Through her words, I came to know her family, the brothers and sisters she had mothered, protected, brought up and guided all those bleak years, and her mother, Fatima, who is still a great beauty and could pass as her older sister. At first they were like characters in a novel for me, shaped by Malika, until I met them one after the other. She hadn't lied. They are all, without exception, dignified, funny, generous, moving and intense, as Malika is too.

Malika is a survivor. She has the survivor's toughness and strength. As a result of having come so close to death, she has a detachment from life that often amazes me. She has no notion of time or space; days, times and arrangements mean nothing to her. The missed appointments, her lateness, her total lack of a sense of direction, her fear of the Métro and crowds and her technophobia still surprise and amuse me.

Despite her modern airs and her mobile phone, which she is never without, she sometimes seems like a Martian lost on Planet Earth. She panics over nothing, doesn't know the codes and is often utterly at a loss. At other times she shows impressive judgement, intuition and an astonishing capacity for analysis. She is touching, fragile and often physically weak—illness, deprivation and isolation have left their mark on her, and yet she is so solid. If those twenty years of prison and suffering have, sadly, done irreparable damage, they have also forged a remarkable soul, an admirable character. I actually wonder which of the two of us has in fact lived the least.

For that whole year, I laughed and cried with her, I nannied her, advised her, tucked her up in bed, comforted her, listened to her, pitied her, bucked her up, pushed her too, sometimes to the point of exhaustion. But the relationship has never been one-way. What Malika has given me, and for always, is immeasurable. She is probably not even aware of it. She has taught me that courage, strength, determination and human dignity can survive even the most extreme and brutal conditions. She has taught me that hope and faith in life can move mountains (or dig tunnels with bare hands). She has often forced me to look deep inside myself, to question my ideas about life. She has even made me want to discover the Morocco that she describes with such warmth and passion, without rancour for its people, even though they deserted her. I'm sure I will go there with her . . . one day.

Writing this story was, of course, for me a means of speaking out against the arbitrary, the callous persecution of a mother and her six children. Words cannot describe the revulsion I feel for what this family has suffered, as I do for all violations of human rights on this earth. One result of turning a blind eye to the horrors of the world, because you can stand only so much, is that you end up forgetting that each individual who is subjected to heinous suffering is your fellow, your equal, and that you could have been in their shoes, and that he or she could one day have become your friend.

And yet this book is not an indictment. History will be the judge of the crimes, and that is not our intention. Nor is it an exposé. I have transcribed what I heard, over the days: Malika's raw testimony, with her hesitations, her uncertainties, things she drew a veil over, but also, most of the time, her relentless precision.

What I wanted to convey, what we convey together, with her words and mine, with her sentiments and our shared emotion, is above all the incredible journey of a woman of my generation, incarcerated from earliest childhood, first in a palace and then in prisons, and who is now trying to live her life. In going as far as I could with her, I hope, like all those who now love her and surround her, to have helped her rediscover her appetite for living.

January 1999 Michèle Fitoussi

PART ONE

ALLÉE DES PRINCESSES

1

MY BELOVED MOTHER

From the living room come the strains of mambo and cha-cha music, the percussion and guitars punctuated by the arrival of the guests. Laughter and conversation fill the rooms, wafting up to the bedroom where I am finding it hard to get to sleep.

Invisible in the doorway, my thumb jammed in my mouth, I stand gazing at the women in their evening dresses made by the great couturiers, vying with each other in beauty and elegance. I admire their lacquered chignons, sparkling jewels and sophisticated make-up. They look like the princesses from my favourite fairy stories that I so want to be like when I grow up. Which I am longing to do . . .

Suddenly she appears, the most beautiful of all in my eyes, wearing a white, low-cut dress that emphasizes the curve of her neck. My heart thumping, I watch her greeting the guests and smiling, kissing her friends, bowing her graceful neck before strangers in dinner jackets. Soon she will dance, sing, clap her hands and party till dawn, as she always does when my parents give a party at home.

She will forget me for a few hours, while I fight against sleep in my little bed, thinking constantly of her, the sheen of her skin, her soft hair where I love to bury my face, her perfume, her warmth. Mummy.

My beloved mother from whom, in my childhood paradise, I cannot imagine ever being separated.

There is a bond between my mother and me that comes from a shared destiny made up of abandonment and loneliness. Her own mother died in childbirth when she was barely four years old. I in turn was torn from her gentle embrace at the age of five to be adopted by King Muhammad V. Perhaps that closeness has been cemented by our both having been deprived of our mother's affection in childhood, our proximity in age—she was seventeen when I was born—our incredible physical resemblance and by our savagely destroyed chances of fulfilment as women. Like me, my mother has always had the grave look of those to whom fate has been cruel.

When her mother died, at the beginning of the Second World War, her father, Abdelkader Chenna, an officer in the French army, had just received orders to join his regiment in Syria. It was impossible for him to take his daughter and young son with him. He placed the two motherless children in a convent run by French nuns in Meknès, where he lived at the time, so that they would receive a good education. The little boy succumbed to diphtheria. My mother, who adored her brother, found it hard to get over this loss, which left her alone amid strangers. She was to have many other sorrows in her life.

The nuns set out to turn this pretty little Fatima sent to them by Heaven into a perfect Christian. She learned to make the sign of the cross and worship the Virgin Mary, Jesus and all the saints. Then my grandfather came to fetch her and take her home. A devout Muslim who had already made the pilgrimage to Mecca, he nearly swallowed his medals with rage.

It wasn't good for a career soldier to bring up such a young girl alone. His friends urged him to remarry. He chose a very young woman from high society, whom he married primarily for her talents as a cordon-bleu cook. Khadija's skill at making *pastilla*—my grandfather's favourite dish—was unrivalled. My mother couldn't bear sharing her beloved father with a stranger only a few years older than she was. The birth of a sister, Fawzia, then a brother, Azzedine, made her even more jealous.

Her ambition was to escape as quickly as possible from a home where she was unhappy and where her father kept her shut away, as was traditional for girls. But she had nowhere to go that could give her the warmth she lacked. Her mother's family, wealthy Berbers from the Middle Atlas region, were nearly all dead. My great-grandparents had produced four daughters whose beauty was legendary for miles around. Three had died in their teens. The fourth, my grandmother, Yamna, married her neighbour, the handsome Abdelkader Chenna, whose land bordered on her family's.

He had to kidnap her to wed her, in true fairy-tale tradition. All I know about her is that she was a competent woman, modern and resourceful, who liked clothes, travelling and driving. At fifteen she was already a mother. At eighteen she hosted a literary salon in Syria, where my grandfather had followed his regiment. At nineteen she was dead.

My mother and her young uncle, fruit of my great-grandfather's late marriage to a black slave, were soon the only survivors of the entire family. The corn-growing lands and gold amassed over the generations made her a rich heiress, although less wealthy than her uncle, who received the larger share of the fortune, in accordance with Moroccan custom. She owned apartment buildings, villas and an entire district of the old town of Salé, an ancient fortified corsair town near Rabat. My grandfather was appointed trustee until she came of age. Unfortunately, he mismanaged the money and frittered away bigger sums than he made. However, there was still a considerable fortune when my mother came into her inheritance.

By her early teens, my mother was already very beautiful. Her father's officer friends who came to the house were not indifferent to her huge black eyes, delicate face, olive complexion and prettily curvaceous little body. She was not averse to their attentions. She wanted to get married and have a family. A young officer back from Indochina with a chestful of medals became a regular visitor to the house. My grandfather, who knew him from before, had met him again at the mess. Charmed by the officer's intelligence and his reputation for bravery at the front, he befriended him and invited him home. Concealed behind a curtain, my mother watched him throughout the dinner. The officer was aware of her little game and their eyes met. He was struck by the intensity of her gaze. She admired him in his magnificent white uniform.

My grandfather tried to persuade his new friend not to return to Indochina. The young officer was moved by his arguments and doubtless also by his daughter's beauty. A few days later, my father (for it was he) came to ask for her hand in marriage. My grandfather was taken by surprise and, to be honest, his response bordered on irritation.

'Fatima is only a child,' he protested. 'Is it appropriate to think of marriage at fifteen?'

Abdelkader was still traumatized by the death of Yamna, his dearly beloved first wife, which he attributed to a series of early pregnancies in close succession. But in the end he gave in, especially as my mother had greeted her suitor's request with enthusiasm. She didn't know him, at least not yet, but she felt she had to leave home. He courted her assiduously.

She soon fell in love with him.

There was a sixteen-year age difference between my parents. Muhammad Oufkir, my father, was born on 29 September 1920, at Ain-Chair in the Tafilalet region, which is the stronghold of the Berbers of the Atlas mountains in Morocco. His name, Oufkir, means 'the impoverished'. In his family, there was always food and shelter for the beggar or the needy, who were plentiful in these rugged, wilderness areas. At the age of seven, he lost his father, Ahmed Oufkir, chief of his village and later appointed *pasha*—provincial governor—of Bou-Denib by Lyautey, then Resident General under the French protectorate.

He had a solitary, probably rather sad childhood. He studied at the Berber secondary school in Azrou, near Meknès. After that, the army became his family. At nineteen he entered the prestigious military academy of Dar-Beida, and at twenty-one he enlisted as reserve second lieutenant in the French army. He was wounded in Italy, convalesced in France and earned his captain's stripes in Indochina. When he met my mother, he was aide-de-camp to General Duval, commander of the French troops in Morocco. He was beginning to tire of garrison life. He, the career soldier who frequented brothels and gaming houses, was moved by the childlike innocence of his betrothed. He immediately showed himself to be gentle and considerate.

Muhammad Oufkir and Fatima Chenna were married on 29 June 1952. They moved into a very simple little house, in keeping with Captain Oufkir's modest pay. My father played Pygmalion to my mother: he taught her how to dress and how to behave at table and in society. With all the dignity of her sixteen years, she took her role as officer's wife very seriously. They were happy and madly in love. My mother, who dreamed of having eight children, immediately became pregnant.

I was born on 2 April 1953, in a maternity hospital run by nuns. My father was wild with joy. It didn't matter that I was a girl, I was the apple of his eye, his little queen (my name, Malika, is Arabic for 'queen'). Like my mother, he wanted above all else to have a family. They were not in complete agreement over the number of children to come. My father wanted to stop at three. Two years later, my sister Myriam was born, on 20 January 1955, and three years after her came my brother Raouf, on 30 January 1958. A memorable party was given to celebrate the birth of the first boy.

I have nothing but happy memories of my early years. My parents lavished love on me, and my home was peaceful. I saw little of my father. He came home late and was often away. His career was progressing rapidly. By 1955 he had risen to the rank of major in the French army, when he left to become King Muhammad V's chief aide-de-camp, after playing an instrumental role in bringing the King back from exile. By the time Muhammad V died in February 1961, he had become head of the police. But I was in no doubt as to the depth of his affection for me. When he was home, he showed how much he loved me. His absences didn't affect me.

The centre of my world was my mother. I loved her and I admired her. She was beautiful, refined, the model of femininity. Smelling her fragrance or stroking her skin was enough to make me happy. I followed her like a shadow. She loved the cinema and went nearly every day, sometimes to two or three showings. From the age of six months, I went with her in my carrycot. These trips to the cinema at such a young age probably explain my passion for the seventh art. She took me to her hairdresser and asked him to give me a perm. She wanted a little girl with ringlets, like Scarlett O'Hara. But, alas, with the first gust of wind, my pretty hairdo flopped.

I went with her to visit her friends, on shopping trips, horseriding and to the Turkish baths, where I suffered agonies when I had to get undressed in public. I watched her dress, do her hair and outline her eyes with kohl. I danced with her to the wild rock music of our shared idol, Elvis Presley. At those moments, we were practically the same age.

Life revolved around me. I was spoiled, dressed like a little princess at the most elegant boutiques: Le Bon Génie in Geneva and La Châtelaine in Paris. My mother was stylish and extravagant, unlike my father who was bored by material possessions. Money slipped through her fingers. She was capable of selling an apartment block to buy herself the entire collection of Dior or St Laurent, her favourite couturiers, and would spend twenty or thirty thousand francs at the slightest whim.

In 1957, we moved from the captain's little house to the aptly named Allée des Princesses—princesses' avenue—in Souissi, the residential district of Rabat. The villa opened onto a wild garden where there were orange, lemon and mandarin trees. I played with Leila, a slightly older cousin, whom my mother had adopted.

A few years later, when I no longer lived with my family, my father, who was now Minister of the Interior to King Hassan II, had another villa built, again in the Allée des Princesses. My parents now had two more children, Mouna-Inan, born on 17 February 1962, who changed her name to Maria in prison, and Soukaina, a year later, on 22 July 1963.

My family was very close to the royal family. My parents were the only outsiders allowed to enter the Palace and wander around freely. My father, chief of Muhammad V's aides-de-camp, had won the trust of the old king, and my mother had known the sovereign since childhood. Before her father's second marriage, she had lived in Meknès for a while, at the home of one of the King's sisters, and he had been a regular visitor. Muhammad V had noticed the beauty of the little girl, who was eight at the time. He had immediately developed a fondness for her that did not diminish over the years.

He saw her again in 1952, during his silver jubilee celebrations. His aides-de-camp and their wives were invited to attend the ceremony. After that, like my father, my mother had her own privileged access to the Palace. The King trusted her. He enjoyed her company, but this austere man was much too principled to allow himself the slightest ambiguity towards a married woman.

My mother became the friend of the King's two wives who demanded to see her daily. She became part of their cloistered world. The two queens were shut away in the harem. My mother bought them clothes and cosmetics, and told them everything that was going on outside, in the minutest detail. They were avid to hear all about her life, her children and her marriage.

Rivals for the King's affections, the two women were as different from each other as can be imagined. The first, Lalla Aabla, known as the Queen Mother, or Oum Sidi, mother of the master, was the mother of the crown prince, Moulay Hassan. The other, Lalla Bahia, who had a wild nature and was stunningly beautiful, was the mother of the King's favourite daughter, little Princess Amina, born in exile in Madagascar in 1954, to the surprise of the queen who had thought she was infertile.

Whereas Lalla Aabla, accustomed to the intrigues of the harem, was adept at the art of diplomacy, Lalla Bahia had little regard for the polite small talk and dissembling that were de rigueur at court. Caught between the two of them, my mother soon learned the art of compromise, for at the Palace neutrality was impossible. You had to choose your camp.

Moulay Hassan, also called Smiyet Sidi, 'the almost master', lived in a neighbouring house and often came to visit us, as did the princesses, his sisters, and his brother, Prince Moulay Abdallah. I was told to greet them with deference. One evening during Ramadan, after breaking the fast, my mother was lying down in her sitting room, surrounded by some of her friends. I was playing around in the house. As I crossed the corridor, I saw a strange man coming out of the kitchen. Overawed by his imposing presence, I froze in my tracks. He smiled at me and kissed me.

'Go and tell your mother I'm here.'

I ran to tell her. She immediately prostrated herself before this strange man.

It was King Muhammad V, who had dropped in to see her unannounced, as he was sometimes wont to do. He told her he had taken the liberty of entering the kitchen because he had smelled something burning. The cook had left the teapot on a burner and it was beginning to melt. His Majesty had saved us from a fire.

I was five when my mother took me to the Palace for the first time. The King's two wives and all his concubines insisted on meeting me. It was lunchtime when we walked into one of the King's dining rooms, which was full of women from the harem strolling around gracefully, trailing behind them the long glittering trains of their kaftans. The blaze of brilliant colours and the incessant chattering made me think of an aviary of exotic birds.

The room was enormous, with balconies along its entire length and mosaics decorating the walls. I'd never seen such a huge room. At one end, majestically standing on a dais, was the royal throne. To one side rose a mountain of gifts, still in their wrappings, that had been presented to the sovereign at receptions and ceremonies or during official visits. At the other end of the room, in an alcove, the King's table was set European style, with china plates, crystal glasses and silver cutlery. His concubines sat at his feet, on the brown-carpeted floor, around oblong tables for eight. Their crockery was of the plainest, and it was not unusual to see them serving the dishes cooked for them by their own slaves onto tin plates.

The Queen Mother presided over the table nearest that of the King, surrounded by the concubines of the moment, those called in Arabic *moulet naba*, 'those whose turn it is'. They were therefore more heavily made up and better dressed than the others, and exuded an air of superiority. As for those who had enjoyed royal favour the previous day, or the day before that, they affected a disdainful, self-satisfied look, and noisily chewed on gum arabic.

I clung to my mother's kaftan in awe, but I was dying to rush around. Suddenly the room filled with a joyous clamour. The women were greeting someone I wasn't able to see. Weaving in and out of their legs, I glimpsed a little girl in a white dress, with a huge bow at the back. I thought she was gorgeous with her black ringlets, milky complexion and tiny freckles sprinkled over her impish face. I found my olive skin and straight hair extremely ordinary in comparison.

I was relieved to see a child of my own age at last, but I was puzzled. Why was she entitled to so much attention? We were introduced to each other, and we kissed shyly. Then I discovered that this pretty little girl was Princess Amina, known as Lalla Mina, the cherished daughter of the King and Lalla Bahia.

Then there was a fresh commotion. King Muhammad V made his entrance from the left, in accordance with custom. When it was her turn to greet him, my mother kissed his hand and introduced me to him. He gave me a simple hug and said a few kind words. Then everyone flocked to the tables and the King sat down alone at his. The slaves served the meal and the most exquisite dishes filed past.

As soon as I'd gulped down a few mouthfuls, I slipped away to play with Lalla Mina. For a brief moment, we got along perfectly. But soon a shriek shattered the harmony. The Princess had savagely bitten my forearm. I ran back sobbing, trying to catch my mother's eye. Embarrassed, she discreetly signalled to me to be quiet. Indignant at this lack of sympathy, I then rushed at Lalla Mina and sank my teeth into her cheek.

Now it was the Princess's turn to howl so loudly that the entire court rose. I felt a menace hovering over me, as if the entire gathering was going to advance on me and attack me. The little girl sought her father's eyes, but in vain. So she rolled on the floor and screamed even louder. Ashamed, I took refuge in my mother's arms.

The King intervened at last. He picked me up and asked me to tell him what had happened.

'She insulted my father,' I sobbed, 'so I insulted her father and bit her cheek.'

The court was shocked at my words, but the King thought it was very funny. He made me repeat the sacrilegious insults several times. Then the Princess and I were split up, but we carried on darting each other defiant glances.

At the end of the meal, Muhammad V came over to my mother:

'Fatima, I'm going to ask you something that you can't refuse me,' he said. 'I can think of no-one better as a playmate, as a sister for Lalla Mina, than your daughter. I would like to adopt Malika. But I promise you that you will be able to come and see her whenever you wish.'

Adoption was common at the Palace. Childless concubines adopted orphans, impoverished little girls, earthquake victims. Other girls came to court at adolescence to become ladies' companions. But it was rare for a child adopted by a sovereign to become, like me, almost the equal of a princess.

Doubtless I owe the privileged, almost filial relationship I had with Muhammad V, and later with Hassan II, to my ambition and strong will. During all those years spent at the Palace, I strove to win their affection, to become part of their lives and make myself indispensable. I didn't want to remain unnoticed.

What happened next is a blur in my mind, as if I were the victim of a kidnapping. I remember my mother leaving hurriedly, then I was bundled into a car and driven to the Villa Yasmina where Lalla Mina lived with her governess, Jeanne Rieffel.

Tearing me away from my mother meant tearing me away from life. I cried, screamed and stamped my feet. The governess forced me into the guest room and double-locked the door. I sobbed all night.

My parents never spoke to me of this period. If there were explanations, I've forgotten them. Did my mother cry until dawn, as I did? Did she open the door to my room from time to time, did she sniff my clothes, did she sit on my bed, did she miss me? I have never dared ask her.

As time went by, this separation became something I accepted, despite my grief. I loved my mother so much and was so unhappy being away from her that each of her visits was a terrible ordeal. The few times she dropped in to see me, she would arrive at twelve and leave at two. When the governess told me she was coming, my joy was matched in intensity only by the immediate pain that followed it.

The night before one of her visits, I couldn't sleep. In the morning, I couldn't concentrate in class. The hours dragged by interminably. At half-past twelve I came out of school and the ritual would begin. Mother was there. I galloped down the stairs to the sitting room and stopped before going in because I could smell her perfume, Je Reviens, by Worth. That first moment belonged to me. I buried my face in her jacket hanging on the coat rack.

My mother was sitting on the sofa. Why did she greet me so calmly? Weren't we supposed to be reunited amid heartbreak and tears? So I would check myself and kiss her frostily. But then, during the few minutes the governess allowed us to be alone together, I would furtively kiss her hand and stroke her forearm. I showered her with a thousand gestures of love and affection that had become foreign to me yet for which I was still starving.

At the table, the governess monopolized my mother and prevented me from talking to her. I didn't eat. I watched her, drinking in her words, following the movement of her lips. I took in as many details as I could and replayed them every night before falling asleep, in the solitude of my room. I was so proud of her beauty, her elegance and her youth. Lalla Mina admired her too and that filled me with joy.

But the minutes ticked by and I had to leave for school again. Her visits became less frequent and I felt more and more distant from her. My home was no longer in the Alleé des Princesses, but at the Royal Palace of Rabat. I lived a cloistered existence, never seeing beyond the Palace walls and those of the other royal palaces where we were taken for holidays.

I saw the lives of others, real life, through the windows of the magnificent cars that drove us from one place to another. My own life was luxurious and protected from the world—it belonged to another century, another mentality, other customs.

It took me eleven years to escape from it.

2

THE KING'S PALACE

1958–1969

DURING THE REIGN OF MUHAMMAD V

The King didn't want his favourite daughter to be brought up in the confined atmosphere of Sidi (the Master)'s Palace. He had the Villa Yasmina done up for her. It was a paradise for well-brought-up children, shielded from the brutality of the world, a fairy-tale realm of luxury, calm and beautiful stories. There I was taught the art of being a princess.

The pleasantly large, white house was ten minutes from the Palace on the road to Zaers. You were driven through the gates and on to the main building, where Lalla Mina and Jeanne Rieffel, her governess, lived. Their apartments were on the first floor, together with the kitchen, the bathroom, the reception room dominated by the grand piano, the dining room, the TV room, the guest room and Lalla Mina's room next to that of the governess. The whole place was decorated in a modern, comfortable style, with floral chintz sofas and curtains, thick carpets and corner divans.

On the ground floor was a huge playroom filled with a vast number of toys, bicycles, billiards, miniature cars and garages, cuddly toys, dolls and their accessories, dressing-up clothes and a cinema for our private use. The house stood in a splendid garden, with thousands of different varieties of flowers—jasmine, honeysuckle, roses, dahlias, pansies, camellias, bougainvillaea, sweet peas. The avenues were lined with mandarin, orange, lemon and palm trees. For the Princess's entertainment, there was a climbing frame with swings and slides.

Lalla Mina, who loved animals, had her own zoo. There was a tiny enclosure where monkeys frolicked, and it had sheep, a squirrel brought back from a trip to Italy, pigeons and a goat. She even had her own stables behind the house, with looseboxes and a riding school. Also behind the house, there was a huge orchard with hundreds of fruit trees. We even had our own little primary school at the Villa Yasmina. The head teacher was called Madame Hugon and our teacher, Mademoiselle Capel. I have fond memories of Mademoiselle.

At first I slept in the guest room, near the Princess's bedroom. A year before the death of the King, two little girls of humble origins, Rashida and Fawzia, selected from among the top pupils in the country, came to join us and to be brought up with Lalla Mina. At that point I moved with them into a little house in the garden, next to the zoo. Two rooms opened out onto a patio with a glass ceiling. From now on I would share a room with Rashida.

Our timetable remained unchanged from the time of Muhammad V to that of Hassan II. Every morning, at around six thirty, the King would come over and wake us up. First he went into Lalla Mina's room then he would come into mine. He pulled back the sheets, took me by the feet and playfully tugged me towards him.

From the outset he made no distinction between his daughter and me, displaying the same kindly affection towards both of us. The King adored his daughter. He was not very demonstrative, but from the way he looked at her it was clear how much he loved her.

He was a constant and regular presence in our lives. He shared our breakfast and then stayed with us until it was time for school. He would come back around eleven thirty, sit in on our Arabic class and then go off again.

We ate in the house under the supervision of Jeanne Rieffel, the Alsatian governess recommended to the King by the Comte de Paris, after she had brought up his own children. Rieffel was an authoritarian spinster who must once have been very pretty: she had lively, big blue eyes and ash-grey hair, and held her head gracefully. I was in awe of her and I hated her. She wasn't nasty, but she knew nothing about teaching or psychology. She ruled us with a rod of iron and was forever punishing us and bullying us, because it was character building, or so she thought.

'A person is judged by their manners, not by their learning.'

I can still hear that menacing phrase, which she repeated to us daily in her Teutonic accent. On this subject she was constantly at war with Madame Hugon, our head teacher, who pushed us to succeed academically.

Muhammad V was an austere king who maintained moral discipline at court too. He was very religious, and was idolized by his people. Every Friday, at the end of the morning, he rode out of the great gate of the Palace on horseback to attend the mosque, which was in the Palace grounds. He wore a white jellabah, his ceremonial dress, and a red tarboosh on his head. Slaves held a big velvet canopy over him, to shield him from the sun. He crossed the Palace complex surrounded by the finest stallions from his stables, which pranced to the beat of the Royal Guards' drums. The ecstatic crowds lined the avenues cheering their king. People were so devoted to him that they would fling themselves to the ground to collect the dung from his horses.

Lalla Mina and I would be driven in the car to see him, and as soon as he appeared we would applaud him enthusiastically.

After prayer, he returned to the Palace in a horse-drawn coach. This vision of the King on horseback was like something out of a fairy tale. I never tired of it.

Nevertheless, diversions were few and far between under his reign. We holidayed in the royal palaces, in Fez, at Ifrane in the Atlas mountains, or by the sea at Wallidia. The King's favourite pastime was *pétanque*—bowls—which he played with his chauffeur, a decorator and a steward who had followed him when he was in exile in Madagascar from 1953 to 1955. After school, we would go and cheer him on.

Lalla Mina was a very spoilt child. While her father was alive, heads of state from all over the world sent her thousands of toys, which piled up in the playroom. At Christmas she received so many that the governess confiscated some to give to the poor. Walt Disney had designed an American car especially for her. The interior was decorated with all his cartoon characters and he had added a tiny kitchen and all the furniture for a doll's house. We were often filmed and photographed: magazines from all over the world were interested in the Princess's day-to-day life.

Muhammad V died suddenly at the age of fifty-two, on 26 February 1961. He died on the operating table during routine surgery. I was only seven years old, but I clearly remember the Palace in mourning and the grief of the little Princess. The morning he died, I found her in our garden, sobbing among the flower beds. I hugged her lovingly, not daring to say a word.

I felt great compassion for her. Her sorrow affected me as deeply as if it had been my own. Wasn't she like a sister to me? I had loved Muhammad V because he had always been fair and kind towards me. But he wasn't my father and I felt a pang at the thought that one day I too could lose my father.

At the Palace everyone was dressed in white, the colour of mourning. I was only a little girl, not yet fully acquainted with all the royal customs, and I found all the goings-on strange and confusing. In one room was the *aamara*, the chorus of slaves rhythmically banging tambourins—long, narrow drums. Others chanted:

'The King is dead, long live the King . . .'

Five days later, they rejoiced at the coronation of the new King, Hassan II, at the age of thirty-two. Not far away, in the room where Muhammad V's coffin lay, his concubines wept noisily.

On the death of the King, my mother naturally thought of taking me back, but the subtleties and sensibilities of the Palace always complicated the simplest actions. My return home would have implied that my mother showed less deference to Hassan II than she had shown his father. And besides, in these tragic circumstances, how could she have been so heartless as to deprive Lalla Mina of my comforting presence? The time wasn't right.

Nor would the time ever be right in the years that followed.

Eventually I became a commodity: the more influential my father became politically, the more I was used as a pawn between him and the King. If my father happened to broach the subject of bringing me home, was it because he questioned the way the King was raising me?

Long years passed before I could insist, on my own, on my wish to go home.

THE EDUCATION OF A PRINCESS

When he was still crown prince, the young King had promised to treat Lalla Mina as his daughter. On the death of Muhammad V, the Palace was in a state of uncertainty: would he keep his promise? He did.

The Princess's status remained unchanged and our lives went on almost as before. Hassan II did not come to wake us up in the morning or join us for breakfast or for our lessons, as his father had been in the habit of doing, but he always came to the end-of-year prize-giving at our little school.

We sang, we danced, we read poetry, recited surats—verses—from the Koran, and performed plays in French and Arabic. The King would sit in the front row, surrounded by his concubines, a few ministers and his court. This special effort—for it was an effort for him—was sacred. He made it out of respect for his father and out of love for his little sister. Hassan II did not yet have children of his own and the Princess and I had no hesitation in demanding his full attention.

We slipped into his car at the slightest opportunity, went horse-riding with him, watched him play golf, cheered him on at tennis and went on holiday with him. We even attended Cabinet meetings. We were two mischievous eight-year-olds seizing any chance to laugh and have fun, and forget the pomp of the Palace.

As in the past, we were woken up at half-past six. We washed, dressed, prayed, made our beds, tidied our rooms and polished our shoes. The governess would arrive unannounced and check that everything was impeccable. Around seven thirty, breakfast was served in the dining room. When we started secondary school, every morning at eight o'clock a car followed by an escort drove us to the lycée in the Palace grounds. Outstanding teachers were recruited from all over the kingdom. Some of the King's ministers also gave us lessons.

Half a dozen girls, among the best students from each province, came to join our group of four, Lalla Mina, Rashida, Fawzia and me. The teaching was in French and Arabic, and later in English. Our curriculum included history, grammar, literature, maths, languages and even religion. Since Muhammad V's time, it had been customary to educate the princesses up to the baccalaureate. One of his daughters, Princess Lalla Aisha, was so brilliant that her brother Hassan II appointed her ambassador to London and Rome.

A rebellious and rather unruly pupil, I loved playing tricks on my teachers, and this was reflected in my grades. Our Koran teacher, an elderly gentleman with an aloof manner, had taught Hassan II. When he entered the classroom, he insisted that we rush towards him to kiss his hand. It was my job to remove his burnous and hang it up at the back of the classroom. He taught us classical Arabic, which was one of my favourite subjects. The calligraphy was similar to drawing, at which I excelled. And I also liked to hear him chant the surats in his deep, steady voice.

This holy man believed firmly in spirits. He claimed that jinns were part of us, day and night. I didn't believe in supernatural forces, but since he seemed so convinced of their existence I decided to play a prank on him.

One morning, I took advantage of a moment when he was at the blackboard and slipped inside the clothes hanging on the coat stand, my feet wedged firmly under its feet. When he turned round, the coat stand began to walk. He started to shake from head to foot. The closer I advanced towards the desk, the more frightened he was, and the louder he chanted verses of the Koran. Unable to control myself, I burst out laughing. He was convulsed with rage. I had dared to humiliate a patriarch who was revered by all, even by His Majesty.

The Palace had a good laugh over this prank. The King too laughed heartily, even though he was disconcerted by the fury of the old man, who accused me of not believing in God.

I was incorrigible, continually getting into trouble: I sawed off the legs of the English teacher's chair, set bees on the teacher who was allergic . . . Each time, Madame Hugon, our head teacher, went and complained to the King. My weekly reports were full of scathing comments: 'disobedient, rebellious pupil', 'clowns around', 'always talking'.

I would take my report to the King while he was eating. I stood there quaking, awaiting my punishment, speechless with dread.

One day he turned to his concubines:

'I don't understand. They tell me she's talkative, but I can't get a word out of her.'

The whole room burst out laughing: they knew me well.

At half-past twelve, morning classes ended. The car took us to the golf course to meet the King. Sometimes we had lunch at the Palace, but generally we returned to the Villa Yasmina. While we waited for lunch to be served, we would go into the playroom. This was a precious time when I would play the piano, or make sketches of all the film and music-hall stars I used to dream about.

The governess would call us for lunch at around one o'clock, repeating the same old formula in her hateful accent.

'Go to the toilet, do a wee-wee or a poo-poo, wash your botties and your hands. Hurry up, young ladies . . .'

During the meal, we were made to speak German. I couldn't stand the language because it was Rieffel's, but that wasn't the only thing that was an ordeal for me.

I hated the insipid food we were served at the villa, which was supposedly good for us. I dreamed of *tagines*, soups, meatballs, Moroccan pancakes and cakes dripping with honey. The Queen Mother and Lalla Bahia, who knew about my weakness, had all sorts of succulent dishes brought to us once a week, but Rieffel never allowed us to taste them. She was so sadistic that she would allow the dishes to be presented to us at table and then order them to be sent back.

Instead we were given meat salads and spinach gratin, boiled fish and steamed potatoes sprinkled with parsley. I hated the meat, bread and vegetables. I liked only the hard-boiled eggs we were given occasionally, and above all I loved Moroccan dishes. To all intents and purposes, I ate nothing. Rieffel tried to force us to swallow every mouthful. I invented hundreds of ploys to avoid eating, and lived in fear of being banned from watching films as punishment for my misdemeanours.

After lunch we had a brief moment of freedom before setting off for school again. Around half-past six, when our lessons were over, we would return to the Palace to see the King. If he was holding a Cabinet meeting, we visited Oum Sidi, the Queen Mother, who was our ally against Rieffel. She would find all sorts of pretexts for waylaying the governess and we seized the chance to slip away.

Dinner was served at around eight o'clock at the villa. During exam time, I worked long into the night. Otherwise we would go to bed at nine o'clock at the latest. We weren't allowed to watch television or even to read, we had to put the lights out straight away. I would secretly listen to a little transistor radio that I kept hidden under my pillow.

From my bed, I had a view over the patio. I had chosen to be by the window so that I could look at the sky and the stars, which I found comforting. The night was my kingdom, my haven of peace. Nobody could disturb my thoughts. I escaped into a life of make-believe, where I was free at last. I didn't sleep much; I cried and I thought of my mother, missing her a little more each day.

I was fraught with contradictory feelings. I wasn't unhappy. Lalla Mina loved me like a sister and I returned her love. The King, the Queen Mother, Lalla Bahia, and the concubines lavished affection on me even though they were never demonstrative. I had a dream childhood, with everything I wanted and more.

But I missed my family terribly. I had learned of the birth of my little sisters through the Palace. Myriam and Raouf were complete strangers to me. I knew nothing about them, their likes and dislikes, their games or their friends. When, exceptionally, the governess allowed me to go home for the afternoon, the next few days would be unbearable. I couldn't eat or sleep, and my grief would subside only after days and nights of secret tears.

Twice I was able to spend a few days' holiday with them, but then someone would come to fetch me back on some pretext or other. Lalla Mina missed me.

Sometimes I saw my father at the Palace, but our contact was too brief. He was not expansive, and displays of emotion made him uncomfortable. But a look or a squeeze of the hand was enough to make me understand that he loved me. Often I sensed his sadness at not being able to bring me up himself. As time went by, I learned that my father was a very important man, but I had to grow up a bit more before I was fully able to appreciate his political role. I lived in such seclusion that I had no idea what was going on in the world. I did not even understand the Ben Barka affair.[1] I was barely aware that security around me had been stepped up. I heard my father's name crop up over and over again on the radio, without grasping what was going on.

Above all, I was plagued by the urge to telephone my mother. Whenever I was anywhere near a phone, I had to try and contact her. Monsieur and Madame Bringard, the steward and housekeeper, lived in a little house at the villa gate. Opposite it was Monsieur Bringard's office with one of those precious telephones. Sometimes I would slip out of my room in the middle of the night and sneak across the patio, without making a sound, because Rieffel watched us from her window. I'd walk through the garden, skirting round the many guards stationed there, enter the steward's office and grab the telephone, trembling.

During the day, I would contrive all sorts of ways to shut myself

[1]On 29 October 1965, Mehdi Ben Barka, King Hassan II's former mathematics teacher, leader of the Moroccan opposition and founder of the Union Nationale des Forces Populaires, spokesman for the Third World, was kidnapped outside the Brasserie Lipp in Paris by two French police officers, Souchon and Viotot, and taken to a villa in Fontenay-le-Vicomte. He was never seen again.

General Oufkir, then Minister of the Interior, and Colonel Ahmed Dlimi, Director of National Security, were accused by the French of being behind the kidnapping and killing of Ben Barka. An international arrest warrant was launched against them. Dlimi gave himself up to the French authorities and was acquitted in June 1967. General Oufkir was sentenced in his absence to life imprisonment. In Morocco, he received a tribute from the King 'for his unwavering loyalty to our person'.

away and call my mother. But then, after all that cunning, when I heard her voice at the other end and there were other voices in the background, I couldn't think of anything to say to her. I was painfully aware that my family had their own lives in which I no longer had a place.

Weekends varied a little from our strict schedule. On Saturdays, the German lesson lasted all morning. The governess taught us her language with the aid of frequent punishments and slaps. Then Lalla Mina, who was mad about horses, went off to her stables and I would go down to the playroom to draw, listen to music, or play the accordion or the drums. Like all little girls everywhere in the world, we also liked playing with dolls and make-believe tea parties. We entertained our guests in a prettily decorated hut, serving them leaves in silver bowls.

If we had enjoyed a particular film the previous week, I re-enacted it. We delved into chests full of dressing-up clothes to create the characters. I was always the director and I cast the parts and wrote the scripts. We went through a *Carmelites* phase, then *The Sound of Music*, *Romulus and Remus* and *The Three Musketeers*.

After lunch we went for a walk in the country, to 'get a breath of fresh air', at the governess's insistence. Every Saturday, and sometimes during the week when the King wasn't available, we would leave Rabat. We would be dropped off some distance from the Palace so that we had to walk for two or three hours to get home, with the car and the escort crawling along behind us.

On the way there, the minute I sensed that Rieffel had dozed off, I would give the chauffeur a knowing look and he would switch on the radio. Then I'd wait for my favourite songs, rock 'n' roll, the twist, pop music—anything but those awful German *Lieder* that the governess made us sing. It was even more of a treat because it was forbidden.

Saturday evening was one of my favourite times because we were shown old movies. But best of all I liked the Palace cinema. There we were allowed to watch as many of the recent films as we wanted, without Rieffel censoring them. On Saturdays during Ramadan, the kitchens would prepare wonderful refreshments for us, which we would eat with the King and the concubines, watching films until daybreak. Needless to say, on Sundays everyone had a lie-in.

When Lalla Mina's father was still alive, Pandit Nehru had given her a baby elephant. The animal was kept in the magnificent park of the Dar-es-Salem palace, which was on the road to Rabat, surrounded by nature. When we were little, we often used to go there at lunchtime to feed the ducks on the lake.

The baby elephant became our favourite plaything. He was gentle and affectionate, gobbling up the crusts of bread we slid under his trunk. We went to see him every day and our greatest treat was to ride around the park on his back, accompanied by his mahout, who had come all the way from India. But the elephant driver wanted to go home. After he left, a Moroccan groom looked after the animal and began to ill-treat him. Provoked to the limit, the elephant attacked his tormentor. He had to be put down. Lalla Mina and I were inconsolable.

Our love of animals was boundless. At the stables, among the horses, lived a little white camel, Zazate, given to us by the governor of Ouarzazate when we had visited the south with Moulay Ahmed Alaoui, the King's cousin. This intelligent man who was passionately interested in Moroccan culture had been given the task of teaching us about the country when we reached our teens.

For two or three years, during the holidays, he took us to villages and little towns, deserts and mountains. Before each visit, he gave us a lesson in geography and history. Thanks to him, I discovered the region of my paternal ancestors, the *sharifa*, direct descendants of the Prophet. In these deserts of the south, inhabited by the 'Blue Men', I was greeted even more enthusiastically than Princess Lalla Mina. They organized a camel fantasia in our honour, with races, trick riding and elaborate costumes.

Zazate came to live with us. We kept her in one of the stalls at the Villa Yasmina stables, next to the Princess's stallion. On Saturday afternoons I sometimes gave in to Lalla Mina and agreed to go riding with her. I preferred to mount the camel, and we had great fun. Sometimes she asked me to take a horse, and challenged me to a race.

These were moments of intense happiness. I felt free, light. I loved galloping in the wind, feeling the branches brush my face. I had the feeling I no longer belonged to anybody. I was myself at last, with no restraints or obligations. I was starting to understand the joys of riding.

For the holidays, other than trips with Moulay Ahmed, we had the choice of the many palaces in the kingdom: Tangier and Marrakesh in the spring, or the palace at Fez, restored by Hassan II and now one of the most magnificent in the country.

The place I loved best of all was Ifrane, in the Atlas. It was like arriving in the Haute Savoie region of France. The houses were of red brick, just like in *Snow White*, and in winter the mountainsides were covered in snow. We threw ourselves into skiing with delight. Lalla Mina and I stayed in a huge, six-storey villa where King Muhammad V had lived when he was crown prince. A twisting road wound its way up through the pine forest to the royal castle, perched on the summit and surrounded by a fairy-tale park. Hassan II had done it up in luxurious style, like most of his palaces.

In July 1969, for his fortieth birthday, he arranged a performance of *Swan Lake* on Ifrane's lake. It was an unforgettable sight, like something out of *The Arabian Nights*. When Nasser came to visit him, the King organized a big party in his honour. At neighbouring Michlifen, in the middle of the forest, there was an extinct volcano with a huge crater. In the winter we used to go skiing on its slopes. From the comfort of a huge marquee erected specially for the occasion, Nasser witnessed the unforgettable spectacle of a horseback fantasia in the middle of the crater.

At Ifrane, we went panther hunting by helicopter at night, or we went after boar and hare in open jeeps. I always sat next to the King, aware that these were very special moments.

LIFE INSIDE THE PALACE

The Palace was our world, our favourite playground. We never tired of racing down the corridors, exploring the alcoves and patios, slipping in wherever we were allowed, into the King's apartment, the harem or the kitchens. Lalla Mina would open a door and poke her cheeky little face around it, and I would venture in too, with a mischievous grin. People caught sight of us, they called out to us . . . we were pampered, kissed, made a fuss of and fed, our every whim satisfied.

The Royal Palace was surrounded by walls as old as the city of Rabat itself. Originally, they were the walls of the ancient stables where the horses were tethered—the word Rabat means 'tethered'. A road ran from one side to the other. The complex included the mosque with its little mausoleum, the married slaves' quarters, the headquarters of the Department of Protocol and of the Royal Guard and, a little further, the garage, one of my favourite haunts, where the King's superb collection of cars was lined up. A huge gate opened onto the Palace, which was as big as a city, with its own private hospital, golf course, steam baths, lycée, souks, playing fields and the big zoo which the Princess and I visited so frequently.

Several massive, opulently decorated buildings linked by endless corridors constituted the living quarters. These comprised the palace of Hassan II, who was forever moving from one wing to another as the fancy took him, that of Muhammad V, too big and gloomy for our liking, the concubines' palaces where each had her own apartment, and those built by the late king for Oum Sidi and Lalla Bahia.

The passages that led to the queens' palaces stretched for two kilometres. We always ran down them, for there were so many things to see and do. Each queen had a cinema, a summer garden and a winter garden, and Italian salons decorated with exquisite frescoes. The windows overlooked a huge patio a thousand metres square and the swimming pool which took up the whole esplanade.

Lalla Bahia, whom we called Mamaya, slept in an imposing four-poster bed draped with white silk. In private, she often wore silk wraps and mules with bobbles that emphasized her tiny feet. A real

Hollywood star. She spent hours in her white marble bathroom crammed with beauty products.

I loved watching her smear Nivea onto her face, then spend ages wiping it off with piles of fine white cotton towels specifically for that purpose. 'My girl,' she would say in her sensual voice, 'no cream, even the most expensive, is as effective as this.' Judging by her perfect milk-white complexion, she knew what she was talking about.

Lalla Mina and I spent hours sitting on the floor in her drawing room, looking at her photo albums which traced the history of the royal family: the births of the princesses, Muhammad V's exile and return, the King and his sisters' weddings, birthdays and anniversaries. Mamaya was neither maternal nor demonstrative towards her daughter. Oum Sidi showed the little Princess a lot more warmth and affection but she could also be strict. I was very fond of the Queen Mother; I admired her bearing, her haughty air and her restrained, reserved personality.

We often used to visit the kitchens to gorge ourselves on everything that Rieffel forbade us to eat at the villa. Or we would career along the endless corridors that led to the concubines' apartments or the slaves' quarters. Slaves, known as *aabid*, have lived at the palace in Rabat for generations. They are the descendants of the black slaves bought from African slave traders. Their great-great-grandchildren still serve the King, in each of his Moroccan palaces. They belong to the royal family but are free to marry outsiders and leave the Palace if they so wish. In practice, they rarely do so.

According to custom, whenever there was a royal wedding at the Palace, around forty slave couples would be married on the same day. They would then go and live in the married slaves' quarters, in little houses built specially for them. Their children in turn became slaves. Only the 'fire slaves', whose job was to administer corporal punishment, had a specific duty. The rest formed an army of interchangeable servants at their master's beck and call, paid a pittance. Some answered to the King's wife, others to the concubines, and others depended on the King himself.

The women worked in the kitchens, did the housework and

ironing, and were nannies, seamstresses and even third-class concubines. The men were in charge of the garage, waited at table or kept watch, like stone statues, in every corner of the Palace, or in the niches of its countless corridors. The unmarried and widowed slaves lived inside the Palace, in a special wing. They lived alone, or shared little alcoves closed off by curtains called *koubas*, on either side of an avenue in the open air. They cooked the best dishes in the Palace, over calor gas stoves. Despite their paltry means, their *koubas* were spick and span, and they themselves were always immaculate.

All day the slaves listened to oriental music on their transistor radios with the volume on full. They were all tuned in to the same station, which created a striking stereo effect. Delicious smells of cooking wafted from their *koubas*. To attract our attention, they would call us, appealing to our weak spot:

'Lalla Mina, Smiyet Lalla, come . . . I've made a *tagine*, lovely pancakes . . .'

Some would make *hashisha*, hashish jam, cooked for hours in little saucepans over calor gas stoves. Sometimes I'd steal a pot from them to share with Lalla Mina in secret, and we would giggle hysterically for hours on end.

Mountains of shoes piled up outside the concubines' doors, for at the Palace everyone went barefoot on the carpets. You kicked off your shoes before walking on them, and put them back on again afterwards. I always found those heaps of shoes comical.

On my arrival at the Palace, I had been adopted by Muhammad V's harem. After his death, I witnessed the arrival of that of Hassan II. I knew all those women well; I was admitted into their private sphere, I shared their confidences. Muhammad V's concubines went to live in an exquisite place that Hassan II had built especially for them, a little village of white houses surrounded by gardens, just opposite our lycée. They had their own swimming pools, souks, steam baths, a private hospital and a cinema. They continued to serve the new sovereign, giving him advice and supporting him, and played an important role, whatever people say to the contrary.

Hassan II's concubines were very young girls, chosen from all over the country for their beauty. The eldest were not yet seventeen. They were clumsy, awkward and uncertain, not knowing how to behave. They were installed in the former apartments of Muhammad V's concubines.

They were immediately taken in hand by the older women, who taught them about Palace life, etiquette, tradition and habits. They prepared them for their lives as women, for the sexuality of a concubine is not like that of ordinary mortals. Jealously guarded secrets were passed on from harem to harem. Their names were changed. Fatihas and Khadijas, often daughters of the lower classes, became Noor Sbah, 'light of dawn', or Shem's Ddoha, 'setting sun'. After their training, they were married to the King in groups of three or four, in his palace at Fez, amid sumptuous festivities where I enthusiastically joined in the dancing and singing. The King was happy. At that time he was an heir full of hope, not yet embittered by political strife.

Hassan II added new concubines to his harem until the beginning of the Seventies, around forty in all, who joined his father's forty or so wives. They followed him everywhere around the Palace, from his dressing room to the Turkish bath, the hairdresser's and to gym classes. They formed cliques: the older women, the plotters, the teases, the playful ones, the smutty ones . . . their aim was to attract his attention, to be his favourites of the moment. When they succeeded, it was a triumph—until, that is, another clique won his favours and they were cast aside like yesterday's fashion.

The most highly regarded concubines had the status of childless wife, for as a rule they were not allowed to have children. Only the King's wife can give him heirs. Then came the housekeepers, whose job was to supervise the running of the Palace and to maintain the traditions that the King valued.

Muhammad V had a concubine whose job it was, on feast days, to dress him in his ceremonial costume, a white jellabah and trousers. After his death, she continued with Hassan II. This special ceremony took place in a room at the Palace comprising a vast white marble patio with a bubbling fountain in the middle. Three sides of the room were lined with *koubas* paved with brightly coloured *zellige*—

mosaic tiles—and decorated with silk carpets, cushions and precious fabrics, brocades and velvet. These *koubas* were separated from the patio by a taffeta or velvet curtain. This architectural feature was repeated throughout the Palace in Rabat, and in all the other royal palaces.

On the days when he attended the mosque, Hassan II would enter his *kouba* followed by the concubine who was carrying his costume. Those of his wives who so wished were allowed to accompany him. When he was dressed, the concubine in charge of incense would burn little fragrant incense sticks. Another brought an exquisite inlaid chest on a velvet cushion of emerald green, the colour of the Palace. In the chest were rows of little bottles of essential oils—amber, musk, sandalwood and jasmine—which came from Mecca. The King would pour a few drops of the chosen fragrance onto a wad of cotton wool and dab it behind his ears. Then he threw it onto the floor.

That was the signal for the scramble to begin. All the concubines fought over that wad of cotton wool and passed it from hand to hand to catch a whiff of the precious scent mingled with that of their lord and master. I would always try to be the first to pick it up so I could steep myself in his perfume before the others.

When the King returned from the mosque, the voices of the male slaves announced his arrival, chanting non-stop:

'May God give him long life.'

Then the *aamara*—the slaves' choir—began to beat their tambourines to the rhythm of the chant. It was forbidden to approach the King before he had washed his hands. When his return from the mosque coincided with the end of Ramadan or the feast of Eid, Hassan II would sit in front of the *kouba*, on a majestic throne-like chair. On those days, all the concubines who had been punished or repudiated were allowed to throw themselves at his feet and ask his pardon.

Every evening, before dinner, the bath concubine washed the King's feet with soaps and perfumes, in accordance with a precise ritual. Another concubine was in charge of the sandalwood ceremony, which took place at every festival, every religious holiday and at all wakes and funerals. The sandalwood from Mecca smouldered continuously in a precious engraved silver burner filled with glowing charcoal.

The concubine presented little pieces of sandalwood to the King, which he threw into this container. It was then taken into all the rooms, to purify them. The scent of sandalwood permeated the entire Palace. Sandalwood powder was put in the vacuum cleaners; sandalwood was burned in the oriental censers—*mbhehhra*—carried from room to room by the slaves. All the apartments, cars and even the Palace's inhabitants themselves were impregnated with this fragrance.

Naima, the concubine who held the keys to the outside, was a very lively girl, the only one of the women to have any contact with 'outsiders', and especially with men—from gardeners and decorators to guards and members of the Cabinet. She was also responsible for the newspapers, which she brought to the King every day.

Hassan II had introduced a ritual at the close of the afternoon. He had his hands and scalp massaged in a tiny *kouba* that dated back to Muhammad V's day. We all attended the session, sitting cross-legged at his feet, commenting on every stage with great bursts of laughter. Then I would go and kiss his hands; their skin was so soft. The hairdresser and the manicurist were French, as were the two gym coaches who gave the concubines lessons on the esplanade of their palace.

The King was always looking for new entertainments to amuse all his wives, some of whom were still children. He had multi-saddle bicycles brought over from the United States. For several weeks, the vast corridors of the palace at Fez echoed with our laughter. We were a sight pedalling behind him in single file.

During their training, the concubines, like the slaves, wore bottle-green, grey or brown kaftans, decorated with silk braid in matching tones. They rolled up the sleeves to the elbows and held them in place with huge widths of elastic. Around their waists, another piece of fabric, the *tehmila*, was worn like an apron. Once they became confirmed concubines, they were at last allowed to wear kaftans in all the colours of the rainbow.

The King took an interest in every detail of their dress. He decided on the style of the ceremonial kaftans, the colours, the fabrics and the belts. It was wonderful watching the concubines swish around the Palace, dressed in their brilliantly coloured outfits. Every hue was permitted, from the brightest shades to the subtlest pastels. They were graceful in the way they moved, wore their heavy clothes and rolled up their sleeves or the hems of their robes. You would think they were dancing.

Tradition required them always to wear kaftans inside the Palace. Outside, on the beach, on the golf course, at the tennis courts or on horseback, they dressed in the latest European fashions. Fabrics were brought in from Europe, and the King chose these too.

Whenever they travelled by car—in huge limousines with curtained windows—from one palace to another or on trips, the concubines wore special black or navy-blue jellabahs, which looked like coats with round hoods. Their faces were gracefully concealed under dark muslin veils.

When we were on holiday in Marrakesh, Hassan II announced that we were to go out with him, which put us all in a cheerful mood; we so rarely had the opportunity to go into the town with him! We were given traditional jellabahs, and horse-drawn carriages were sent for us. Dressed up in a slave's jellabah, the King drove our carriage himself. In the medina, he haggled over the gifts he bought us. Nobody recognized him. I remember my delight and our fits of giggles.

It was almost impossible for the women to go anywhere without the King, except on rare occasions. I have vivid memories of an official visit to Yugoslavia, in the early Sixties, with the Queen Mother, Oum Sidi, and a few of her concubine friends. Marshal Tito had provided us with a castle outside Belgrade which looked as though it belonged to Count Dracula.

Noor Sbah, one of the most mischievous concubines, pulled a dark stocking over her face and wandered down the gloomy corridors, holding a candle and knocking at all the bedroom doors. This childish prank caused shrieks of terror throughout the castle, and gales of laughter from Lalla Mina and me, who had secretly followed her.

At the end of our stay, the Queen Mother wanted to slip off discreetly to Italy without telling the King. But journalists were waiting for us in Trieste and the incognito trip was shelved.

In recent years, the concubines' caged regime has become more relaxed. They go about unveiled, and without curtains at the windows of their cars. Queen Latifa is allowed to travel around alone, and she has her own cars, chauffeurs and guards, which was not the case when she married Hassan II.

In the year that followed Muhammad V's death, the King, then aged thirty-three, was expected to get married. The most prominent Berber family in the country sent two young beauties—first cousins—to the Palace: Latifa, aged fifteen, and Fatima, who was thirteen. They were subjected to the same training as the other concubines who had arrived at the same time, from all the provinces of Morocco.

But it was already clear that the King would choose one of the two girls. It was not a decision to be taken lightly. The legitimate wife would be the mother of the King's children, the mother, above all, of the heir to the throne. For political reasons, to maintain a delicate balance between the different Moroccan tribes, she had to be a Berber, like all the monarchs' wives, like the Queen Mother, Lalla Aabla, and like Lalla Bahia.

Fatima was tall and well proportioned, with white skin, pale eyes and a madonna-like face. Latifa was smaller, with irregular features and a prominent nose, but she had huge brown eyes and luxuriant hair. She did not have her cousin's spectacular beauty, but she already had a very strong personality.

The two girls were scarcely older than me, but I considered them to be already women. I happened to be next to the King when he received their family, one of the most distinguished in the land. He conducted himself with humility and deference, like a son-in-law rather than a monarch, confronted with these traditional Berbers who did not bother with appearances. The women wore white veils and the men wore jellabahs. Their modesty and dignity and the simplicity of their dress seemed out of place in this *Arabian Nights* décor.

Fatima fell head over heels in love with the King. Latifa, who was prouder and less demonstrative, waited for the King to make his choice. The King was not indifferent to the beauty and freshness of the younger girl, or to her passionate, spontaneous love. But he also liked the charisma of the older girl. Only those close to them were aware of the rivalry that existed between the two cousins. The older concubines tried to influence the King to choose Fatima, who was more docile and easier to manipulate. They tried to force nature's hand so that she would fall pregnant straight away. The birth of an heir would make the marriage official, but this did not transpire.

One day, Latifa took the initiative and addressed the King.

'Sidi, I will never agree to being just a concubine in your harem.'

If he wouldn't allow her to be the mother of his children, she added, she would rather go home. She was not belittling the status of a concubine, or even the idea of sharing, or anonymity. It was just that Latifa wanted to be a mother. The King liked her strong will; he preferred women with character to women who were too pretty, and Latifa had plenty of spunk. All of five foot two inches tall, she inspired respect without even needing to open her mouth. He chose her for his wife. Her cousin Fatima remained a concubine in the harem.

These customs seemed natural to me. They didn't shock me because that was how I was brought up. I was too young and too ignorant to be aware that they were medieval. For me, the King's wedding was a spectacular show, and I loved all the pomp and ceremony. But I was also very happy. I felt truly involved in everything that affected my adoptive father, directly or indirectly.

The following year, on 26 August 1963, Latifa produced a little girl, Lalla Meriem, who was born in Rome. The baptism celebrations were lavish, with days and days of music, dancing and refined banquets where we were served the rarest dishes. Latifa was triumphant. The birth of the little girl confirmed her status as Queen.

Latifa had four more children: Sidi Muhammad, the crown prince, born in 1964, followed by Lalla Hasmma, Lalla Asmaa and Moulay Rashid. Each time she was pregnant, the King was ruthlessly strict about her diet. She had to eat healthily, which meant lots of vegetables, and avoid sugar and fat. He was merciless and she was starving.

She was pregnant with Moulay Rashid when she begged me:

'I want some *coiffes du caïd*. Now.'

It was not an easy craving to satisfy. The Queen wanted pancakes that took hours to prepare. They looked like turbans dipped in honey, hence their name. At that time I was living at home, but I still came to visit the princesses and the concubines.

I ran home and asked Achoura, our governess, who was an outstanding cook, to make the pancakes. When she found out who they were for, she wanted to take a lot of trouble over them and arrange them on silver dishes. But I didn't have much time; Latifa had said 'now'. Above all, I didn't want to be seen, for the King would be likely to throw one of his dreaded temper tantrums.

I placed the pancakes on an ordinary plate wrapped in a simple dishcloth, and returned to the Palace. I went a long way round to avoid bumping into anyone, but I soon found myself face to face with the old concubines. They wanted to know where I was going. I lied, saying I was going to visit the Queen Mother. Such lovely smells came from the dish I was carrying that they asked me what it was for. I claimed the pancakes were for Lalla Mina, but they weren't fooled.

'Whatever you do, don't take any pancakes to Latifa. Someone could be using you, they might have poisoned them without your knowing, and then you'd be in serious trouble.'

Their words brought home to me a fact of Palace life that I had wanted to forget. There, people were afraid of potions, charms, curses and black magic. And indeed, a year later, a jealous courtesan was accused of trying to poison Latifa.

The concubines, especially the elder ones, were very pious women. Five times a day, for the five ritual prayers, they knelt on their little silk mats brought to them by a slave and prayed facing Mecca. Afterwards they would spend a long time on religious devotions, reading or reciting surats from the Koran.

I hated spending too much time with them, except to contemplate

Lalla Bahia's sublime face, prettily veiled with muslin. I wasn't a good Muslim. I liked only the traditions and the pomp of religious ceremonies, and there were plenty of celebrations at the Palace, which Hassan II had updated to suit modern tastes.

The twenty-seventh night of Ramadan, called the Night of Destiny, is dedicated to prayer, as soon as the fast has been broken. That night God supposedly grants our wishes. We would all go and pray with the King in the Palace mosque. He would install himself in the front and his wives would kneel behind him.

Incapable of meditating in silence, I played the clown. Oum Sidi and Lalla Bahia couldn't help laughing. The King heard them and guessed that I was pulling faces. He tried to concentrate but I could see him growing angry. Whenever he became irritated, he would pluck at his sleeves to show his annoyance. Then he would be certain to scold me. But that didn't prevent me doing it again.

The feast of Mawlid, which marks the Prophet's birthday, was celebrated every year in the slaves' quarters. Huge wooden platters would be piled high with mountains of black *zematta* sprinkled with icing sugar. This special dish reserved for baptisms was made from durum wheat flour cooked for two days and mixed with melted butter, nutmeg, gum arabic, pure honey, cinnamon, sesame and toasted ground almonds. It was absolutely delicious.

From early morning, the *aamara* could be heard chanting psalms, accompanied by musicians playing the lute and the violin. We arrived at the end of the avenue and climbed the stairs leading to a balcony overlooking the slaves' quarters. The women were decked out in their coloured kaftans. Any colour was permitted except black or white.

Latifa, the King's wife, was the most elegant, and the most bejewelled. Her gems were by far the most magnificent. The King's sisters and his sister-in-law, Lamia, the wife of his brother, Moulay Abdallah, wore kaftans with the same motif as his, but in different hues. They all wore gold belts decorated with precious stones, earrings, necklaces, tiaras and pearls in their chignons.

From our balcony, we then witnessed the most incredible sight. All the sick slaves, the epileptics, asthmatics and rheumatism sufferers, came out of their *koubas* and began to dance before us, swaying to the rhythm of the *aamara*'s religious chants.

They would go into a trance to rid themselves of their jinns, the evil spirits that were the cause of all their diseases. A slave arrived bearing a goblet overflowing with prickly pear skins. They grabbed these skins with both hands, without seeming to feel the prickles, kneaded them and rubbed their bodies with them, concentrating on the afflicted parts. Others drank boiling water straight from the pot without feeling the slightest pain. Afterwards they never had any marks on them.

This Mawlid ceremony traditionally took place at the Meknès palace. According to Oum Sidi, in Muhammad V's day even more dramatic scenes took place.

'We saw injured slaves arrive who had fractured their skulls with their axes,' she would tell us, while Lalla Mina and I shuddered in horror.

At the Rabat palace, Hassan II kept a tighter rein on the situation.

Latifa and I began to dance to the beat; we wanted to go into a trance too. But the King gave his wife a furious reprimand.

'Your rank does not permit you to behave like them. You are impervious to the devil and possession.'

That was how the Palace explained the world. Jinns attacked slaves, who were born into servitude, and spared princesses. Everyone had their place and that was that. It was all for the best, and for all eternity.

There were other festivals that delighted us. There was the Kohl festival, which coincided with the ripening of the grapes, when little girls were allowed to wear make-up. The applicator used to draw a kohl line under the eyelid was first dipped into a grape to moisten it. Then every little girl would wait in turn to be made up like a woman, giggling and larking about.

For the water festival, we had to spray everyone who came within reach. It was a very joyful day spent perched high up on balconies, or hidden in dark crannies on the lookout for victims. The King had great fun and we were often in cahoots. He would walk under a balcony with his wives and step out of the way at the last minute, so that Lalla Mina and I could pour a bucket of water over his entourage. They would shriek and threaten to do the same to us. The three of us would laugh our heads off, and the others would eventually join in.

I also loved Ashisha Ghadra, the children's festival. On the big patio surrounded by *koubas*, there would be around ten of us little girls cooking over tiny charcoal braziers, assisted by our respective nannies. We dressed up in little housewives' kaftans, our sleeves rolled up to the elbows and held in place with elastic like the grown-ups. All the crockery and kitchenware were on a small scale. Then the King would come and sample our cooking, give his verdict and hand out prizes, kissing the winners.

The King wasn't a great eater but he loved making up recipes. He often had a kitchen set up in the Palace dining room and concocted dishes himself that we all tasted in turn. The result was sometimes dubious, but we had no choice. We had to eat it all up, exclaiming and smiling:

'Sidi, how delicious!'

But he couldn't bear us to put on weight. He had promised Lalla Mina a surprise if she managed to lose her puppy fat. During a stay in Tangier she secretly went on a diet and told him she'd lost four kilos. He kept his promise and told us he was going to perform Hatefa. He took up his position on the balcony overlooking a large patio. Beside him, two slave concubines carried little boxes filled with large copper coins, rarely used, worth at that time between ten and fifty francs. Oum Sidi, Lalla Bahia, Latifa and the concubines were gathered below with the two of us in their midst, all waiting for him to shower us with the coins. He laughed until tears ran down his face, watching us crawl around on all fours picking up the money. Most of the concubines larked about, vying to catch his attention. I kept silent for once, busily piling up the coins.

When the King came down, he asked each of us how many coins we'd collected. The concubines pointed to me.

'She's got the most,' they said, half laughing, half accusingly.

He asked me to show him my spoils. I opened my skirt, in which I'd gathered my treasure. There was a huge heap of coins.

'You've done well,' he said. 'But who are you going to give them to?'

'I'm going to give them to my mummy.'

My answer irked him a little. He couldn't bear being left out.

Sadly for me, Rieffel confiscated the coins.

'You're too young to handle so much money,' she said.

At twelve we had our ears pierced, during a special ceremony that was as important as baptism or marriage. Our initiation into the world of women was celebrated with the chanting of the *aamara* and the ululating of the concubines and slaves. Lalla Mina was afraid it would hurt too much and hid, making me do likewise. But the King grew angry. He found me and made me go first, to set an example to his sister, whose cowardice made him furious. Then the women came and congratulated us with effusive embraces and ululations, while the musicians banged their drums enthusiastically.

Whereas Muhammad V's Palace had been closed to the outside, Hassan II flung the doors wide open. Religious ceremonies were celebrated in the intimacy of his harem, but the King often threw public parties to which he invited high society, officers and foreign dignitaries on official visits.

We were always very excited at the prospect of meeting 'people from outside', strangers to the Palace, although we despised them so much that we didn't want to mix with them. We stayed together and formed a united front against intruders. When there was a performance, the King sat in the front row, his wife next to him, his mother behind him and the rest of us in serried ranks behind them.

During these parties and official visits, I often met heads of state and leading foreign figures. Nasser told my father that I had a lovely smile, the King of Jordan did a bit of trout fishing at Ifrane, and the Shah and the Shahbanu of Iran and Baudouin and Fabiola of Belgium came on official visits. At the risk of sounding presumptuous, I have to say they didn't make much of an impression on me. Despite their elevated rank, they were 'outsiders'.

Very occasionally we escaped from the Palace to visit Moulay Abdallah, the King's younger brother, who lived with his wife Lamia on an estate in the Agdal district. Tall, rugged and elegant, with black hair and velvet eyes like Rudolph Valentino, Moulay Abdallah set female hearts fluttering with his dashing looks and his kindness. His circle included film stars, and the international jet set. Every year, on his birthday, they all converged on his home.

But he was above all our confidant and friend. He knew how to listen to us, advise and comfort us with great humanity. For our entertainment he would bring in a rhythm 'n' blues band, invite a few friends over, and we would launch into a wild afternoon of dancing and fun. He took us motorbiking on the beach on a specially marked-out track, giving us a brief sense of freedom that was only relative as we were always watched by dozens of armed guards.

We would sometimes go and wake him up in the morning. He'd entertain us from his bed, and we'd chat about this and that. He gave me a lot of clothes from his wardrobe—suits, cashmere and silk sweaters and bespoke shirts, for my two uncles, Azzedine and Wahid, my mother's younger brothers. He also gave me a favourite pair of sunglasses as a token of his affection.

It was a great honour to wear clothes that had belonged to the sovereign and his family. The King gave his clothes to the men closest to him, his advisers and some of his ministers. On returning home, I always found it strange to see my father wearing shirts bearing the royal monogram.

THE KING AND I

Arguments frequently broke out between the concubines. There were countless factions, and all the women were quick to add fuel to the flames when a quarrel was in the air. One day I got into a row over something stupid with a concubine who was known for her spiteful tongue. I asked her furiously:

'Who do you think you are?'

'I know who I am,' she retorted haughtily. 'I am Sidi's concubine.'

'So what?' I retorted. '*I*'m his daughter.'

I felt very close to the King. I considered him as a second father. He was authoritarian and I respected him, but he was also accessible. When I kissed his hand as a sign of submission, I would immediately turn his palm over and press it to my lips to demonstrate my affection. In return, he pressed his hand to my mouth to show that he understood my gesture and that it was reciprocal.

Lalla Mina, the King and I had great fun together, especially during the early years of his reign, before the birth of his children. He sometimes spent entire evenings with us at the Villa Yasmina.

I would sit at the piano and play old songs which we'd all sing in unison. I had persuaded Lalla Mina to ask for a drum kit for her birthday. We had set it up in the playroom. I would bang on the big drums while the King danced with his sister.

I had wanted to learn ballet but the doctors were opposed to the idea. At the time Lalla Mina was only seven years old and they thought it might impede her development. Besides, the Princess had only one passion and that was horses. Her life revolved around them.

The King arranged for us to have riding lessons, which I hated because they were imposed on me. He wanted to make me an accomplished rider, like my father, and as he himself was. But each time I went near a horse, it was torture. I tried every trick in the book to avoid the torment of the riding school.

The day before, I would pretend to have a fever or diarrhoea, but the King wasn't fooled. So I would engineer a spectacular fall from my horse. I faked unconsciousness or screamed that I'd broken my arm or my leg. I'd be rushed to the Palace hospital, where the concubines would bring me sweets after the doctor had seen me.

The King heard about my ruses, but he was intransigent.

'She can kill herself on horseback, I don't care. But if she falls off, she must get back on again at once.'

He didn't understand how I could be so cowardly.

One Friday, we were told that we were going to the royal stables at Temara, around twenty kilometres from Rabat. We rode with Colonel Laforêt, a Frenchman who managed the stables, and a whole staff of officers. The women followed, wearing riding gear—

jodhpurs, boots and hard hats: they mounted like men, but they weren't as fast as our little group.

They took us to the riding school. All the King's horses waited in a magnificent line. At the end stood a ridiculously small donkey. I realized immediately that it was meant for me. Nothing could have made me happier. The King thought he would humiliate me by giving me such a ludicrous mount while the court paraded around on the splendid stallions.

'That's for you, scaredy-cat,' he said.

I found it hard to conceal my relief. But the day ended in disaster. I can't remember why, but I was locked in the stable cellar for a good two hours, which caused me untold terror.

We often used to go to the Fez spa, famous for its sulphur springs, an excellent cure for rheumatism and asthma. The King and his concubines would go there to take the waters.

One day, I was clowning around in the pool when the King walked past. I was wearing only a little pair of panties.

'Take them off,' he ordered severely.

Covering myself up to bathe meant that I was afraid of male eyes. My attitude was hurtful to His Majesty, the only man allowed into this female universe. It meant that I had something to be ashamed of.

But I was eleven years old and, King or not, I was very modest. I refused. My disobedience earned me a slap. He yanked my panties off himself. In tears, I stayed in the pool until nightfall for fear someone might see me naked.

We visited Casablanca less often. The King didn't like his palace there, nor did he like the town, which was a symbol, in his eyes, of riots and disturbances. Nor could he stand the humid climate, which irritated his chronic sinusitis. We would stay in his father's villa and bathe from the private beach. There, everyone was naked, including the King and all his wives. I eventually got used to taking my clothes off in his presence.

In the villa in Casablanca I had discovered a room where, as in all his royal palaces, there was a mountain of unopened presents, still in their wrapping. The King never had time to open them. I was dying to steal at least one, not so much to possess it, but out of curiosity. It was the afternoon and everyone was having a nap. During my attempted theft, I knocked over a few packages and they clattered onto the marble floor. It was my misfortune that the room where the King lay resting was nearby. He had a little cough that I would recognize among thousands.

I froze.

'Where is that devil?' he asked, wide awake.

He already knew the answer. The 'devil' could only be me.

I cast frantically about me for somewhere to hide and ended up squeezing inside the goods lift. But then there was no way out. By chance, he planted himself in front of it and asked the slaves, then his wives, to look everywhere for me. It was turning into a game.

Hidden in my cubbyhole, I was petrified; my legs had turned to jelly and he showed no sign of budging. His people came back empty-handed. Only then did it occur to him to look into my hiding place. He ordered me to come out, which I did, quaking. This time the escapade ended in laughter.

But the King could be horribly strict. At the age of eight, in Temara, I was given a special punishment called *falakha* for some stupid prank that Lalla Mina and I had played. Two fire slaves slung each of us across their shoulders, our heads and legs dangling on either side, while the king thrashed the soles of our bare feet with a whip.

When I reached the age of fifteen, I received my first real punishment. It was the day we brought home our school reports, and I put them on his table before joining the concubines who were making fun of me. They knew my marks weren't brilliant and that I was likely to get a beating. I pretended to laugh with them, but I didn't feel very proud of myself. My heart was thumping. But I tried to look bravely in the King's direction.

He held out his hands and the reports were brought to him. He leafed through Lalla Mina's, and then, in a heavy silence, he picked up mine and examined it closely for what seemed like an eternity. Then he looked up and asked for the fire slaves to be called in.

His words sent a shiver through the assembly. All eyes were turned to me, full of pity for the punishment I was about to receive. The

King motioned me to approach. He grabbed me by the ear, lectured me, and then signalled to the fire slaves. I was made to lie down in front of him, on the carpet. Three men held me by the wrists and three by the ankles. The chief slave grabbed his whip and awaited the King's orders. It was up to His Majesty to decide on the number of strokes.

I was lucky in my misfortune. The King ordered only thirty strokes, but he would not leave it to anybody else to carry out the punishment. Someone brought him a little stool to sit on, to bring him down to my level. You could hear a pin drop in the room. Everybody held their breath, not daring to speak or move. The King had even forbidden Latifa, Oum Sidi and Lalla Bahia to intervene on my behalf.

Amid total silence, he began to beat me. One, two, then three strokes. I let out a little cry, then another equally feeble whimper. The third stroke intrigued him: he had struck me so hard I should have screamed. He stopped, leaned towards me and pressed his hands on my buttocks. He felt a triple layer of fabric acting as padding. Knowing that I wouldn't be spared the whip this time, I had taken precautions and protected my bottom with nappies and woollen jumpers. I was wearing a full skirt that hid all these layers.

The King gave a cry of rage. In the room everyone else began to laugh and in the end he joined in the general mirth. Then I threw myself at his feet:

'Sidi, I promise I won't do it again.'

At the Palace, everyone remarked on my audacity in defying the King. The entire court, from the concubines to the slaves, had heard what had happened.

The following week, my report was just as bad. Worse, even, if that was possible. The King said nothing at the time, but a little later he asked me to accompany him. He had to go outside the Palace. There was nothing unusual in his request; we often used to follow him on his errands, so I wasn't on my guard. We were driven to the Alleé des Princesses, to the house where he had lived before ascending the throne.

I loved that villa. I felt at home there, especially as we had to drive past my parents' house to reach it. That put me in a good mood. I was so unprepared that I didn't immediately realize why the King ordered me to get undressed.

He made me go into a small room where slaves dressed me in a thin jellabah. I received a cruel whipping that made me cry with pain for weeks. I still have the scars on my buttocks. My parents would never have treated me like that. I missed them bitterly.

Another time my report was so bad that the Head of Protocol took pity on me and promised to talk to the King on my behalf. He threw himself at the King's feet on the way to the golf course and asked him not to punish me.

The King looked at him frostily.

'Who do you think you are, daring to intervene on her behalf?'

The poor Head of Protocol was convulsed with shame. He was crushed, lower than a worm. He was whipped in my place.

Nobody escaped the royal punishment when the King thought they deserved it. With us, it was his way of acting as a father. In fact he took such a paternal interest in Lalla Mina and me that he was involved in every detail of our upbringing. When he saw that we had grown into two pretty young ladies of fifteen, he decided to dress us to suit his taste, which wasn't bad but, alas, a bit too proper for our liking. He had a dressmaker come to the Palace and ordered an entire wardrobe from her, complete with stockings, knickers and bras. He even attended the fittings and decided on the length of the skirts.

I begged him to shorten my skirts, but he was adamant. The hemline had to reach the knee. So I chose fine woollen fabrics which allowed me to hitch up the waist and secure it under a little belt the minute I was outside the Palace gates. At last I could run around as I pleased, without hindrance. When I gallivanted along the corridors like that, everyone watched me, laughing at my daring. It was considered unseemly to bare one's ankles.

But this was the Sixties, mini-skirts were in fashion and, despite our limited contacts with the outside world, we were aware of these crucial sartorial details thanks to the few newspapers and French magazines I flicked through when I managed to elude the governess's watchful eye: *Salut les copains*, *Jours de France*, *Point de vue* and *Paris-Match*. Latifa and the concubines dressed in the latest Western fashions whenever they had the opportunity. I delighted in everything they wore.

One day, when I was running down one of the longest corridors, my skirt hitched halfway up my thighs, I couldn't resist the temptation to pause and admire myself in a big mirror hanging on the wall. Then I saw the King coming towards me.

In a panic, I began tugging at the fabric. He came over, undid the belt and pulled down my skirt:

'You can even make it into a kaftan if you want,' he said.

Two days later, our dear dressmaker arrived. We were in the middle of dinner. The King called me and ordered me to undress, which I did with great reluctance. She asked me to try on some suits that he had ordered. The first one was a tailored woollen suit with a Fifties-style straight, very tight skirt.

The King came over, took the pins from the dressmaker's hands and felt the fabric, commenting on how thick it was. It was impossible to hike it up as I'd done with the woollen dresses. He signalled to me to walk up and down the room and watched me for a long time. Then he ordered a pair of very high-heeled shoes to go with the suit.

A concubine broke in saying that I was already very tall. Men wouldn't be interested in me if I was a head taller than them. He dismissed her views with a wave.

'High heels will exercise your knees,' he explained. 'They'll give you shapely thighs and pretty calves, like a woman.'

A LONELY ADOLESCENCE

Rieffel hated men.

'They're monsters,' she would say, 'they are the root of all women's misery. You must avoid them like the plague, or cholera.'

She deluged us with decrees: never find yourself in a corridor with a man, never be familiar with male members of staff or any other individual of the opposite sex. In the car, we weren't allowed to turn round and stare, and I was often slapped to punish my curiosity.

When we had an opportunity to go into the centre of town, she wouldn't allow us out of the car.

These precautions to protect us from the devil were virtually useless. Men were not allowed into the Palace, except for my father, who came only on certain occasions, Moulay Ahmed Alaoui, the King's cousin, and a dozen or so old bores hand-picked for their extensive culture, intelligence, sharp wit and devoutness.

At the table, they conducted subtle arguments over the King's policies or launched into battles of wits citing the great Arab poets, like at the court of the Sultan Haroun al Rashid. Apart from the slaves and servants, who didn't count, they were the only specimens of the opposite sex we encountered. Except the King, of course.

But it was a man, a chief mullah, who gave us sex education lessons through the Koran. He taught us that women exist purely for seduction and submission, that their bodies serve first and foremost to satisfy men's desires. He gave us a crude outline of sexual relations, drawing the vagina and penis with exaggerated precision on the blackboard. For girls of our age, this was deeply shocking. We had been brought up in extreme modesty and to hear a man, a religious leader to boot, talking to us about sex, especially in those terms, just added to our confusion.

Nor could we rely on Rieffel to soften the mullah's words. In her view, the whole subject was taboo. We weren't allowed to mention it, we had to pretend 'it' didn't exist. I remember my first period, when I was twelve, as a difficult time, not so much for the physical discomfort as for the terrible feeling of shame and isolation. Our nannies were in charge of teaching us hygiene—how to wear the protective sanitary towels made of cloth, how to wash them, and how to wash ourselves too. These women had complete power over us. Even in the presence of a dozen people, they would take us into a corner and make us take down our knickers, and if they were soiled we were violently punished. Mine inserted a key in my vagina and twisted it until I screamed. Or she would pinch me in the most sensitive places, like the inside thigh.

I needed a mother or an older sister who would listen to me, who could explain the changes taking place in my body, reassure me and tell me about the joys of becoming a woman, but all I got at that crucial point of a young girl's life was cruelty and humiliation. The concubines helped me a bit, but their support was ambivalent. At first, they celebrated my entry into their clique. Now I could understand their conversations, feel involved. They would no longer stop talking in my hearing or ask me to leave when they had secrets to confide.

But two years later, their attitude changed. I had become a young woman of marriageable age, a potential rival to the younger ones. Our relations changed imperceptibly. They scrutinized my body when I was in a swimsuit, in the summer, at the palace in Skhirat, when I dressed Western-style or wore make-up. They didn't say anything specific to me, but made remarks, goading me. I had become a threat; the King might choose me for a wife.

What right had I to wish for a better fate than theirs? I don't think the idea occurred to the King, but their jealousy was persistent.

I was a tormented soul. Outwardly, I was smiling, happy, funny and mischievous, but all it took was a word, or a whiff of perfume that reminded me of my mother, and I would clam up. Each day, the governess made me more aware that I was different from Princess Lalla Mina. I wasn't allowed to dress like her, or to wear my hair long because hers was frizzy.

My mother brought me back the latest fashions from Paris and London, and had them sent to the Villa Yasmina. The governess would allow me to wear them for one day. The next day she'd come and fetch them, call in a dressmaker who would copy some models for the Princess, and the suitcases would vanish.

Over the years, my unhappiness turned into a feeling of rebellion that was difficult to articulate. The Princess and I were fond of each other. At the Palace I was shown a great deal of affection. But when you are adopted, you are cut off from your past, from your roots; people do all they can to persuade you that you no longer have a family of your own. You are just one among many. The harem was full of anonymous women. But I had a father, a mother and a family that I would see again one day.

At night, in bed, I dreamed of freedom. I went over images from my favourite films and tried to conjure up the world. I made up stories which I forced my room-mates to listen to in the dark. If I later found it easier to adjust to prison than my brothers and sisters, it is because I was used to being shut up. I had always been able to live in a confined space, occupy my time and fall back on my own resources.

But I missed my mother terribly; I suffered so much from loneliness that twice I tried to commit suicide. The first time I was ten. I decided to put an end to my life in the big sunflower field behind the garden of the Villa Yasmina. I pricked the end of my thumb with a sharpened bamboo stick to make the blood spurt out, then I mixed sand in the cut to cause an infection and waited, my eyes closed and my heart racing. Death was slow in coming, so I got up after a few minutes.

Every day I rubbed the wound with earth, hoping that it would get worse and that I would be sent to the Palace hospital, which would bring my mother running to my bedside. And that is what happened. So I did benefit a little from this bungled suicide.

The second time I was twelve, and I wanted to throw myself from the sixth floor of the villa at Ifrane. But it was frighteningly high and I was put off by the fear of hurting myself. These attempts should not be dismissed as harmless pranks. I felt uneasy at the Palace and was frequently unhappy. Obsessed with the idea of putting an end to it all, I lacked only the courage. Or rather, I already had a furious determination to survive.

I was permanently torn between East and West. At my parents' house and at the Villa Yasmina we spoke French, but at the Palace Arabic was the rule. We spoke a court dialect that was old-fashioned and highly refined, with very specific expressions, intonations and gestures. I have never managed to rid myself of it; later my family would tease me about it and it never failed to inspire respect in my fellow Moroccans. Wherever I go in Morocco, I am always asked if I belong to *Dar-el-Mahzran*—the house of power.

At the villa, our governess taught us table manners and how to behave in company, how to serve, entertain, cook, curtsey and become young ladies fit for European high society.

At the Palace, they were intent on making us women as soon as we reached puberty. Etiquette was dinned into us; we were taught not to make any gaffes, and how to conduct ourselves at court and in the harem, how to wear Moroccan dress, to be submissive and to prostrate ourselves. The emphasis was on obedience and on the most superficial aspects of femininity. We were nothing compared with our elders, and as women we were less than nothing. I was taught when to speak and when to hold my tongue. I learned to read between the lines and to make caution a rule and a secret weapon.

At the beginning of adolescence, when my character was not yet fully formed, I could have been attracted by the court, the beautiful clothes, the jewels and the flamboyant concubines whose sole concern was to pamper their bodies and please their lord and master. But those moments of envy were brief. I knew that I wasn't made that way and never would be. I felt oppressed. The older I grew, the more I felt like a prisoner. I belonged body and soul to the Palace and I was suffocating.

When we travelled by road, followed by our escort, I tried to make the most of that moment of freedom. I would look inside the cars we passed, at a couple with children or a young man on a moped. I found myself envying their freedom. And then another set of gates would open and close behind us and I was once again inside, a woman of the 'indoors'.

It was sometimes hard for me to draw the boundary between my two worlds, my two upbringings. I knew that one day soon I would have to choose. I came from an ordinary family with principles and values that were different from those of the Palace. But my real life was subject to the power of an absolute monarch who ruled by divine right. I lived in the harem, surrounded by slaves, in a feminine world ruled by that one man. Everything that went on at the Palace eventually seemed normal to me, whereas in fact court life, with its excesses, opulence and pomp, its omnipotence and all-pervasive fear, was truly outside the norms.

And yet at the Palace I was protected. This little community living in the past preserved me from the dangers of the wider world. But, deep down inside, I was a European. I was often shocked by what went on within the Palace walls, by the cruelty and severity of the sentences and punishments.

Concubines were beaten, repudiated, banished, and disappeared for ever in the depths of the prison-palaces, like the one at Meknès. They were stripped of all their wealth and lived there like wraiths.

Hajar and Qamar, two Turkish concubines who had belonged to the Sultan Yussef ben-Yussef, Muhammad V's father, had been shut up there on the death of their master. Prince Moulay Abdallah took pity on them and had them brought to live in his house in Rabat, so they could have a peaceful old age. When I met these two little elderly ladies with auburn hair, white skin and blue eyes, who spoke a strange Arabic dialect, I realized just how feudal this life was, and that these practices were barbaric. I felt that I had stumbled across an unknown underground world, which was not mine but which existed in the shadows. I would try to find out the reasons for punishments, and what had happened to the guilty.

I strained my ears, but the wind carried only sighs and whispers.

LEAVING THE PALACE

My mother, who could no longer bear my father's repeated infidelities, had threatened to leave him numerous times. The opportunity presented itself in the shape of a young officer from the north, with whom she fell head over heels in love.

She left home, made my father give her custody of Maria and Soukaina, respectively aged two and one, and sent Raouf and Myriam off to a select boarding school in Gstaad, Switzerland. She rented a little villa in Agdal, the student district of Rabat, opened a ready-to-wear boutique, which soon became a must for the smart set, and changed her life completely. She now associated with intellectuals and artists.

My mother didn't care about what people would say. She was happy, in love, and more beautiful than ever. She needed to go through this stage. She had married too young and had missed out on her teens. She was reliving them with her dashing officer.

The King arranged for my father to remarry and told me about it himself. I knew only that my parents had got divorced, but I didn't know why. I was eleven years old but nobody explained anything to me, as if I were still incapable of understanding. The court merely gave me sympathetic looks.

The wedding was celebrated in great style, at the palace in Marrakesh. I resented the King for arranging it, and for having removed my mother from the court. Overnight she had been forgotten; the doors had closed on Fatima Chenna, the divorcee. In society circles, they were all vying with each other to invite the new Madame Oufkir, whose name was also Fatima, organizing endless parties in her honour. I nicknamed her 'the twit', she was so stupid.

I was traumatized by this betrayal. It taught me a lot about human nature. My mother had been popular, adored, and yet she was brushed aside like a troublesome insect. What had happened to her could happen to me one day . . .

After the wedding, my father wanted to see me. He had me come to the house, where I didn't recognize anything any more. I refused to kiss him and told him I hated him. He didn't have the right to destroy a family. This made him uncomfortable, and he tried to justify himself. I realized that I had hurt him and took advantage of it to be even more brutal.

'I still love your mother,' he confided in a broken voice.

But I didn't understand anything of the intricacies of adult affairs. How could he love one woman and marry another? And who could I turn to for an explanation? Mimi and Raouf were in the Swiss mountains, my little sisters were too young, and Lalla Mina wouldn't have understood. I felt lost, lonelier than ever. I felt I was somehow betraying my mother.

My father was telling the truth. His feelings towards my mother hadn't changed; he couldn't bear to lose her. He watched her, threatened her and spent whole nights in the car, opposite her house. The young officer was sent to the remotest parts of the country and was chosen for the most dangerous missions. He was ordered to resign, but he refused.

The chief-of-staff told him he was crazy to have stolen the wife of the most powerful man in the kingdom.

'Now she's mine,' he replied arrogantly.

On the occasion of an official visit by the King to the south of the country, my father asked my mother to help him organize a reception in his native village. That was how they got back together again.

My father obtained a divorce and they remarried. My mother was very fond of him deep down. She often used to tell me that my father had made her what she was. She truly loved him, and still does today. Never, even during our bleakest moments, did I hear her complain about the fate we had to endure because of him.

My mother was pregnant again. Throughout her pregnancy, my father kept saying:

'The best present you could give me would be a son who looks like me.'

The child born from their reconciliation came into the world on 27 February 1969, the day of the big earthquake. The King named him Abdellatif, 'the spared'. The earthquake was exceptionally violent but few people were killed. My father didn't have a chance to get to know his son, who was only three when he died.

Now an adult, Abdellatif is the spitting image of our father.

My parents had already been back together again for some time, but their story remained the main topic of conversation at court. The concubines loved a nice meaty scandal they could get their teeth into. Throughout the Palace people whispered, murmured and gossiped. As far as Rieffel was concerned, my mother was a fallen woman, a whore.

One day, when the whole court was at the Palace hospital, waiting for news of Oum Sidi who was having an operation on her gall bladder, I overheard the governess maligning my mother to one of the court ladies. I began to shriek at them. The King heard me from the other end of the corridor and rushed over. He shot me a look telling me to be quiet, out of respect for his mother, but I carried on shouting.

My tantrum had an effect on him. He held me by the back of the neck, to calm me down, and asked me to explain. Sobbing, I replied that I wanted to go home.

'I've got a family,' I said. 'I'm heartbroken that I don't see them.'

I added that Lalla Mina was an ungrateful wretch, and I knew it, even though I'd always done my utmost to please her.

To my amazement, the King agreed.

'I'm not saying you're wrong,' he replied. 'The Alaouites are known for their ingratitude.'

I realized that my outspokenness had wounded his pride. He couldn't ask me to stay any longer. That evening, I was back home.

I had tried to run away before this. I had discovered a little door near the outbuildings, and in the daytime, far from prying eyes, I had managed to burrow under the wire fencing. One evening I finally managed to get through to the other side. But I was overwhelmed by my freedom; I wasn't ready for it yet. I didn't know where to go. Fear of an unknown world made me retrace my steps. The next day I wrote a desperate letter to my father, telling him I was going to run away. Over the phone, he reasoned with me and swore he would do everything within his power to bring me back home.

There were other reasons why I wanted to leave. The King wanted to marry me to a general's son whom I didn't like. If I stayed any longer, I would lose my chance. I would never be able to live the life I so yearned for, embark on lengthy studies, travel, become an actress or a film director.

In my final weeks at the Palace, I spent my time talking to the concubines and trying to open their eyes to their sad fate. My words, far from making them think, made them laugh until they cried. Yet these women were clear-sighted: they knew exactly what their life entailed, what they had lost and what they had gained in exchange.

During the first six months that followed my homecoming, I slept at home at night and continued to live at the Palace and study at the lycée by day. My position was delicate. I was sad at the idea of having rejected the concubines' life, and I could see they resented it, especially the older ones. They had told me time and time again that I must never leave or abandon Lalla Mina. I felt uncomfortable, guilty. But relieved. And happy.

Once the school year ended, I wanted to keep away from the Palace. The Department of Protocol was always calling to invite me but I refused each time. Nevertheless my father made me go, out of respect and courtesy.

I burst into tears, terrified at the thought that they might make me go back.

3

THE OUFKIR HOUSE

1969–1972

MY HOMECOMING

I returned home at nightfall. I remember the darkness and the feeling of intense happiness that surged through me. I was going to make up for lost time, regain my childhood. My place was here, with my family, in these peaceful surroundings that would now be mine.

Mother was in London, my father still at the ministry, and the children with their governesses. I was greeted by unfamiliar household staff, whose excessive deference embarrassed me.

I wandered around the house, stroked the walls and ran my hands over the furniture. I lingered in front of the pictures on the wall, the family photos from which I was missing. They charted the passing of the years: my brothers and sisters as toddlers, my father in full dress uniform, my mother in elegant outfits that I'd never seen her wear.

I opened the cupboards in her room and her perfume made me reel. I rediscovered the habits of my early childhood, when I used to bury my face in her jacket and immerse myself in her smell. In the living room, I dared to sit in my father's place, on his favourite settee. I curled up on the cushion where he was in the habit of sitting. Stroking his lighter, I cried tears of joy mingled with sadness.

I had missed home throughout my life at the Palace. But it was only on returning that I realized just how desperately.

Our house was in the Allée des Princesses, like the previous one. My father had bought the land with his pension from the French army and had taken out a loan to build the villa. It was huge, comfortable and, above all, welcoming. From the gate a drive led to the house whose external walls were a red ochre colour, like those of the villas of Marrakesh. On one side of the drive was a sloping lawn surrounded by a cypress hedge to protect our privacy. On the other, my mother had created a Japanese garden with loose stones and dwarf trees. We had a swimming pool, a tennis court, a cinema, a sauna and a garage with about ten cars.

However, there was nothing pretentious or flashy about it. My parents appreciated the comfort that money brings, but hated ostentation. My mother, whose refinement was inborn, had decorated all the rooms tastefully but simply.

Everyone who came to our house exaggerated when they described it. It was said to be one of the most beautiful residences in Rabat. That wasn't true. The living room, where we congregated most often, was quite small, with a low round table in the centre, in the traditional Moroccan style. We ate lunch and dinner there and watched television. My bedroom on the first floor, decorated in bijou English style, was ready for my homecoming.

Later, despite my father's initial opposition, I was allowed to live separately from the main house, in a studio apartment between the swimming pool and the sauna. The flat was tiny and contained only a built-in bed, two bookshelves and a bathroom, but because it was away from the house I felt a little more independent.

It took me a long time to become part of this unknown family. During the first few months I was an observer, studying each individual's tempo. My brother Abdellatif was a newborn baby. He took up all my time when I came home from school. I found it hard to rebuild a relationship with my brother Raouf and my three sisters, to create a complicity we had never had. It was easier with my mother. We immediately slipped back into our old ways. Being apart had not damaged our strong bond.

There was a pleasant atmosphere in my home. It was a real home, full of life and laughter. But since my father had become a leading figure in the kingdom—Hassan II had made him Minister of the Interior in 1964—the atmosphere had become less warm. Our family privacy suffered.

At home, the flatterers and hangers-on were even more deferential towards my father than they were at the Palace. The men waited humbly to see my father. The women came in the hope of copying my mother's latest outfits. The smart set considered her the arbiter of style. We lived in full view of a court that governed our lives and our time.

Sometimes we had the chance to eat lunch together, as a family. But most of the time the courtiers settled down and made themselves at home in the little sitting room where my father held meetings with the ministers and officers. When their wives arrived, they would all go up to the first floor, to the big drawing room, to have a drink and chat. The adults dined late, and it wasn't unusual to have thirty or so guests at the table.

At home, we weren't so much aware of the grandeur as of my father's power. I didn't know that side of him so well. At the Palace, I had vaguely learned that he was someone important; the Queen Mother was particularly fond of him, the courtiers revered him and the King spent a lot of time with him.

On my return home, I discovered that people were also afraid of him, that they criticized him, that he was seen as a cruel man. My friends saw him as public enemy number one. The mere mention of his name sent a chill down their spines.

At the Lycée Lalla Aicha where my parents had chosen to send me after I left the lycée at the Palace, the girls respected and envied me, but they whispered behind my back and pointed at me. One student called me a murderer's daughter, because of the Ben Barka affair, about which I still knew nothing. I didn't know what to say back to them. With the naivety of my age, it wasn't my father I condemned during our political arguments, but the Government and Repression, with a capital G and a capital R.

I adored my father. I felt that people didn't see his sensitivity, generosity and kindness. He was a calm, discreet man, seemingly more restrained than my mother, who didn't mince her words. In actual fact, he was much more acerbic and scathing than she was. His instinct was very sound and he relied on no-one but himself, at the risk of making mistakes or upsetting others, for tact wasn't his strong point.

Naturally wary, he could sometimes be very quick-tempered, despite his normal composure. He was quite temperamental. Sometimes, when he was cheerful and relaxed, he would display a subtle sense of humour and have everybody in stitches. At other times he would sink into a profound silence that nobody could coax him out of. Distant and unapproachable, at those times he resembled a sphinx.

His tastes were simple, but he had a very generous soul. Even when all he had to live on was his captain's pay, he was capable of blowing it all in one evening by taking my mother to a restaurant. He was handsome, proud and charismatic. When he walked into a room, he eclipsed everyone else. Modest to the point of prudery, he never kissed Mother in our presence. He would put his arm around her affectionately or fondly squeeze her hand.

My parents had a loving, respectful relationship. They never raised their voices or argued, whatever their quarrels or their problems. They admired each other enormously. And yet they were very different.

My mother was an artist, a bohemian, a spendthrift, generous and home-loving. She was a happy person, who loved life, loved a party and would sing the entire repertoire of classical oriental music at the top of her voice. She had a wonderful voice. She loved the movies, and fast cars that she drove herself, screeching through the streets of Rabat at top speed. She was self-taught, read copiously and was interested in everything.

Her uncompromising nature earned her enemies. She was outspoken, direct, impatient and temperamental; she lacked flexibility. Unlike the flatterers who surrounded her, or who lived at the Palace where she was a frequent visitor, she was neither calculating nor manipulative; she didn't play games. She was forthright, almost too much so. She was maternal towards us, and never showed a preference for any one of her children, even though I can flatter myself that I had a special bond with her. She spent more time with us than my father, despite her busy schedule.

My father did remain accessible, however, on condition that we made the effort to approach him. He had a unique relationship with each of his six children.

Myriam, who was fourteen at the time, was often ill. She suffered from epilepsy. My parents had consulted doctors all over the world, but in vain. Her fits were violent and dramatic. Was it this ailment that made my father distant towards her? I remember one occasion when she'd altered the marks in her school report. My mother noticed and asked my father to punish her. But he was incapable of raising his hand to us. He asked Mimi to go into the drawing room with him. He would pretend to beat her and she was to cry out at regular intervals to convince my mother he was really chastising her.

Eleven-year-old Raouf was the eldest son, the heir. He was a young god, horribly pampered by all the women in the house and universally adored. The guards clicked their heels in his presence. He hero-worshipped my father.

And my father adored him, but their relationship was difficult. As a teenager, Raouf was very good-looking, with an almost feminine beauty, long hair, an olive complexion and high cheekbones. My father was doubly strict, almost aggressive towards him, he was so terrified of his heir becoming a homosexual.

This fear was ill founded. My brother was already popular with girls, and he was just as interested in them. After the coup d'état at the Skhirat palace in 1971, when several hundred courtiers, officers and guests were massacred during the King's birthday celebrations by a band of mutinous NCOs, Raouf wouldn't let my father out of his sight. He had wangled his way into being part of the escort. As he had learned to drive at thirteen, he often took the chauffeur's place and went out in the evening with my father. He would sit and wait patiently until his meetings were over, sometimes late into the night.

Maria and Soukaina, respectively aged seven and six, had very different characters. The lively and independent Maria charmed my father, but she was difficult to pin down. Even in those days she didn't express her feelings. Soukaina, on the other hand, was sweet and affectionate. She would snuggle up to my father, sucking her thumb, or would sing him songs in a comical voice that made him laugh until tears ran down his face.

She spent her time lying flat on the floor on her stomach, doodling on paper. My father was convinced she would become a painter or a writer.

As for Abdellatif, still in nappies, he was the apple of everyone's eye. My father's wish had been fulfilled. His baby son looked like him.

Abdellatif had nearly died as an infant, when he came near to being devoured by a lion cub given to my father as a present and which he had brought home. The animal had been romping freely on the lawn; first it attacked two Yorkshire terriers before going for the baby who was playing nearby. It nudged him like a ball while the nannies looked on helplessly, then held him in its paws and bared its fangs as soon as anyone tried to approach. We had to call my father so he could see the danger for himself. The cub eventually let go of its prey and was banished to play with its fellow cubs in the zoo.

MY FATHER AND ME

We were friends, allies. I charmed and provoked him, but never overstepped certain boundaries. I was careful, however, not to show him fear or servile deference; I was far too much of a rebel.

In the mornings, he would call me to adjust his tie or button up his collar. I was proud of this ritual, and so was he. One day I was having trouble doing up his shirt and I teased him, saying he'd developed a double chin. He was very vain, and immediately took action: a game of tennis at the house with his friend, General Driss Ben Omar, a sauna and a few light dietary restrictions. Unfortunately, these excellent resolutions didn't last long.

When he was going on a trip, he would ask me to pack his suitcase. He would then boast about it to his ministers. He'd say to me with a little smile:

'Dress me like one of your rock stars. I want to be "with it".'

At around one o'clock, when he arrived home from the ministry or the staff headquarters, he would go into the big drawing room, settle down on his sofa, always in the same place, ask for a beer and drink it slowly. I'd be finishing lunch and would go up to see him, often with Soukaina who adored him. I looked after him, served him and stayed with him until it was time to leave for school again. I liked to stroke the scar on his right hand, the result of a car accident.

He had installed a grand piano in the big drawing room, and he would ask me to play when we had guests. He was very proud of my musical accomplishments. I complied a little reluctantly: I didn't like this role of the young lady of the house.

A few weeks after my return, I accompanied my parents on an official visit to Spain, for the Seville Fair. It was an opportunity to get close to them, to become their daughter again, and even their only child, as my brothers and sisters had stayed behind in Rabat. I experienced my first real moment of family happiness on this trip. Together we attended all the parties given by the Spanish aristocracy, and danced wild flamencos till dawn.

I discovered a cheerful, jovial father, a night owl who adored love songs and pretty Gypsy women. An authoritarian father too. One evening he forbade me to go out dressed in a see-through Indian top that I was wearing without a bra, as was the fashion at the time. He was annoyed by such immodesty.

Our close relationship was not without its ups and downs. I was sixteen and a born rebel, resistant to all forms of authority. I had been kept in check for too many long years. Later, I fought another battle to be allowed to wear mini-skirts. I refused to be chauffeur-driven to and from school. I wanted to live a normal life, which wasn't easy when you were General Oufkir's daughter.

I couldn't wait for my eighteenth birthday when I'd be able to take my driving test. My bodyguard, whose driving was somewhat erratic, had taught me the rudiments. But I had no notion of the highway code. I obtained my driving licence thanks to my police escort who asked the examiner to give it to me.

Every day I met up with a group of friends, much to my father's disapproval. He thought that some of them, like Sabah, my closest ally, were too forward. Véronique and Claudine were in my class at the Lycée Lalla Aicha. Véronique's parents, ardent Trotskyists, were members of the extremist left-wing opposition party led by Abraham Serfaty. (He was imprisoned in 1972 and not released until 1991.) They lived hippie-style in a house in Rabat, not far from ours, with a neglected garden overrun by dogs—Alsatians, Dobermanns and bulldogs. The children were left to their own devices. It was the opposite of my life, but that did not get in the way of our budding friendship.

Véronique often used to invite me to lunch, despite her parents' misgivings about me. They did not hesitate to goad me and make allusions about my father. In the end I told them that I could not defend him politically, but that he was my father and I would not stand by and hear him insulted.

My male friends included Ouezzine Aherdane, son of a Berber party leader who had several times been a minister under Muhammad V and Hassan II; Maurice Serfaty, the son of Abraham Serfaty; Driss Bahnini, the son of the former prime minister; another who was the son of a businessman and many more besides. Ouezzine sported a Bob Dylan look, with long hair and floral shirts. He drove a souped-up VW Beetle which he repainted when he felt like it: on Monday it was lime green, on Tuesday candy pink. Then he moved on to a convertible Mustang.

I would gladly have swapped my chauffeur-driven limousines for his old bangers. One afternoon when we were playing truant, we were all in Ouezzine's car, laughing and clowning around. At the traffic lights a car drew up alongside. Inside was my father, glaring at us. Petrified, the exuberant gang slid to the floor. Ouezzine, who was far too proud to show he was afraid, pulled away looking straight ahead.

I was a frequent guest at Maurice Serfaty's home where I met the activists visiting his father. Even though I was my father's daughter, under surveillance like him but for different reasons, Abraham Serfaty always showed me great trust because I was his son's friend. He had the intelligence not to mix up his children with politics. I was perfectly aware of his activities but it would never have occurred to me to talk to my father about them. And for his part, he would never have banned me from his house.

Above all, my father worried about all the boys surrounding me. He was influenced by his entourage of hypocritical flatterers, who pretended to be concerned about my virginity and my honour. I couldn't care less. Defying them amused me more than anything. Of course, I didn't want to let my father down, but that didn't stop me from sneaking out almost every night to indulge my love of music and dancing.

I was very organized. I would put in a token appearance until ten o'clock, and answer questions about my schoolwork like a model daughter. When dinner was announced, I'd stand up, kiss my parents, say good night to the guests and excuse myself, saying I had to revise for a test the next day. Once in my room, I'd slip into a mini-skirt or shorts and doll myself up to the nines. After stuffing a bolster topped by a wig between the sheets, I'd sneak out.

It wasn't easy: our lives were stifling. We were under constant surveillance. There was no question of going out without an escort. There were guards all over the place, and among them several informers. The switchboard operators who worked at the house in shifts were also informers. But one of them had agreed to help me sneak out.

My mother's two younger brothers, Azzedine and Wahid, who were aged twenty and seventeen, would be waiting for me in their car. We drove off to meet our friends in the fashionable nightclubs. Azzedine kept a jealous eye on me and wouldn't allow anyone near me.

I danced till dawn and in the morning I woke up at seven to go to school. But I made it a point of honour to pass my exams. One evening, while I was getting ready, I heard the two wooden window frames open softly. In the dark, I could make out my father. Somebody had informed on me. That evening I stayed quietly in bed. He never breathed a word to me of what he knew.

We spent the summer at the beach, near Rabat. My parents owned two chalets there, much simpler than the ones the bourgeoisie built which often looked like mini-palaces. My parents' chalets were real beach houses. They lived in one and let us have the other. They wanted me to stay with them but I refused, pretending I had to revise for my exams. In fact I wanted to carry on sneaking out at night, which once again turned out to be fraught with complications. There were jeeps and police all over the place, and a round-the-clock army patrol.

I often woke up at midday. One day, after lunch, to which I had turned up still puffy-eyed, my father, who pretended to believe that my exhaustion was the result of sitting up all night studying, suggested I go out with him for a drive. I so rarely had the opportunity to be alone with him that I happily agreed.

He drove for a while in silence, then he asked me if I had heard of a nightclub called La Cage. I denied it vehemently, feeling a little ashamed. That was where I danced till dawn. He pulled up opposite the place.

'You don't recognize it?'

I pretended not to understand, and he didn't press the matter.

Another day, he announced in front of everybody that someone had seen me in a club in Casablanca. Luckily it wasn't true, and I was able to protest my innocence in good faith.

'One evening I'm seen in Casablanca, and the next it'll be at La Cage.'

'I believe you about Casablanca, but I'm not so sure about La Cage.'

The first time he took me to London, he caught me smoking in the toilets of the Playboy Club. He waited until I came out and declared that I could smoke in his company rather than hiding. A little later, he had a discussion in front of me with General Ben Omar, a strict man who brought up his children to fear him. My father repeated that he didn't like secretiveness. He'd rather see me smoking than listen to me lying to him, a statement which shocked the good general.

My father had terrible table manners and chewed his food noisily. Nobody in his entourage dared say anything to him about it, and it didn't bother my mother. He also hated fussy food. Like me, he only liked eggs, preferably fried. On an official visit to Agadir, he dropped in to see one of his best friends, Henry Friedman who owned the

Casbah d'Agadir, a sort of forerunner of the Club Med. It is still there today.

Of all my father's friends, Henry was the only one who was able to tell him a few home truths. A Jew from Eastern Europe with red hair and blue eyes and a croaking, broken voice, he was a six-foot colossus who weighed twenty stone. There was always a cigar screwed into his mouth. A concentration camp survivor, he was full of the joys of life, but also had an authoritarian side. He loved eating. Starvation and the horrors of the camps had given him a profound respect for food, and he was an excellent cook. On this occasion he had prepared a table full of appetizing dishes for my father.

My father inspected the spread.

'Look, I'm sorry, Henry,' he finally said, 'but I don't like all that. I want two fried eggs.'

Henry lost his temper and shouted at my father, who remained very calm. The servants quaked at the sight of General Oufkir being given a dressing down, but Henry, red as a beetroot, just continued. The angrier Henry became, the more my father's little smile grew. He was delighted to have provoked him.

At home, I couldn't bear sitting down to meals with him. My strict German-style upbringing made it hard for me to stand the slightest breach of good manners. When I ate with the children, I couldn't help reprimanding them. They were obviously well brought up, but not refined enough for my liking. I taught them how to fillet a sole and to chew slowly. I couldn't get used to their manners and they made fun of mine, instilled by Rieffel, the governess, and honed by the unparalleled sophistication of Palace life. I have never been able to shake them off.

During a dinner with some of my father's closest officers, I was soon exasperated by his noisy chewing. I stared at him. He looked up and stared back. We had understood each other without a word. Then he began to chew even more noisily, defying me. I imitated him and said:

'We can't hear a thing around here, you're making so much noise.'

All the officers laid down their knives and forks. They disapproved of me; I was rude, wild and disrespectful. But he said nothing.

Another time he had decided to stop smoking. He arrived from staff headquarters, his pockets full of chewing gum. He knew that I hated the sound of someone chewing. He opened the packet, stuffed all the chewing gum in his mouth and looked me in the eye. I sustained his gaze.

On another occasion he was in the sitting room with some ministers, talking politics. I went into the next room and put some music on loudly. He asked me to turn down the volume. I obeyed, and then a few minutes later I turned it up again. Those were the sort of little games we played all the time.

At the end of the year, my marks weren't good enough for me to go up to the next class. My nocturnal escapades had taken their toll. I decided to opt for the humanities baccalaureate and asked my parents to send me to boarding school. That way I thought I'd have more freedom.

In September they enrolled Raouf, Myriam and me at the Lycée Paul Valéry in Meknès. I hadn't shed my habit of sneaking out at night, and I did so more often than I should have, which frequently landed me in hot water. Once I even received a good clout when, instead of going back to school in the morning, I played hookey with Sabah and spent a whole day in Rabat.

A SPOILED TEENAGER

I dreamed of a normal life but I had no idea what that meant. My world was so easy. I just had to snap my fingers and anything I wanted was mine without any effort on my part. Travel? I flew first class the way others took the bus. Clothes? I bought up couturiers' collections in every major European city and, if need be, I borrowed my mother's Saint Laurent outfits. Fun? My life was an endless round of parties and balls, with guests straight out of the society gossip columns. Holidays? I had a choice, the world was my oyster. I took everything for granted, money, luxury, power, royalty and subservience. The people around me were so eager to please that even if you had black eyes, they would compliment you on how blue they were if they were ordered to do so.

My parents invited all of Morocco's high society to my eighteenth birthday ball—Prince Moulay Abdallah, Princess Lamia, the entire government, a heavy sprinkling of military and a few stars.

And I? Spoiled child that I was, I sulked. Dress fittings bored me. Dior gowns weren't for me, nor were posh hairdos. So I scowled and threw tantrums. The hairdresser who had spent two hours creating a complicated chignon, with endless backcombing and lacquer, swore he'd never come back and do my hair when he saw how unimpressed I was with his masterpiece. Before he'd even finished packing up his things, I had rinsed my hair and let it down over my shoulders. I deserved a good slap.

I had to greet all the guests with my parents, bend over backwards in my efforts to be amiable and act the perfect young lady of marriageable age. I opened the ball with Prince Moulay Abdallah, made small talk with the elderly ladies, smiled at my grandfather, at the generals, the ministers . . . I managed to play my part for most of the evening.

But when the Jamaican band launched into the first reggae number, little madam Malika let herself go on the dance floor. I threw off my lovely white chiffon dress embroidered with roses, slipped on a pair of jeans and a T-shirt, and danced barefoot until I dropped, all night, mostly with my father.

So I actually ended up enjoying the party I had been dreading. I'd been showered with gifts, including some splendid jewellery. I'd been complimented on my beauty and my parents were delighted. And I'd had fun. For a long time, even during my early years in prison, I kept a little album of photos taken that night. It was confiscated, along with everything else, but I managed to get it back when I was released. The faces of the generals who were at the party and who were executed after the Skhirat coup had been circled with green biro.

What do young girls dream of? Most of them dream of love. I dreamed of stardom. The movies remained my great passion, the love of my life, from the days when I used to re-enact all the films I liked for Lalla Mina and my schoolfriends at the royal lycée. To be a film star, that's what I longed for. I'd seize any opportunity to mix with the world of razzmatazz and glitter. In London, where my mother had a house near Hyde Park, I met the Greek actress Irene Pappas. She was starring in a film being shot in London. I immediately got ideas into my head. Luckily for me, my two uncles, Azzedine and Wahid, were supposed to be chaperoning me. In fact, they were enjoying themselves as much as I was.

We met up in the vast apartment Irene had rented. We danced the *sirtaki*, drank vodka and champagne and laughed and sang till dawn, when we were driven home in Maseratis and Lamborghinis by the son of King Fahd of Saudi Arabia, or by a young Greek actor, Yorgo. That was how I was supposed to be learning English.

Paris fascinated me. I'd jump at any chance to beg my parents to send me there. Once again I needed a chaperone. My cousin Leila Chenna, my childhood playmate, was entrusted with the task. I was overjoyed, and settled into her home. A little older than me, Leila was the most beautiful girl of her generation. Her looks had brought her luck: she had become an actress. The Algerian director Muhammad Lakhdar Hamina had fallen passionately in love with her and had given her a part in most of his films, including the famous *Chronicle of the Burning Years* which won the Palme d'Or at the Cannes film festival. She had also played in a James Bond movie.

Leila embodied my dream. She had succeeded in the movies and she was independent. She was friendly with the actors I admired most. And she wasn't selfish. She introduced me to Alain Delon, the star of stars, the actor women worshipped. I wasn't particularly impressed. In the eyes of the temperamental, spontaneous seventeen-year-old that I was at the time, he was already a mature man. Almost old. There could be no question of anything between us other than friendship, maybe ambiguous at times but always platonic. I saw him a few times in Paris and then in New York and Mexico where he was shooting Joseph Losey's *The Assassination of Trotsky*, co-starring Romy Schneider. He taught me to play Yahtzee.

Alain was very fond of me, but respected the fact that I was a young lady, full of virtuous principles. He liked my 'shy virgin' side. He often used to phone me in Rabat. My father, alerted by his hangers-on who were always quick to panic when it came to my reputation, was concerned about this relationship. There was no need. Alain was a real friend, one of the most faithful. He later proved that he had never forgotten me.

Jacques Perrin was a regular visitor to Leila's apartment. He had just produced Costa Gavras's *Z*. He was greatly admired and celebrated . . . and gorgeous . . . I had a brief, casual flirtation with him. I was probably a little bit in love with him. But I wasn't yet ready to belong to anyone. I was too intoxicated by my new-found freedom.

America was the land of my dreams. I spent a memorable Christmas holiday over there; New York and Hollywood were the highlights. In the Big Apple, I became friends with Marvin Dayan, the nephew of Moshe Dayan, the Israeli Minister of Defence. This delighted my father and shocked some of his ministers. As for Los Angeles, that is one of my best memories. I was accompanying Princess Nehza, the King's youngest sister, and with her I was invited to meet the whole of Hollywood. We went to dinners and parties, each more amazing than the last. I met all the world's biggest movie stars and celebrities of the day, Zsa-Zsa Gabor, Edward G. Robinson and scores of others. I was overawed, intimidated, but at the same time dazzled. Although I was aware that I was able to mix in such illustrious company because of my name, which opened every door as if by magic, I was still dazed by it all.

At one of these parties I even fell head over heels in love with a screen cowboy, Stuart Whitman, who had only to turn his blue eyes in my direction for me to go into raptures. I confided my crush to the woman sitting next to me on the sofa, a stunning French model. She listened to me very seriously.

'I understand,' she said, smiling. 'You're right, he's gorgeous.'

I was about to go on to enumerate all his charms, when I saw Nehza glaring at me. She motioned me to join her.

'Malika, you're behaving badly. Not only are you staring brazenly at that man, but worse, you're doing it in front of his wife.'

His wife was my beautiful neighbour. She had the grace not to hold my confession against me, and invited me to her house several times. She had been charmed by my naivety. I became friends with her and her husband who was touched by my futile love.

At their Malibu home I became friends with the delightful Brigitte Fossey, an officer's daughter like myself, and the mother of a four-month-old baby girl called Marie. A little later, Steve McQueen, whom I met in a Los Angeles nightclub where I was dancing with Dean Martin's son, invited me to go buggying in the Californian desert. He knew my parents. We spent an unforgettable day together, careering around the dunes. I have never laughed so much.

I was so keen to become an actress that I nearly managed to wring a film contract out of an American agent, a friend of my father's. Over the phone, my father had to use all his powers of persuasion to discourage me.

'Malika, sit your baccalaureate and then I'll send you to the States and you can do as you please.'

I obeyed the voice of reason. When I think that Hollywood awaited me . . .

With hindsight, I look back at the girl I was with amusement, and also a certain fondness. I wasn't too stupid but I was very spoiled, and my genuine attempts at rebellion would probably have gone on for a long time. My destiny was already mapped out: marriage to a wealthy husband at twenty, a life of luxury and boredom, of sleeping around, infidelities, frustration and dissatisfaction drowned in alcohol or drugs. It was a fate identical to that of so many other unhappy Moroccan society girls I know.

At least my ordeal has spared me that miserable fate. Of course, I have lost years that I will never get back. Only now am I just beginning to live, on the verge of old age. It is painful and unfair. But today I have a different attitude to life: it can't be constructed from superficial things, no matter how attractive they may appear. Neither wealth nor appearances have any importance now.

Pain gave me new life. It took a long time for me to die as Malika, General Oufkir's eldest daughter, the child of a powerful figure, of a past. I've gained an identity. My own identity. And that is priceless.

If there had not been all that waste, all that horror . . . I'd almost venture to say that my suffering made me grow. In any case, it changed me. For the better. It's as well to make the best of things.

THE SKHIRAT COUP

Summer 1971 looked especially promising. Although I'd frittered away my school year, I achieved a good grade in French. I had a place at college to complete my humanities studies. A long two-month holiday lay ahead, and I had plans to go out a lot, swim, see my friends and travel. At one o'clock in the afternoon of 10 July I was still asleep. The previous evening my father had taken the whole family to a restaurant, which was an unusual thing for him to do. It had been a wonderful evening, with lots of laughter. After we got home, I continued to party all night, which was why I was enjoying a lie-in. Life was pleasant and calm. What could happen to us?

I had a rude awakening. Bodyguards were rushing around all over the villa; the staff were frantic. Fighter planes could be heard roaring in the sky. There was an atmosphere of disaster. The danger was real: there had been a coup at the Skhirat palace where the King was holding three days of non-stop festivities to celebrate his forty-second birthday.

My father was unreachable and my mother was having lunch with a friend, Sylvia Doukkali, who had a beach villa. Raouf had gone into town on his motorbike with friends. Worried about my brother and unsure what to do, I finally decided to go and join my mother. The news of the incident had taken Sylvia's guests by surprise, and some of them were still in their swimming costumes. Her house was only a few kilometres from Skhirat, and as my mother and I were getting into the car to drive back to Rabat, I saw convoys of military trucks heading in the opposite direction.

It was impossible to return home, so we decided to spend the night in a little house we owned in town. Sylvia Doukkali accompanied us. She was distraught. Her husband Lharbi, who was the King's private secretary, hadn't come home and she hadn't heard a word from him.

It later emerged that NCOs from the royal military training college had burst into the palace during the King's birthday celebrations. They massacred hundreds of guests, officers, members of the court and male celebrities from all over the world. The King hid in the toilets. Other rebels took over the radio station and bombed the palaces of Skhirat and Rabat. The King eventually succeeded in bringing the situation under control.

At dawn someone phoned my mother to warn her that Lharbi Doukkali had been one of the first to be massacred at Skhirat. There were more than two hundred dead, a third of them from among the King's guests. The King had managed to put the rebellion down, and thirty-eight mutineers had been killed. Ten officers, including four generals, had been arrested. They were going to be executed later.

The conspiracy had been led by General Medbouh, an officer of integrity, who was appalled at the corruption rife in his country. He was killed at Skhirat by Colonel Ababou, his accomplice. My father pleaded in favour of the acquittal of the 1,081 rebel trainee officers, and obtained it. His role in this first coup was never proven, but the way it was organized and the clemency he showed towards the rebels gave rise to speculation. His relations with King Hassan II broke down after this event.

The attempted coup d'état was like a thunderbolt in my ordered life. I could never have imagined that anyone would challenge the King's authority. Apparently ordinary officers could have killed him if the situation had not swung in his favour. I wasn't mature enough or sufficiently acquainted with the ways of politics to understand what had just happened. I remember above all the atmosphere of panic, and my grief on learning of the death of some of my friends who happened to have been at Skhirat.

Back home the next morning, my mother and I decided to go to the King's villa in the Allée des Princesses, a stone's throw away from ours. The King had taken refuge there with his wives. We were given a warm welcome; it was very moving. Everyone was crying and kissing. But for the first time in my life, I felt a certain unease. I was torn by conflicting loyalties. I had been very frightened for my father, and for the King, but I no longer supported the monarchy, the ruling authorities. I was no longer on their side.

I felt ashamed that people were thanking me for my father's actions. He had helped put down the rebels—but weren't they fighting to rid the country of corruption? Later, talking with my friends, my thinking became more nuanced. I gradually realized that things weren't so black and white, with the goodies on one side and the baddies on the other.

My mother insisted on seeing the King. I knew the house well, and took her to his apartments. Just as we reached his door, he suddenly flung it open. He was so edgy that he jumped back at the sight of us. That made him annoyed with my mother for having given him a fright. The King was so proud that he couldn't bear to be caught unawares by a stranger in a moment of weakness. My opinion didn't count; I was one of them.

My mother wanted to recover Lharbi Doukkali's body, and attempted to persuade the King to let her do so. He began to shout:

'Look at you, going out of your way to help others, dealing with the funeral arrangements for this one and the burial of that one. But mark my words: not one of these people you're so concerned about will lift a finger to help you if anything happens to you.'

But he did agree to let her take the body so Lharbi Doukkali could have a decent burial.

The following days were a nightmare. The ten officers who had been arrested were summarily shot. They had all been close friends of my father's. He came home ashen, his eyes red and his mouth grim. He wore his military combat uniform. He went straight up to his room and lay on his bed. I sat at his feet and took his hand to kiss it. Mother was at his side.

My father grieved over his friends' deaths for a long time. He had not been able to persuade the King to give them a fair trial. He knew that none of them would have been pardoned because they had threatened national security, but he cared about the judicial process. For the first time in his life, he wasn't able to confine himself to the measured language of the politician. He railed against Hassan II. On the day of the funeral of the guests and all those who had died trying to protect their monarch, he exploded again. The King had followed the funeral procession wearing one of his favourite check jackets. My father accused him of having no respect for the dead.

Nnaa, my paternal grandmother, left her palm grove at Ain-Chair and came to our house. I seldom saw her but I was very fond of her. She was an extraordinary person, the soul of dignity, nobility and piety. This sober, straightforward woman of the desert who always wore a plain white kaftan reminded me of a Sioux squaw, with her prominent cheekbones, slanting black eyes and auburn plaits. She was very brave. She caught vipers with her bare hands and, like my father, was an accomplished rider.

My father and his mother greeted each other by kissing hands, as is customary among the people of the south. She said to him, trembling:

'My son, may God protect you. I thought you were dead.'

Coldly he stopped her tears.

'Ma, I won't allow you to cry unless I die like a criminal. But if you consider I have died like a man, please don't shed a single tear.'

A little later I shut myself away with him in the sitting room and blurted out my anger and pain. I couldn't bear the idea that the children of the executed generals had been evicted from their homes and beaten and kicked by the army. I had heard that those orders had come from my father. I demanded an explanation.

He assured me of his innocence and told me he would like to see the children of General Habibi who had been one of his closest friends. So I acted as go-between. After a great deal of hesitation, the eldest boy agreed to come to our house after dark. My father gave him a briefcase without telling me what was inside.

'I hope that you and your brothers will always conduct yourselves as men worthy of your father.'

He had tears in his eyes as he spoke these words.

Mina, the daughter of General Medbouh, who was assassinated by his accomplice, Colonel Ababou, at Skhirat, was twenty-two, the same age as my uncle Azzedine whom she was dating. She was unable to retrieve the General's body from the Avicenne hospital. Once again I spoke to my father about it, and he gave her money and obtained a new passport for her so that she could get to France. She took the name of her maternal grandfather, Marshal Ammezziane, to avoid difficulties. That shocked me.

Whatever happens to me in my life, I said to myself, I'll always keep my own name.

With each day that went by, I became increasingly convinced that

I would lose my father in tragic circumstances. I couldn't explain this premonition: I just knew it.

I confided my fears to one of my friends, Kamil, the day after the coup d'état.

'This year it's not too bad. But just wait, next year things will be much worse,' I told him.

I said the same to my father:

'Be careful. You'll suffer the same fate as Medbouh.'

He didn't answer.

AFTER SKHIRAT

After the coup my mother went to London to rest, far from the upheavals of court. I took the children to Kabila, a fashionable spa resort in the north of Morocco.

For the first time I was entirely responsible for them and I took my role as the eldest very seriously. At the end of the summer we all returned to Rabat. My father, who usually worked at home, now left the house very early in the morning and returned in the afternoon to receive ministers and officers.

He became even more powerful; he had been appointed Minister of Defence and head of the royal air force. He was in charge of the army, the police and home affairs. But he had become a different man. He seemed broken; a frown never left his face and he denied himself even the smallest pleasures. I think he was still grieving for his friends. He had gone back to his first family, the army, and could no longer stand our extravagant, luxurious life. He hankered for simplicity and restraint.

Our change of lifestyle was radical. At home he instigated a discipline that was almost military. Security was tightened, and there were fewer scroungers and hangers-on. He dictated every detail of our lives: we could no longer watch films or entertain whoever we wanted. Raouf was made to take Arabic lessons from an officer with Islamist convictions. He criticized my way of dressing. I was so shocked by this new attitude that we often had rows.

Unannounced visits from the King became increasingly frequent.

He came near to violating our privacy. I had the impression that there was a widening rift between my father and the King. There no longer seemed to be the same understanding between them. The silent hostility between the two men I loved most in the world grieved and worried me.

I felt ill at ease both at home and outside. The country was in the grip of a strange mood. The monarchy had been knocked off balance. For the first time, the King's divine power had been challenged in the public mind. The sacred person of the unassailable descendant of the Prophet, the emir of the faithful, had come under attack. In January the university students and schoolchildren went on strike. There were riots that my father suppressed with a heavy hand. At the Lycée Lalla Aicha, I found myself increasingly isolated. Nobody other than my closest friends could decently show me any sympathy. However, I continued to take part in lessons; I was a bright student and I wanted to obtain my baccalaureate. But the headmistress herself feared for my safety and advised my parents to withdraw me from her establishment.

After hours of arguing, I managed to persuade them to send me to Paris where they enrolled me at the Lycée Molière, under a false name. Against my wishes I had been obliged to take my mother's name and, with the agreement of Alexandre de Marenches, the head of French Intelligence, I was now Malika Chenna. My parents also agreed to rent an apartment for me a stone's throw from my new school rather than put me in a student hostel.

I was placed under the supervision of an older friend, Bernadette, who had promised to keep an eye on me and prevent me from going out in the evenings. It was a promise she was unable to keep: my powers of persuasion were too great.

I wouldn't allow my mother to buy me furniture reflecting her 'bourgeois' tastes. I didn't want anything expensive for fear my new friends might discover my real identity. She gave me some money, which I spent at the flea market. I felt I was living the ultimate Bohemian lifestyle: eating frozen dishes in a two-bedroom apartment in the 16th arrondissement seemed deliciously 'lefty' to a spoiled brat like me.

Paris was mine and I made sure I went out every night, begging Bernadette not to tell my parents. I became a regular at clubs like Le Castel and Régine's, sometimes staying out all night, but I was determined to get good grades. It was a simple question of pride.

One evening, when I was at a little party at a Moroccan friend's house, Bernadette called me in a state of panic.

'Malika, come home straight away. Your parents keep phoning. It's an emergency.'

It was one o'clock in the morning. Someone drove me home. There was a crowd outside my building in Rue Talma. As I drew near, I realized they were uniformed and plain-clothes police. They were everywhere—in the courtyard, in the lobby, in the trees and on the stairs.

The Moroccan ambassador, who had just arrived, seemed extremely agitated. He explained nothing but told me to grab a suitcase that Bernadette had already packed. I was virtually pushed into his car. I spent the night at the ambassador's residence. Once there, he told me that it was suspected that Colonel Gaddafi had planned to kidnap me.

He asked if I had noticed anything unusual during the previous few days. Something came back to me. Yes, two burly men dressed in black had rung our doorbell, a couple of nights previously, saying that our apartment was for sale and they wanted to view it. Bernadette and I had inspected them through the spyhole and decided they looked too sinister, so we didn't let them in. A little later, I was followed when I was shopping in Rue de la Pompe. Bernadette had been the first to notice.

The Intelligence officers showed me photographs but I refused to recognize anyone. It wasn't my style to be an informer, I had principles . . . I flew to Morocco and stayed for a few days, but I begged my parents to allow me to go back to France. In exchange, I had to agree to heavier security. For several weeks it seemed as if there were police everywhere.

A month before my final exams, I had a very serious car accident and nearly lost an eye. One of my friends, Luc, the son of André Guelfi, a Corsican businessman and close friend of my father's, was at the wheel. He lost control of the vehicle and it hit a lamp-post. I hadn't fastened my seat belt and went through the windscreen.

I was taken to hospital by ambulance. My cheek was cut open, my nose was sliced in three, my eyebrow was torn, my eye was damaged, my throat gashed and my mouth was split in several places. I had a broken wrist, a sprained thumb and, to crown it all, I was suffering from concussion. Lying on a stretcher in casualty, I overheard the comments of the nurses, who thought I was unconscious.

'What a shame! She's completely disfigured! She must have been so pretty! How terrible . . .'

I had two operations on my eye and, luckily, the second one was a success. The King had sent Moulay Abdallah and a few ministers to visit me. My mother was glued to my side. My father phoned continuously. He couldn't come to France himself as he had been sentenced to life imprisonment *in absentia* at the Ben Barka trial. Although those in the know said that President Pompidou was prepared to let him in, as soon as I was able to speak I made him swear not to leave Morocco.

I stayed in hospital for two weeks. When I came out, I wanted to carry on as normal. I was in a lot of pain, and I had to wear huge dark glasses all the time because the light hurt my eyes.

Shortly after I came out, I went to see Professor Mora who had performed the operations. He congratulated me.

'Mademoiselle Oufkir, you are quite a case. Your willpower saved your eye.'

After a few days I had recovered 50 per cent of my vision. Today my face is virtually as it was before the accident. I have been only left with a few scars. I wasn't able to go back to Paris to have the last stitches removed and undergo physiotherapy. In prison, for a long time I suffered from facial tics. Even now, when I'm tired or irritated, a facial nerve sometimes gives an involuntary twitch.

My parents made me go home to Morocco to finish convalescing. I had decided to take my exams in October, at the Lycée Descartes, where resits were held for those who had been unable to take the exams in June.

Events decided otherwise.

THE 1972 COUP D'ÉTAT

The King, who was entertaining President Boumédienne of Algeria, had asked me to go and see him as soon as I got back to Rabat. I felt ugly. My face was puffy and covered in lumpy scars, and there were dark circles under my eyes.

'It's not serious, Malika,' he consoled me. 'Everyone's had a car accident at some time in their lives: Lalla Malika, Lalla Lamia, myself . . . Next month I'll send you to the USA to see the top specialists, and I promise you, very soon it won't show at all.'

It was the beginning of July. My mother wanted me to accompany the family to Kabila for the holidays, but I was determined to revise for my exams. She agreed to let me stay in Rabat with my father so that I could study in peace. He was up to his ears in work; the house had become like staff headquarters. He never went out, and I saw processions of officers and ministers coming and going. The atmosphere was somewhat threatening. But I still went to see him every day, whenever he was able to make time for me, either at lunchtime or at the end of the afternoon.

My mother owned a pretty little maisonette opposite our villa, with a sitting room, a tiny bedroom and a delightful garden. I moved in there to have peace and quiet. I worked flat out, together with a friend who was taking her law finals.

My father decided that we'd go and spend a weekend in Kabila. We took the Mystère 20 plane he used for all his trips. I was anxious. Barely a month after my car crash, he had nearly been killed in a helicopter accident. On another occasion, he had narrowly escaped a bomb attack at an official ceremony that he had been unable to attend. I have always suspected, without ever having any proof, that the King wanted to get rid of him.

The rift between the two men was becoming deeper and deeper. In the middle of a Cabinet meeting, when they had just voted for a substantial increase in the prices of oil, sugar and flour, my father took out his revolver and threatened to shoot himself. I think he dreamed of establishing a constitutional monarchy with the crown prince, Sidi Muhammad, on the throne. The battle for power had begun.

That weekend at Kabila was unusual and, to be honest, completely wild. My father behaved most oddly. He had just made us live through a year of the utmost sobriety, and here he was singing and dancing all day long.

I had brought over the latest pop records from Paris, and from ten in the morning he'd start nagging me:

'Kika, I want to dance, put the music on full blast.'

How many times had I heard him telling me to turn the volume down?

I discovered a different father. A real father. I had forgotten how charming, thoughtful and cheerful he could be, a real live wire. We partied from dawn till dusk. He was joie de vivre itself. The minute he woke, at six, he would go to the beach and lie by the water's edge, alone. And this was the man who normally didn't like the sea. He watched the sun rise or scanned the horizon. My scars had barely healed and I shouldn't have been out in the sun, but I didn't care. It was my way of saying 'I'm fine' and, above all, of being with him. He took a water-skiing lesson, and he couldn't even swim. As a precaution, he put on a wetsuit and wore a huge lifebelt round his waist. He looked so funny that we immediately named him 'Moby Dick, king of the ocean'.

Life was very simple in Kabila. We entertained a lot, but my mother insisted on doing the shopping herself, escorted by the bodyguards. She discussed the menus with the cook. It wasn't her style to snap her fingers and be waited on. My father lived in his swimming trunks. In the evening he slipped on a tunic, like the ones worn by the Blue Men of his native south. But the shadow of power hung over us more than ever. We were surrounded by police and armed guards. Hangers-on sought our table and our company. For our guests, the ultimate way to show off was to be able to let slip 'We had lunch with the Oufkirs . . .'

After three wonderful, frenzied days we flew home. I carried on revising in my little house. One afternoon, at around six, I went to see my father. He was alone. I joined him in our drawing room that looked out onto the garden.

I poured him a whisky and sat beside him, stroking his hand, as usual.

'Will you sing something with me?' he asked suddenly.

'If you like, but what?'

He began to hum:

'*Lundi matin, le roi, sa femme et le p'tit prince, sont venus chez moi pour me serrer la pince* . . . Monday morning, the king, his wife and the li'l prince, came to give my hand a pinch . . .'

From time to time he gave me a sideways glance.

'Come on, sing with me!' he said.

He never told me why he was singing that particular song. I still wonder about it; it was odd, to say the least, and it haunted me for a long time.

One morning, around nine, I was working when I heard him calling me from the garden. Normally he was considerate and would always announce his arrival by telephoning first.

I opened the door and immediately recoiled, struck by the look on his face. He was standing there gazing at me with such love and intensity that I was taken aback, and even upset. I wondered whether he was staring at me like that because of my scars and if he was annoyed with me for being disfigured.

Then he threw his arms around me, hugged me tenderly and asked about my plans. My mother had a house in Casablanca and I had decided to move there to be closer to my friends, the Layachis.

'I'll be much better off there,' I said. 'The girls will give me a hand with my revision. And don't worry, I won't go out at night, I've got to get through my exams. I promise you I'll pass.'

'All right. You know I trust you.'

'Yes, Daddy. I know you trust me. You don't need to worry about me.'

My father, who normally never had any time, always had so many things to do that when he kissed me he would already be elsewhere, hesitated . . .

He looked up, swept the sitting room with his gaze, and let it come to rest on me.

'Darling, you know I love you.'

I was unable to speak.

Then he turned on his heel and left. I just stood there without reacting. The door opened once more. It was him again. He walked over to me and hugged me very tight. At last he left, reluctantly, it seemed.

A little later, I set off for Casablanca.

It was 16 August 1972. At around four o'clock I was at home, in the drawing room of our house in Casablanca, surrounded by my friends. We were laughing and chatting happily.

Prompted by an intuition that I can't explain, I switched on the television. A presenter was announcing that there had been a coup d'état and that the royal plane had been fired on over Tétouan. They didn't know who was responsible for the attack.

I rushed over to the radio to pick up France Inter. I waited to hear someone say that my father was behind the coup. My friends all sat there saying that it had to be him, that they were convinced. But information was hazy, nobody knew anything for certain; it was only speculation that General Oufkir was involved and that the coup had succeeded. Order had not yet been restored.

As soon as she heard the news, my friend Houda Layachi's sister begged her to leave the house with her. She pointed at me hysterically, saying she was afraid the army would surround us, that I would be killed and they would too.

Everybody quickly left, except Houda. I wasn't able to contact any members of my family; all the lines were busy or there was no answer. I just lay there, frantic, not knowing what to do.

Around seven o'clock, the phone rang. It was my father. He had the toneless voice of a man who has decided to commit suicide and is recording his last message. The effect was terrifying. It was as if a ghost was talking to me.

He spoke in a detached voice, telling me he loved me and that he was proud of me. Then he added:

'I ask you to remain calm, whatever happens. Don't leave the house until the escort comes to get you.'

I began to scream.

'Daddy, tell me it's not true, it's not going to be a repeat of last year . . .'

'Malika, listen to me. Please keep calm, you know I trust you.'

He kept going on and on saying things I didn't want to hear. I so wanted him to reassure me, to tell me he wasn't behind the coup. But from the start of our conversation, I understood it was him. And that he was lost.

I couldn't accept his defeat. I sobbed, unable to speak. He said nothing more, and hung up.

That was the last time I heard his voice.

I was unable to sleep. I kept mulling over my father's last words and his strange attitude. Something terrible had happened. I didn't dare pick up the phone in case I received confirmation of my worst fears.

Around three o'clock in the morning, my grandfather called me.

'Malika, get in the car and go back to Rabat.'

'No way. I must do what my father said. Where is he?'

The old man insisted in vain. Around five o'clock, the phone rang again. I was still lying awake, distraught, imagining the worst.

Without beating about the bush, my mother confirmed what I was most afraid to hear:

'Your father's dead. Pack your things and come back to Rabat.'

Then she hung up before I had a chance to reply.

Houda had heard the phone ring. She came into my room looking anxious.

'Well?'

'My father's dead.'

She howled, cried, flung herself into my arms, noisily expressing her grief. I remained detached. That phrase, 'my father's dead', was meaningless. It made no sense. I needed proof.

Then the escort arrived. The police officers, in tears, all offered me their condolences. I replied mechanically. I felt like a zombie, incapable of uttering a word.

I kept saying to myself, over and over again, 'It's not possible, people don't die like that, he can't die.'

I went to the window. For a moment, I clung to that view. The sun was rising above the trees in the garden, promising a splendid morning, like all the days before it.

I tried half-heartedly to convince myself.

'If he were dead, I'd be able to tell. Something would have changed outside.' I wanted to believe it, but in my heart of hearts I knew.

Without him, it simply wasn't possible for life to go on exactly as before.

MY FATHER'S DEATH

On the way back to Rabat, we were stopped at a roadblock. A guard from the escort got out of the car and disclosed my identity. Sobbing police officers rushed over to me.

The scene was repeated throughout the journey. Despite their mourning, I still hoped. Or at least, I pretended to. I persuaded myself he was only wounded. Gravely, no doubt, but he was breathing, he was alive. Perhaps I'd get there in time to talk to him . . .

The crowds outside the house and the cars parked everywhere left me in no further doubt. I was greeted by my father's brother, looking solemn, and my grandfather, who also wore a grave expression. He tried to prevent me from entering the house. I struggled violently.

'Let me in, Baba El Haj, I want to see him. I want to know where he is.'

'A woman is not allowed to see the body of a dead man. They're washing him.'

'I want to see my father's body.'

I barged into the sitting room. The men keeping vigil over the body immediately covered it with a white sheet. Everyone rose to their feet. I demanded to be left alone, then I sat down to contemplate him.

I frantically searched his impassive features for the slightest detail that might reassure me that he had died with dignity. There was a disdainful little smile on his lips, like all those who have been executed. Had he left this life with indifference? And why that smile? Was it contempt for the last person his eyes had dwelt on?

I counted the bullet marks on his body. There were five. The last one, on his neck, sent me into a frenzy of pain. That had been the *coup de grâce*.

But the four previous bullets had surely caused him a lot more pain than the last one. There was one in the liver, one in the lungs, one in the stomach and one in the back.

'Only a coward could have butchered him like that,' I told myself in a rage.

I left the room and took off all my clothes. I slipped on a white jellabah and removed my jewellery. I had to wear mourning to show him that my life had ended at the same time as his.

I asked for his glasses and his military uniform. They had not been found. I began to search everywhere. Opening a drawer, I stumbled on a plastic bag containing his blood-soaked uniform. I was momentarily relieved. It was a little part of him, at least, that we could hold on to. I also found his glasses.

My mother, who had just arrived from Kabila, asked to see his body. My father had been washed and his hair combed, and they had dressed him in an old white jellabah. He lay in a coffin in the private cinema. Only his face was visible. He seemed at peace.

Everybody filed past, offering their condolences. Devastated, Mummy sobbed and repeated over and over:

'They killed him, why? Why?'

The soldiers present were quick to report my mother's words to the King.

The King had food sent to us from the Palace. According to custom, a household in mourning is not allowed to cook. I refused this conciliatory gesture. Besides, was it really an act of kindness? I didn't want to betray my father, trample all over his corpse. Doubtless appeasement pays off in the short term, but the price is too high. Compromise? It was out of the question. I despised the hypocrisy they expected of me. I no longer had any business with the King, even if he was my adoptive father. Even if it already made me suffer.

I was criticized for my behaviour. To justify our imprisonment, some good souls claimed that the King had punished us because I had dared humiliate him by refusing his gift. How could I have reacted otherwise? If I hadn't been his adoptive daughter, if he had been merely a king and not a father, I would probably have been less vehement in my refusal, less proud in my anger. I would have behaved with all the respect due to his rank.

But our relationship was too emotional. In defying him, I wanted to pay him back blow for blow. But in everyone else's eyes, my behaviour had political overtones.

For the three days prior to the funeral, I looked after the children. My mother was too distraught. I had to try to protect them as best I could. Raouf was in shock. He just lay there. He had lost his idol, the man he loved more than anyone else in the world.

The girls wouldn't stop crying. They had been told that their daddy was in heaven, but they couldn't accept that they'd never see him again. Even little Abdellatif understood that something terrible had happened. Our friends came and went, trying to comfort us. Their presence meant a lot, but I was hardly aware of it.

During the day, I was in a daze; there was so much to do, so many things to organize. I didn't have time to feel sorry for myself. Every night, I relived the horror. I kept picturing my father's body. The four bullets in his torso and the fifth one in his neck. I heard his last words to me, that sepulchral voice saying that he loved me. I wept but was unable to sleep.

We didn't want to talk to the press who were harassing us. A journalist questioned my uncle Azzedine.

'Do you think your brother-in-law was the sort of man to commit suicide by shooting himself five times?'

My uncle replied that General Oufkir had been executed. His statement was broadcast that evening on France Inter.

My mother entrusted my father's bloodstained uniform to her friends in Tangier, Mamma Guessous and her husband. It was the only proof of his assassination. She burned another uniform in the boiler of the steam rooms, with the help of her brother Azzedine. The next day, the King sent the chief of police to fetch the uniform. My mother told him she'd burned it. Quaking, the man replied:

'His Majesty warned me: "You'll see, she'll tell you she's burned it."'

The boiler was searched from top to bottom. They had the remains of the fabric analysed. The King understood that the proof of my father's murder had gone up in smoke. But the uniform, the real one, was never found. Had Mamma Guessous been forced to hand it over? We never spoke about it again.

At dawn on the third day, they came to fetch my father's body. As he had been murdered, he had already earned his place in paradise, and so his remains were accompanied by wails of joy from the women mourners.

Hassan II gave orders for him to be buried in his native Tafilalet desert. My mother would have preferred Rabat. She wanted to be able to go and visit his grave. But my father's last wishes were that he should lie under a palm tree in his home village, so my mother gave in. Raouf and the men in my family accompanied my father to his last resting place. At Ain-Chair and all around, the dunes were covered with mourning women. They crowded round the coffin sobbing.

He was given a simple burial, in a little mausoleum near his father. I have never been there. I have a feeling that the day I do go, I will have reached the end of my journey.

The next day, 20 August, we were placed under house arrest. Our staff were fired and we were locked inside the house. My mother's family remained, including my grandfather, and a few of our close friends: Ann Brown, our English governess, Houria, Salem, Fatmi . . . the noose was tightening.

My mother was put through gruelling interrogations, led by Superintendent Yousfi, whom we were to encounter again later, in prison. She had a prophetic dream, which I dismissed at the time, but we often talked about it in prison. We were both galloping on horseback along a road that soon turned into a tunnel whose roof was rapidly closing in on us.

Just as we were about to be crushed, we managed to get out. The horses stopped halfway up a hill. We were overlooking Rabat. This dream became clear a little later: the horses represented life, and the tunnel that was stifling us, prison.

Another terrible death soon struck, bringing us more grief. Azzedine, my young uncle who was so brave, died in a car crash. His car was hit by that of a gendarme. He wasn't killed outright, but lay in a coma for several hours waiting for help that curiously took a long time coming.

I had been very fond of Azzedine. He was my ally in everything, my friend and my brother. He had protected me, made a fuss of me and covered up for me. He was handsome, funny, charming and full of life. I found his accident suspicious, and had the feeling that we weren't being told the truth. My misgivings have never been confirmed, but the doubt lingers in my mind.

There was too much grief, and too many tears. My mother knew the bad times were only just beginning, and asked herself how she could save us. The King hated her. He had declared on the radio that she was the *éminence grise* behind the coup, and that she had pushed my father into it.

What with the uniform incident, our proud attitude and the King's hatred of my mother, it looked certain she would be punished. There was talk of her being banished alone. But we children wouldn't be separated from her at any price. Wherever she went, we would go, all of us together, united against the worst.

Throughout those four months and ten days of mourning when we were prisoners in our own home, I tried to keep up appearances. I gave the children lessons and tried to let them live a normal life. Despite our grief, there were still a few amusing moments which allowed us to laugh and relax a little. Otherwise our burden would have been too crushing.

The place was always full of police officers. They vied with one another to be on guard duty during Ramadan because the food was delicious and we were generous. We found a way of smuggling in our friends who had left the house and wanted to see us.

We asked for some Valium and put it in the tea we gave the guards, and it sent them to sleep. Our friends climbed over the walls and spent a few days with us. The evening they left, we put Valium in the tea again and they left the same way they had come in.

During that period, I often thought about escaping. But we were too closely guarded. Besides, where would we go? I was too young to escape, my grandfather was too old, and my mother too grief-stricken. We were defenceless. I sensed that our fate had already been decided and that it would be tragic.

On 23 December, the mourning period ended. My mother took off her white garb. We were preparing for Christmas; the children deserved a few days of fun. Streamers festooned the walls and lamps, and there was a Christmas tree in the living room. We put presents all around it and tried our best to create a festive atmosphere.

The head of the police arrived late that afternoon and ordered us to pack what we would need for two weeks. We were being taken to the south of Morocco.

They were going to put seals on the front door. Nobody would be able to get into our house.

'You have His Majesty's word,' he added.

I was present during the conversation. I told the children to pack their bags, and I emptied out the cupboards. My mother thought I was mad. We were only going away for two weeks . . .

I gave Houria all the new clothes I'd bought in Paris and hadn't had a chance to wear yet, jewellery, perfumes, handbags and shoes.

'But you won't have anything to wear when you get back . . .'

If I ever come back, I thought, it'll be a miracle.

I also gave her a box containing all my photo albums and letters, including one which meant more to me than anything else. It was a love letter that my father had once sent my mother with a bouquet.

I took most of my things: practical clothing, my novels, all my school books and those of the children and the photo album of my eighteenth birthday ball.

We were allowed to take two people with us. It was not an easy choice. The first person to volunteer was Achoura Chenna, a first cousin of my mother's, a year her senior. She had come to live with her at the age of ten when she had lost her father, my grandfather's brother. As a little girl she had learned to cook and sew. She got married a few months after my mother, to a primary school teacher who was a political activist. The couple had a little girl who died as a baby.

Achoura couldn't have any more children. She preferred to seek a divorce rather than see her husband acquire a second wife. Left alone, she knocked on her cousin's door and was made welcome. She became our governess and shared our lives and our sorrow, to the point of following us into the abyss.

The second, Halima Aboudi, was the younger sister of Fatima, Abdellatif's governess. She had left our house some time before, terrified by what was happening, and had been hired by General Dlimi, my father's right-hand man and head of national security. Halima, at eighteen and a half almost the same age as me, came to offer her condolences and stayed with us during the four months' mourning. When she found out we were leaving, she immediately offered to come with us: she didn't want to be parted from little Abdellatif who was three and a half, and to whom she was already deeply attached.

'I insist on coming with you,' she begged my mother.

Ann Brown, the English governess, and Houria, my friend, also wanted to follow us. It was out of the question. From my years at the Palace, I knew more or less what happened when someone was banished. Yet I was a long way from the grim reality.

We left on Christmas Eve. Three women and six children surrounded by armed police. Maria and Soukaina clung to me in fear. Raouf clenched his fists. Abdellatif sucked his thumb.

I turned round one last time to look at the house and I said goodbye for ever. I wept silently so as not to frighten the children. I wasn't crying only for my father, I was crying for my life, the life that was being taken from me.

The thought of exile was harrowing for all of us, but for me it was worse. I was the only one to sense that this was no temporary measure.

PART TWO

TWENTY YEARS IN PRISON

4

A YEAR IN THE DESERT

25 December 1972–8 November 1973

THE ASSA OASIS

Where were we going? I had no idea. We were travelling at night.

We were in a big American car, which had neither curtains nor blacked-out windows. Our armed escort tried in vain to ease the atmosphere. I attempted to glean some information from the police radio. I still didn't know where we were being taken, but I gathered that police were positioned all along the route and that we were being kept under heavy guard.

In the early hours, after Agadir, the cars stopped in Goulimine, a village on the fringe of the desert. We were taken to the house of the mayor who had been told he would be entertaining General Oufkir's wife and children. He welcomed us ceremoniously and laid on a splendid breakfast.

I didn't know what to think any more. Was I right to fear the worst? Was my father really dead? The mayor spoke of him with respect, he openly paid tribute to him, while the police stayed glued to our sides . . .

I didn't understand. But was there anything to understand? We were entering the realm of the irrational, the arbitrary. This was a country where they locked up young children for their father's crimes. We were entering the world of insanity.

* * *

We stayed with the mayor of Goulimine for twenty-four hours, then we went back on the road and drove into the desert. After dark, the cars came to a halt. The scene was one of wild beauty. The almost full moon lit the arid plateaux and ancient mountains of the High Atlas, whose rounded peaks were silhouetted against the dark sky.

I loved the desert. I had often travelled through it in the days when Moulay Ahmed, the King's cousin, took Lalla Mina and me on educational trips around the country. That time seemed so remote that I wondered whether it had ever existed.

We were made to get out of the car and stand in a line on a patch of wasteland. The police took up positions opposite us, and threatened us with their Kalashnikovs.

My mother contrived to brush against me and whispered:

'Kika, I think this is the end.'

Unfortunately, it was only the beginning.

Subsequent events confirmed my fears. This sudden halt, this charade, was simply a manoeuvre to frighten us and prepare us for what was to come. We got back into the cars and drove for hours more. The journey was extremely arduous, especially for the children: the girls were nine and ten years old, and the baby, three and a half. It was hot, and we were thirsty, hungry and scared. There was nobody to comfort us or appease our gnawing anxiety.

At the end of our journey, we entered a tiny village which we managed to glimpse before the cars drove into an army barracks. I gathered from the police radio that we were in Assa, a remote spot in the middle of the desert, near the Algerian frontier.

In the days of the French Protectorate, these barracks had been a place of exile where the French sent dissidents and politicians who opposed the regime. The buildings were ancient, in a poor state of repair, and in some places the masonry was crumbling.

The next morning we were woken by inhuman screams. A building had collapsed in the night, and seven *mouhazzin*—auxiliary soldiers—were dead under the rubble. We clung to the bars at the windows and saw the bodies being carried away. A bad omen.

The police who had escorted us were all from Rabat. They had great affection for our family and visibly showed their grief for my father. But others awaited us, and they had very different instructions. We were to be treated harshly, like prisoners. We didn't know these men. They had been recruited from the remotest regions of Morocco to avoid any connivance with us. Their superiors, on the other hand, came from Rabat.

We were taken to a mud house inside the barracks. A tiny, wizened old man in a military jellabah stood by a table on which were set out nine round loaves and a few tins of sardines.

This was Bouazza, the camp commander. He wore false teeth that jiggled around; he looked as if he was either going to spit them out or swallow them. Even though I was terrified, I couldn't help smiling inwardly at this comic detail. Bouazza belched and yelled that from now on we must obey his orders and he knew he could break us. And we'd better not complain because he received his orders directly from the King.

I bowed my head. Bouazza was bawling and shouting, but he was only his master's voice. And his master had pronounced his final judgement, in keeping with the logic of the world in which I had been raised. As a loyal subject, I had no option but to accept it and resign myself to submission.

However, Bouazza was out of his depth in this situation. He had been in charge of the military prison of Kenitra for forty years; he had witnessed coups d'état, he had guarded dozens of political prisoners, but he had never had to lock up three women and six children.

His grasp of our case was limited to two things, and he boasted about them out loud:

'Subdue the Oufkirs. King's orders.'

For a long time I remained in a state of shock over our drastic change of lifestyle, the transition from wealth to poverty. And yet this was still luxury compared with what was in store. I was fussy, obsessively fastidious about clean linen and toilet facilities, and this place was a pigsty. I found everything repulsive, the coarse, grey, filthy military blankets thrown over foam mattresses, the horrible walls, the flaking plaster and sandy floors of the little mud house where we and our luggage had been deposited. Luckily, the children's innocent playfulness and the insouciance of my eighteen years helped keep our spirits up. We turned the whole thing into a joke.

The next day I set to work. I explored every corner of the tiny house. There were three narrow rooms with mattresses on the floor, and that was it. There were no cupboards so we arranged our things on sheets. Nor was there any running water. We were given buckets of water for washing, drinking and doing the dishes. In the barracks, we were conscious of the guards everywhere.

As we unpacked, I noted bitterly the contrast between this wretched place and our expensive clothes. We had been allowed to bring around twenty designer suitcases—Vuitton, Hermès and Gucci—filled with pretty things. In our former life, my mother bought her clothes from the Paris couture houses and the children's from Geneva, while I combed the designer stores of Paris, London and Milan.

In the desert, all that suddenly seemed so ludicrous.

My mother had left nearly all her jewellery behind, bringing only a little case with her. We had managed to bring our stereo system with us, our records and shortwave transistor radios that could tune in to stations all over the world.

I distributed water and soap, and asked everyone to help me clean. Then Raouf and I set up the record player. We had a sort of fridge that worked on and off depending on the whim of a temperamental generator. It came on only at night and made an infernal racket. The lights were so dim that we felt as though we were living by candlelight.

Despite everything, in the evenings I would plug in the record player and we'd listen for a while to our LPs playing at the wrong speed, and to the radio. We played cards with the children and made every effort to create an agreeable atmosphere. We even bred scorpions and organized races.

I was living a fairy tale in reverse. I had been brought up as a princess and now I had turned into Cinderella. Gradually, I shed my old habits; I always wore the same old clothes rather than clean trousers and shirts that reminded me too much of the past. The desert teaches you to strip yourself to the bare essentials.

To pass the time, we ate continuously. Our food was rationed because we were a long way from the town, the tracks were rough and bumpy, and the market came only every three weeks. Our rations consisted of bread, oil and honey, but we didn't have anything to complain about yet. It is true, we had goat meat, too pungent for our liking, more often than mutton. But at least we had enough to eat.

In the morning, we lingered over breakfast. We all did the washing up together, and then we started preparing lunch. My mother and I divided the tasks between us. She cooked and I did the washing in a bowl outdoors. Halima and Achoura helped us.

We spent most of the day on the little patio. We would drag tea out for hours, until darkness fell with sudden swiftness. Then we had dinner, followed by long evenings when Mother read us stories before we went to bed. The nights seemed endless . . . It was winter, the house was freezing and we often found it difficult to get to sleep. Gas lamps were our only source of heating.

Everything seemed worse at night, just as it had been during my childhood at the Palace. My only link with the outside world was the radio: Europe 1, RFI, France Inter. I couldn't do without it, and at the same time it was torture. Every song reminded me of a happy moment. I yearned for my friends, my past. Though I knew that dwelling on the past was fatal, I found it too difficult to tear myself away from everything and everyone I loved. I felt as though I had been walled up alive, like in the Middle Ages, and I fought back my screams.

In the dark I could hear my mother sobbing. Alone in her bed, she wept over the loss of her husband more than over the loss of our freedom. Her life as a woman had ended at the age of just thirty-six. By dying, my father had condemned her to solitude. During the day she often read the Koran, and I could see from her sad eyes, always puffy with tears, how much she suffered.

Each day we were allowed to go into the village in the oasis for two hours. I refused, at first to keep my mother company, because she didn't want to go out, but above all to assert myself. I was not going to be dependent on their goodwill.

So Myriam, Achoura, Halima, Mother and I stayed in the house while the children went out, accompanied by a police escort who were always very kind to them. They visited the palm grove where the Blue Men lived, and always came home with their hands full: henna, dates, baskets woven by the women. When they realized that their little visitors came back every day at the same time, the villagers made them tea and gave them bread hot from the oven, and cakes.

Those visits were very important for the children. At last they had a chance to express themselves and talk about their discoveries. It was the school of life. Abdellatif especially seemed thrilled. He wasn't yet four, and everything was a game to him. He was put on the back of a mule for a ride, and he was taken to see the cows, calves and chickens.

A village woman gave us some chicks. There was one each. We gave each bird a name and attributed characters to them. Unsurprisingly, they each mirrored the personality of their owner. Those little creatures helped us while away the time. We talked about them, played with them and tried to get them to sleep in cardboard boxes. In the evening they led us a merry dance when we tried to catch them. They scattered throughout the house squawking, and the children laughed and chased them. They had great fun.

I tried to make them believe that our life was almost normal. I created an imaginary world for them, inventing games and making up stories. I wanted to keep them from worrying. Gamely, they went along with me, but they knew very well that our situation was not as temporary as I would have them believe.

Even Abdellatif knew. I can still picture him, knee-high to a grasshopper, in his little blue tunic, saying with his slight lisp:

'When I'm a big boy I'll have a houth, but not like thith, and it'll have loths of carpeths, not thand.'

I could imagine what the others must have been feeling if this little fellow still had such vivid memories of our past life.

A BRIEF STAY IN AGDZ
28 April–30 May 1973

One morning at the end of April, we were made to leave at the double. We were taken to Agdz, a village in the desert, between Zagora and Ouarzazate. By eavesdropping, we caught snatches of talk suggesting the reason for this sudden departure. The villagers had begun asking questions; they had found out who we were and were outraged that children should be treated in this way.

We drove for eighteen hours without a stop, in vans with blacked-out windows. We were treated more harshly than before. We weren't allowed to get out, not even to pee. We had to take turns to use a small powdered-milk tin without a lid.

At dusk we arrived in a poor village. We were locked up in the mayor's house. We stayed there for a month, in total darkness, without ever being allowed out. Normal life went on outside, simply and peacefully. A fountain, the wind murmuring in the trees, children shouting and playing, women laughing, dogs barking. It was heart-breaking to hear those familiar sounds, so close and yet so far beyond our reach.

To kill time, we were always cooking and eating. My mother made little dishes by candlelight, and I made Moroccan pancakes, a treat for the children. I organized toad races and farting contests, which made them shriek with laughter. For them it was like being at a holiday camp and I was happy to play along at their level.

But I felt wretched about the basic amenities, the filth, the military blankets, the hospital beds lined up in a row and the lack of toilets. I was still a spoiled brat.

To survive, I travelled in my imagination. I would pick up my geography book and sit the children in a circle around me.

'After this,' I'd say, 'we'll all go and live in Canada.'

I dreamed of that country. I described to them in detail the forests, lakes and mountains, the vast snowy expanses, the Mounties and the beaver dams. The more they thought up objections, the more I tried to convince them. Even Mother got caught up in the game:

'No, not Canada,' she'd say. 'It's too cold, and too far. What about the family? How will they come and see us?'

We still had ties.

Bouazza arrived one morning and told us there was an article about us and about him in *Paris-Match*. He seemed very proud to have his name go down in history in this way. That gave us a little hope. If the press were writing about us, that meant we still existed. The world would not tolerate such an injustice for long . . .

We were still full of illusions about human nature.

This new period of incarceration marked an important stage for me. On my arrival at Agdz, I was still a normal person; I hadn't yet developed the mentality of a prisoner. And yet that was how I was treated, and how I would be treated in future, wherever I went. I was now certain that there would be no end to the bad times.

We returned to Assa at the end of May. Our living conditions had changed. Beyond the barracks was a patch of waste ground where, during our absence, a prefabricated hut of the most rudimentary type had been erected. The walls, floor and ceiling were all dun-coloured. But it was more robust than the barracks that threatened to collapse at any moment, which is probably why they'd built it. So, they didn't want us to die. Not yet. We settled in.

The house had a hall, a sitting room, a bathroom with a shower, and a string of rooms leading off a corridor. Everyone had their own bedroom. After the cramped conditions of the last house, this one seemed almost palatial. The view was nothing but sky and, beyond that, the mountains. We were allowed out onto the waste ground, escorted by the guards who kept a constant watch on us.

Fundamentally, this was not so much of a change from our past life. As far back as I could remember, I had never gone out without an escort; I had never opened a window without glimpsing one or several armed police responsible for my safety. Here, instead of protecting us, they were watching us. Excursions to the village were out of the question now. Nor, despite our requests, were we allowed to send or receive letters. We asked a guard to contact my grandfather. He promised he would, but failed to keep his word.

One of the children discovered a trap door, and we decided to explore the basement. Perhaps it would be possible to dig a tunnel? The idea of escaping was already going round in our minds. But we barely had time to descend the ladder before we were covered in hundreds of cockroaches that were swarming over the cellar walls and floor.

With summer, the nightmare began. During the day the thermometer reached 55°C in the shade, and the sun beat down on the corrugated iron roof. At night the heat rose from the sand and rocks where it had accumulated during the day. Above our heads the corrugated iron expanded, making a terrible racket. It was suffocatingly hot, like an oven, and we spent all our evenings and nights outdoors.

To help us sleep a little, we wrapped ourselves in wet sheets that we continually sprinkled with water. We covered the water jugs with wet cloths so as to have cool water. Luckily, they didn't ration our water.

With the dry season came the sandstorms. The gales shattered the window panes and the house was full of sand, which got everywhere, covering our faces and bodies. It brought with it huge, hairy, highly venomous spiders that were indistinguishable from their surroundings. We also tried to avoid the thousands of scorpions that slipped in everywhere, under the beds, on the walls and between our sheets. My mother and I scrubbed the whole place from top to bottom to get rid of them, which made us the laughing stock of the barracks; we didn't know that scorpions love moisture. Bouazza's wife got bitten. He was exasperated because we miraculously avoided their stings.

To make the days pass faster, we slept all morning, which meant we stayed awake till dawn. We fooled around, we played and we told stories. When it finally grew cooler, I organized games to entertain the children. I invented a little town, and gave each person a part to play. Soukaina was the dressmaker, like the ones we had seen in the Jewish quarter at home. Abdellatif was her helper.

Raouf opened a pizzeria, and put up a sign at the entrance that said 'Bobino, the Chip King'. You had to pay to eat there. Maria was the hairdresser, and I played the manicurist/chiropodist/beautician. Mother was our customer who needed her daily beauty treatment, then went for a fitting at the dressmaker's and had lunch at Bobino's.

I had fallen back into my old Palace ways: play-acting the things I was forbidden to experience for myself.

'ZOUAIN ZOUAIN BEZEF'

Bouazza was so intimidated by Rabat that he instigated increasingly harsh disciplinary measures. And he began to abuse us. He threatened my mother and lost control in front of us.

One morning he erupted. He began yelling so loudly that he nearly lost his false teeth.

'I've worked in prisons for forty years but I've never had to guard anyone but men! This is the worst possible thing they could inflict on me: killing a woman and her children! That's not my job, never in my life did I think I'd have to do such a thing!'

He went out, visibly agitated and still ranting. Some time later, he informed us he would soon be leaving the camp. He seemed relieved. Then he told us that in the village there was an extraordinary clairvoyant who could predict the future and was never wrong. No doubt the seer had foretold his impending departure . . .

This was when Bouazza changed his attitude and became kinder to us and, unbelievably, he ended up bringing the clairvoyant to see us.

He was a man of indeterminate age. His face and body were completely twisted, and he was unable to stand or walk. His stomach and chin dragged on the ground, and all his limbs seemed paralysed. Police officers lifted him up and dropped him at our feet like a sack of potatoes.

He was accompanied by a village woman, a Berber with very dark skin. She removed her veil, and placed next to the old man a flat straw sieve containing flour. Customers moved their hands across the flour and the clairvoyant studied the prints closely—even though he was blind.

He spoke to my mother in Berber but she couldn't understand him. The dialect in the Middle Atlas, where she came from, was different from that of the desert. My father was one of the few people who knew all four Berber dialects spoken in Morocco. The man spoke with difficulty, dribbling copiously when he opened his mouth. The woman accompanying him translated. First of all he said I shouldn't expose myself to the sun because of the scars on my face. That impressed us because he couldn't see them. He gave me an ointment.

'Put that on your face, and in time they'll fade. Time is the best healer.'

He explained that I should add dried and powdered chameleons mixed with camel's milk to the ointment. I should put a few drops of this preparation in my nose every day. Having tried it on my damaged skin, I can vouch for its effectiveness.

He talked to us about Mimi and her epilepsy. My parents had consulted the top specialists in France and the United States and knew it was incurable. Now, however, we were really not that interested in one another's health. We wanted to hear what he had to say about our future.

'When will we get out of this hell? When will we see our family and friends again? When will we be able to return to a normal life?'

We plagued him with anxious questions. He gave a long sigh:

'It will take a long time, and it will be terrible. But a miracle will intervene and the whole world will talk about it. You will get what you want in the end . . . But I warn you, it will be a very long time.'

My mother pressed him to be more precise about the time involved, but he wasn't able to tell us. This was something he refused to do since falling prey to evil spirits, the woman told us. He simply added that we had special protection because we were descendants of the Prophet, and that we would never suffer any serious illnesses. His predictions all turned out to be true.

Every time we felt overwhelmed, when we reached the depths

of despair, each time one of us was on the verge of cracking up, we would repeat to ourselves, in Arabic, the words of the blind old man.

'*Zouain zouain bezef*: it will be miraculous, very miraculous.'

This prophecy helped us hold out for twenty years.

During our early years in prison, I dreamed only of the King, never of my father. I relived my life at the Palace, the concubines, my pranks, our laughter, my tête-à-têtes with him, our special moments.

I never revisited happy family scenes, or painful ones, my father's death or the mourning that followed it. There was no resentment in my dreams, no confrontation or rebellion. I had nothing but happy memories of my childhood even though, in a sense, it had been stolen from me.

I would wake up, overcome with shame and guilt. I was troubled, uncomfortable, but I couldn't share this with my family. They wouldn't have understood.

I probably coped better with our twenty-year ordeal than my brothers and sisters, for I already knew, on entering prison, what loneliness and abandonment meant. But I also discovered the heart-breaking pain of knowing one's enemy and being close to him.

It was infinitely painful to me to have been brought up by my persecutor and to have felt, for too long, that ambivalent mixture of love and hatred towards him. At first, my feelings towards the King were complicated, difficult to disentangle. My own father had tried to kill my adoptive father. As a result he was dead. It was a tragedy. My tragedy.

Sometimes I didn't know which one I missed most, which one to grieve for. I was the product of my Palace upbringing; everything I was, I owed to the man who had raised me. But I loved my real father so much. I became confused, continually turning things over in my mind. I tried to understand and constantly imagined how things might have turned out 'if only I hadn't done this' or 'if only I hadn't done that'.

If I still respected Hassan II as my adoptive father, I hated the despot he had become the day he had begun to persecute us.

I hated him for his hatred, I hated him for my ruined life, for my mother's misery and the mutilated childhood of my brothers and sisters.

I hated him for the irreparable crime he had committed in locking up a woman and six children, the youngest of whom was only three, for such a long time and in such inhuman conditions.

5

THE WALLS OF TAMATTAGHT

8 November 1973–26 February 1977

GLAOUI PALACE

A song rose up in the darkness. I led it, and soon my voice was joined by those of Raouf, Mimi, the girls, my mother, Achoura and Halima. The words sang of exile and hope, and of nocturnal departure. It was our story.

'*Vous avez poignardé nos vies*—You have cut through our lives like a knife,' went the chorus, 'but justice will always prevail.'

The first time we heard this song on the radio, we were in Assa. The singers were a very popular band of young Moroccans. Darham, their leader, was married to one of my cousins. We were unaware, as we echoed the chorus, that he had composed the song for us. The police officers escorting us on this third journey, crammed into an armoured truck, also began to sing. I hugged the little ones to me and cried.

We were made to leave Assa at the beginning of winter, with no explanation for this hasty departure. On thinking about it a little later, I believed I understood the reason. The King was preparing the Green March, a peaceful march by hundreds of thousands of Moroccans to reclaim the Western Sahara from Spanish rule. We had to be moved away from the south, my family's birthplace, where we had too much support.

In the truck that was taking us to our new destination, the guards had laid a red carpet on the floor, and there were pitchers of water for the children. Our youth and ebullience still triumphed, and in spite of the gloom, the dust and our anxiety, we tried to be light-hearted. Mimi was our favourite target. Despite the gruesome conditions in which we were travelling, she managed to sleep, snoring with her mouth open, her face covered in sand which got in everywhere. She was such a comical sight that we couldn't help laughing and making fun of her.

At one halt, I saw a cavalcade of cars and motorbikes drive by. A car rally was being held in the desert. We were only a few metres from the competitors but they couldn't see us, couldn't hear us and had no inkling of our existence. Life was going on, a stone's throw away, and nobody knew, or wanted to know.

After a long and exhausting journey like the previous ones, we arrived at Tamattaght, far beyond Ouarzazate. Each place was more remote than the last, further and further removed from our former life. We were installed in a huge fort that majestically dominated the desert, a ruined palace whose high walls blocked out the sky.

You could still see vestiges of past splendours, hand-painted walls and ceilings in pastel tones and gold. Tamattaght palace had belonged to the pasha El Glaoui of Marrakesh who had lived in even greater luxury than the legitimate sovereign.

We entered the fort through a huge blue door. The nine of us were given two rooms to live in, on the first floor. Below, a cavern with a beaten-earth floor served as our kitchen. We stored our provisions and trophies in another pokey little room: the place was riddled with horned asps and scorpions, and each time we caught one, we put it in a large bottle filled with alcohol. Halima found a huge python coiled up on itself, which scared us less than it terrified the guards. They rushed out of the room.

We washed downstairs by the fire that was kept alight during the day. My mother had contrived an ingenious sauna system. We made a sort of Indian tee-pee with five thick reeds tied with a rope and covered in plastic sheeting over which we placed our blankets. Mother heated stones until they were white hot and placed them in a little bucket inside the tent. She sprinkled water over them and the stones gave off a delicious heat. Each of us had our 'shower' in turn, first of all Mother with Abdellatif, then the little ones and me, then Mimi, followed by Raouf and lastly Achoura and Halima. For us, it was like going to the *hammam*, the Turkish baths, which was always a joyful occasion.

Very high, steep stairs led to the two main rooms. At the top of the steps, a door opened onto a very long corridor, as narrow as a coffin. At the end was a tiny room where we stored our luggage. This room was windowless, but we were to discover later, when we found an opening, that it faced an oasis.

We had to go up another three steps to reach our domain: a room with a concrete floor, lit by narrow skylights and flanked by two 'alcoves', in actual fact two high-ceilinged, dark, cramped corridors. These were our bedrooms. There was a washbasin and a hole serving as a toilet. In the room, pompously named 'the patio', we arranged tables for lessons, a rug where Abdellatif played, and a mattress where my mother spent the day listening to the radio and reading.

The furniture was pretty basic, but we tried, with the scant means at our disposal, to brighten up the place. The bedside tables were simply Coca-Cola crates that we covered with pretty fabrics; we hung photos on the walls and scattered mirrors and trinkets around to make it cosier.

Initially we all slept in the first alcove, on straw mattresses on the floor. In winter, it was so cold that we warmed our hands over gas lamps. In summer, the heat was stifling. The desert overwhelmed us. We often had visitors: huge rats, made aggressive by hunger. We killed them with clubs. When Raouf threw a bucket of water over one, the rat went crazy and hurled itself at my brother, biting his face.

Our nights were turbulent. My mother was worried; every night, when she read by the light of the gas lamp, she felt a breath on her cheek, a presence at her side. Raouf had terrible nightmares.

Around four o'clock in the morning, I would hear footsteps, muttering, people carrying empty buckets to and from the toilets and up and down the stairs. These ghosts terrified me. One evening, when I had installed myself in the middle of the room, I distinctly felt a woman as small as an elf lying down on top of me and squeezing me until I choked. I woke the others. Nobody was able to get back to sleep and Mother had to read us the Koran until dawn to chase away the spectres.

We told this story to one of the more sympathetic police officers. He believed us, and told us that the place was cursed because it had been built over a cemetery. Had we suffered a collective hallucination? Do the souls of the dead come back to haunt us? It was one thing to rebel against tangible enemies, but fighting against supernatural beings was well beyond our resources.

We moved to the other alcove. The ghosts—if indeed they were ghosts—still came, but they were much less in evidence. My mother still felt a breath on her cheek but she got used to it and, after a few months, our nocturnal visitors disappeared altogether.

I devoted the first few days to getting us settled in and organizing our life. I wanted to protect the children and provide them with a structure. In this unreal existence, cut off from everyone and everything, I imposed a routine that was as normal as possible.

Our day revolved around lessons. I took my role as teacher very seriously. I instigated three different levels. The two little girls were in the juniors, Raouf in the senior school and Mimi in the top class. We woke up at about seven, washed and had breakfast before starting work at eight thirty. I gave the little ones a French dictation and then asked them to make a summary, give an analysis of the text and answer some grammar questions.

Then I gave them some work to do on their own, and did the same with Raouf and Mimi. I improvised as I went along, filled in the gaps and went over anything they hadn't understood.

I made each of them learn five or six new words a day, along with the dictionary definition, and then use them in sentences or a little essay. Eventually I added English and Arabic as well. Raouf was in charge of maths; we went over the syllabus together and he taught it to the children.

Meanwhile, my mother cooked lunch. We weren't rationed, but

we had no fruit, butter, cream, eggs or sweets for the children. Then she looked after little Abdellatif. She taught him the alphabet and played with him as if he were at nursery school. Achoura and Halima helped Mother with the cooking, cleaning and laundry, and looked after our supplies. When they had a spare moment, Halima knitted and Achoura, who couldn't read or write, revised the French lessons I gave her.

After our morning classes, we washed our hands, stretched our legs and sat down to eat. School resumed at two, which gave my mother a chance to rest and listen to the radio. On Saturdays there were no lessons, but we chose a discussion topic and debated it all morning.

Raouf and the little ones were particularly interested in the First World War. They also loved geography, and we went on imaginary journeys all over the world. We talked about Ludwig II of Bavaria who fascinated me, about his country and its history. It wasn't a conventional education, but they preferred it that way.

Around six o'clock we went 'outside', to let off steam. We were allowed out into a gloomy little courtyard, surrounded by high ramparts, which gave us the feeling of being walled in. But that was our only opportunity to get any fresh air. We spread out a carpet, lit a small charcoal brazier, and Mother made pancakes. We relished this break, which was also a way of enjoying being together as a family.

Then it was bath time, then dinner and compulsory reading. The girls had no trouble reading. Raouf was more reluctant. He would read only war stories, adventure books and tales of pilots or soldiers in the Indochina war. We read until ten o'clock during the week, later at weekends.

At night, bats came and perched on our heads. At first they terrified us; later we waited eagerly for them to create a great commotion.

Once a month we organized a show, which we rehearsed enthusiastically. I would make up two plays, one in French and one in Arabic. I was barely twenty years old and I had incredible energy. I used the others, their youthfulness and naivety, to help me fulfil my childhood dreams. I was alternately playwright, director, choreographer and conductor—creating something at last.

My father and King Hassan II. AFP

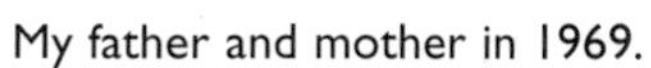

My father and mother in 1969.

OPPOSITE TOP: King Hassan II with Princess Lalla Mina and (right) me at age eight.

OPPOSITE BOTTOM: The Royal Palace at Rabat.

Camera Press/Nicole Herzog Verrey

TOP: Heady days of freedom: me at age seventeen.

BOTTOM: At eighteen, the would-be film actress.

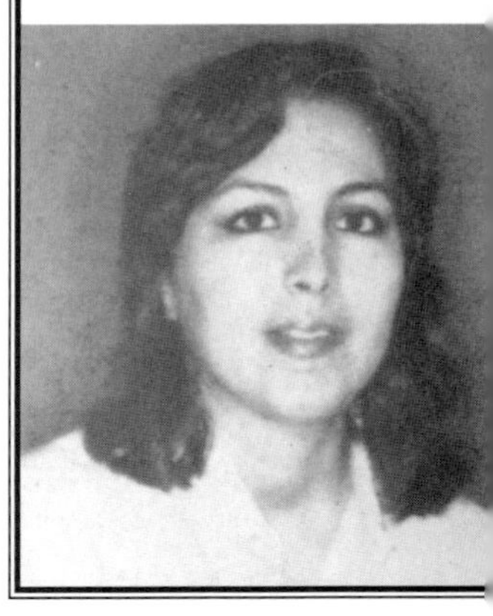

Tamattaght, 1974: pictures smuggled out of gaol.

TOP: (left to right) Abdellatif, Maria, Malika, Raouf, Myriam and Soukaina.

BOTTOM: Mother with Abdellatif.

Mugshots after our recapture. AFP/Popperfoto

TOP: (left to right) Abdellatif, Fatima, Myriam, Maria.

BOTTOM: Malika, Achoura, Soukaina, Raouf.

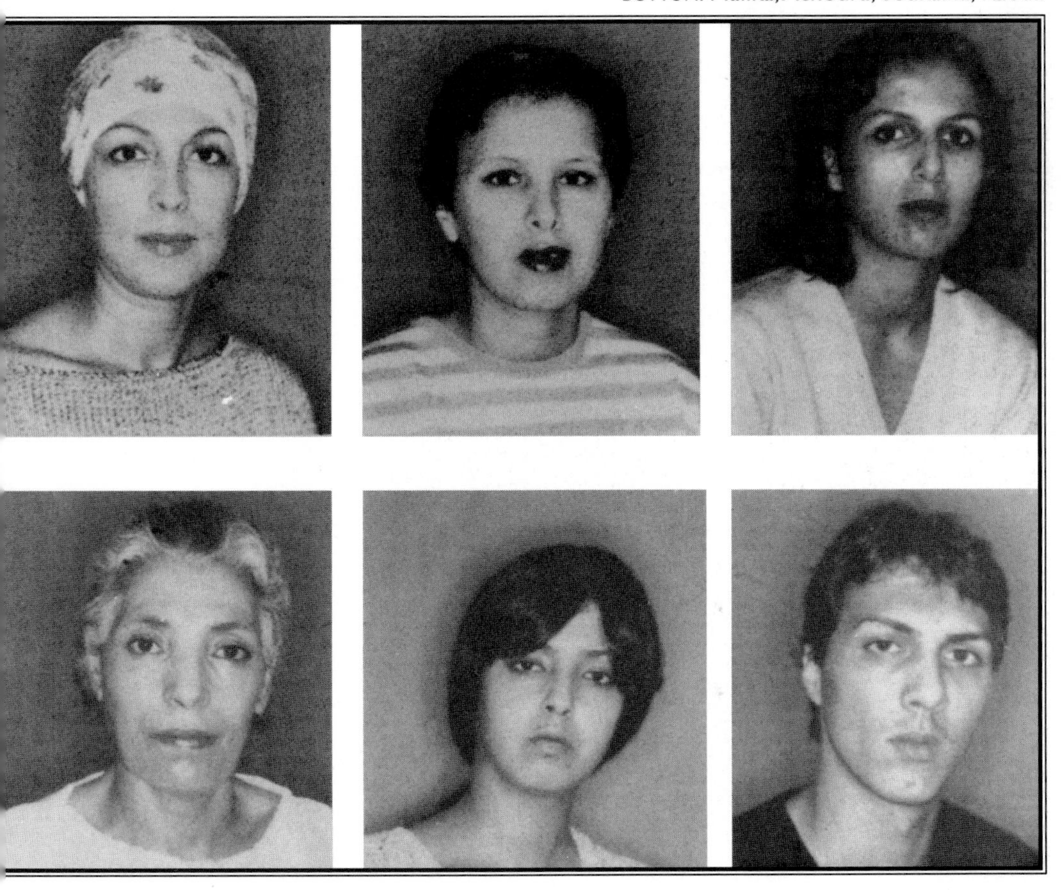

LEFT: After release from house arrest, but still not free: 1994.

BELOW: Maria arrives at Orly airport via Spain, June 1996. Reuters/Popperfoto

My wedding to Eric in Paris, 10 October 1998. © Arnaud Février

Mother and me. © Arnaud Février

We sang, we danced, we mimed. Our sole audience was Mother; we put on these shows for her. We took great pains over the details, delving into our store of clothes to make costumes.

I gave Achoura a Mireille Mathieu haircut when she was going to sing one of her songs. The poor darling knew hardly a word of French: she was such a sight all dressed in black, miming the words and executing the poses and dance steps we'd made her rehearse over and over again. The effect was irresistibly comical.

Frequently I would swap roles round. I would put on a man's jellabah and draw a little goatee beard under my chin, while Raouf would play my wife. With his tall stature, hairy calves, false bosoms under a Moroccan dress and exaggeratedly effeminate gestures, he had Mother in stitches for the entire two-hour duration of the show. Seeing her happy, even for a brief moment, was our finest reward.

Sometimes, on Saturday evenings, we would recreate the casino of Monte Carlo. Soukaina and Raouf, the artists of the family, made a roulette wheel and drew a gaming table, and from memory my mother helped us put the numbers down in the right order. A dried chick pea served as a ball. Raouf played Grace Kelly, and I was Prince Rainier. He wore a plunge-backed evening dress, and make-up and his hair was elaborately coiffed. If his resemblance to the princess wasn't obvious, he still looked magnificent. We also constructed shops, as we had done in Assa, but on a grander scale, and we even made a Monopoly set. I taught them Yahtzee which I'd played with Alain Delon.

I would often tell the children stories about the highlights of my teenage years. My memories rarely left me; they were all I had to ward off despair. I couldn't help reliving them again and again in my mind. Each of us had our own stories to tell the others, to prove we'd lived, despite our tender ages, except Abdellatif, who had experienced nothing. But over the years, our different stories became entangled, changed and distorted. My brothers and sisters appropriated mine. That was how we protected ourselves against the emptiness that threatened us.

* * *

We had to learn to live together, in wretched, cramped, insalubrious conditions, in darkness, isolation and confinement. The children were growing and it wasn't always easy. Despite all my efforts, they were very much aware that their life was unjust and abnormal. Raouf internalized his anguish. He was fifteen when we arrived at Tamattaght. He had not yet got over the loss of his father at an age when a boy probably needs his father most. He couldn't even avenge him, and thus he grew up unable to express himself, surrounded by women and children. He was the most profoundly bereft of us all.

Soukaina was going through a difficult adolescence. She was depressed, switching from sadness to joy, from anxiety to depression. Every day, she slipped a letter under my pillow, telling me she loved me, confiding her anxieties, doubts, wants and needs. Then we would talk about them and I would try to comfort her.

Contact with Maria was not so easy despite our fondness for each other. She was so fragile that the slightest shock would devastate her. When something upset her, she wouldn't eat, speak or move. The horror of her situation was reflected in her eyes; she seemed literally shattered.

Overwhelmed by her illness, Myriam had tremendous difficulty coping with grief, prison and our living conditions. She was doped up with Mogadon which we were able to procure thanks to the guards, but despite everything, her epileptic fits continued with increasing frequency. Poor Mimi, it was awful, and we were unable to do anything to help her. During one particularly violent fit, she spilled a saucepan of boiling milk over her thigh. Because she received no medical attention, the burn took months to heal.

We all spoiled little Abdellatif outrageously in our efforts to make up for the childhood he would never have. He received more than his fair share of attention, love and cuddles. We made him toys from wood and cardboard, and told him stories, fairy tales and lies. We clumsily tried to protect him, molly-coddling him so much that, on his release, he was unable to cope for himself. We desperately tried to save him from the present rather than prepare him for the future. But did we have a choice?

⋆ ⋆ ⋆

The seer was right: we were protected. We suffered a whole series of acute illnesses and each time we survived. I nearly died of peritonitis. I was delirious with fever for weeks. My mother didn't leave my bedside, bathing my brow to try to bring my temperature down.

One of our male nurses gave me aspirin, the only remedy available. Seeing that my condition was not improving, the camp commander consulted Rabat, but to no avail. Alone I fought the excruciating pain, before falling into a coma. When my temperature subsided, I had grown painfully thin and lost all my hair. But I survived.

We were cut off, but thanks to my grandfather, Baba el Haj as we called him, we did receive letters and books. Since our disappearance, the old man had battled like the devil himself to make contact with us and send us a few things to make life easier, with no regard for his own safety, for it was fatal to have anything to do with the Oufkirs.

After knocking at every door and writing to foreign heads of state, to French president Giscard d'Estaing and to humanitarian organizations, my grandfather appealed to Prince Moulay Abdallah. He asked if we could be permitted to receive letters and books.

The Prince hadn't forgotten us. Once again he showed his profound humaneness by granting my grandfather's petition and allowing him to send us regular packages of novels, articles and textbooks. When the big box of books arrived at Tamattaght, we were as thrilled as children around a Christmas tree . . . It was proof that someone in the outside world still loved us.

As a result of this kindness, the Prince was punished by the King. He was put under house arrest. But Moulay Abdallah did not give up. On his deathbed, he was still begging his brother the King to free us.

With the box of books, we received a censored letter in which Baba el Haj gave us cautious news. Thanks to the complicity of the guards who acted as go-betweens, we were able to receive other letters from our family and friends.

Mamma Khadija, my grandfather's wife, delivered these clandestine letters and collected ours, turning up at the secret rendezvous on a moped. She managed to elude the round-the-clock surveillance placed on all our family and friends. She too had joined the resistance. She did not play this role of messenger for long: she died of grief a few years after our imprisonment.

In Paris, I had nearly become engaged to a young man, Ali Layachi. He sent me several letters, full of the passionate outpourings of a young man in love. I answered the first letters, but his ardour soon irritated me. He had absolutely no idea of our plight. I tried to explain to him the gulf that now existed between us.

'There are those who are inside, and those who have remained outside,' I wrote. 'A whole world has come between us, walls have come between us, in fact, everything has come between us.'

I stopped writing to him and ended the relationship. In our daily nightmare, there was no room for dreams of the future, even less for love. And yet I was at that age.

The other letters did us more harm than good. Even though we waited for them eagerly because they were our only link with the outside world, we were shocked by the selfishness and the tactlessness of those who wrote to us. Not knowing what to tell us, they described their humdrum little lives, Christmas Eve with foie gras and champagne, their travels, parties and happy events; all the pleasures that make up the fabric of an ordinary life and which we were denied.

RASPUTIN

Of the twenty-five policemen under orders to guard us day and night, around three-quarters had previously done security duty at our house in Rabat. They had known my father, directly or indirectly, they respected my mother and they loved us all in a paternal way. They brought us fresh eggs, treats for the children, good meat and batteries for the radio. When they went to do their shopping, each one would buy us a little cake or sweet which they would smuggle in when they gave us our daily water ration.

One of them gave Abdellatif a baby pigeon. Soon they brought us more. Those pigeons had babies . . . Within a few weeks, we had become real pigeon breeders. We kept them in cardboard boxes against one of the patio walls. Our life revolved around them. We each had our own bird, and we gave them names and personalities, as we had done with our chicks.

We spent hours watching them, especially on Sunday mornings when there were no lessons. One of the females was called Halima. We watched her and a male doing a courtship dance, kissing, pecking each other affectionately and mating.

But prisoners are still prisoners, and despite our love for our pigeons, we never failed to check their little boxes to steal their eggs. Then Mother would make us an orange tart, much to the chagrin of Maria, who was so crazy about animals that we nicknamed her 'Brigitte Bardot'.

Five or six months after our arrival in Tamattaght, the police threw a potato over the wall with a note inside it to warn us that there was going to be a search. Colonel Benaich had arrived from Rabat, under the direct orders of the Minister of the Interior. This man had lost his brother, the King's personal physician, in the Skhirat coup and he blamed my father for his death. Needless to say he had no love for the Oufkir family.

He barged in, thrusting us aside. I was still in my night-shirt and I felt violated. Even though it was absurd, I still found myself saying, as I always had done when someone hurt me:

'If only my father were here, he would never have dared . . .'

He entered the second alcove, which we used as a classroom when it was too cold to stay in the main room. We had hung up a photo of my father that was very special to all of us, the one of him entering Italy with his regiment. Benaich gave orders for the picture to be torn down from the wall and then he stamped on it. He did the same with our other photos, our knick-knacks, our paltry furniture, the jars we kept our trophies in. He confiscated the books I hadn't had time to hide after receiving the warning.

By the time he left, the patio looked like a battlefield. We stood rooted to the spot, afraid, distraught, and incredulous too in the face of such violence. It began to dawn on us that we were there for a long time and that there would be no respite from our suffering. We were prisoners, there was no other word for it.

Until then, we had been treated relatively well. We had enough to eat, and were able to stay in touch with the outside world through music and the radio.

Benaich's arrival changed our lives. The police who had been guarding us now had orders to persecute us. Who had given the order to treat us with such brutality? Who had an interest in tightening the noose? We had no answers.

The *mouhazzin*—mindless, disciplined auxiliary forces—obeyed this new regime. The police, who were more sympathetic, retaliated by setting up a proper aid network. The older generation had resisted the French during the Protectorate. They were used to taking all sorts of risks while covering their tracks. They knew the system well, and acted in such a way as to ensure maximum safety.

They warned us when a search had been ordered by throwing a carrot or potato over the wall. This gave us time to hide our most precious belongings, especially the radio, to prevent them being confiscated. Some of them went to Rabat to see our grandparents. They carried letters, brought Mogadon for Mimi, and money that enabled us to improve our lives a little.

Every two weeks, when the guards opened the gates to bring us provisions, I sat in the courtyard with Raouf and tried to catch a glimpse of the landscape outside the walls. When we had arrived at the fort, it had been dark. We knew nothing of our whereabouts. The ramparts surrounding us blocked our view.

Each time the gate opened, we saw a strange little man who seemed to be trying to convey a message to us with his eyes. His appearance was bizarre: he had a beard and long hair, and his piercing black stare was like that of a drug addict. He made me think of a tiny Rasputin. We didn't understand what he wanted, and we found him extremely odd.

One morning, one of the policemen came in and discreetly whispered to us that we should ask for a male nurse. He glanced over at Rasputin. We were suspicious, and pretended not to understand. A little later, however, confronted with the bearded fellow's mute insistence, we beckoned him to come in.

He was from the same village as my maternal grandmother, loyal like all Berbers, and wanted only to help us. The night after our first meeting, we heard the sound of something dropping into the courtyard. We rushed out. A huge sack of flour had just landed on the ground. Rasputin was sending signals by flashing his torch behind the wall.

The guards who used to bring us treats did so in dribs and drabs: a steak, a box of eggs, a little flour or sweets that were passed from one pocket to another. With Rasputin, supplies arrived on an almost industrial scale: sacks of flour, rice, semolina and sugar, drums of oil, a hundred and fifty eggs . . .

To deliver all these provisions to us, Rasputin and his friends had to drag them from the oasis to the foot of the fort, enter the ruins and make their way to our section, clambering over the boulders at the risk of causing a rock slide. Then they had to tie the sacks to a rope and sling them over the wall—and all with the utmost discretion. Squads of police and auxiliary forces were watching every square inch of our prison and the surrounding countryside.

The delivery took up most of the night. When it was finished, the nurse came over by the same method as the sacks, accompanied by two young policemen who were overawed but proud to shake our hands. We showed them up to our quarters, and sat in the corridor where we had placed some benches. Each time they brought us food—in other words, whenever they had the opportunity—we would sit and talk until daybreak.

These exchanges meant a lot to us, especially to Raouf, who desperately needed male company. We drank tea and ate the cakes they brought us. The little ones were overexcited. Abdellatif refused to go to bed; he snuggled up to me, fighting off sleep, but these moments were important to him too. We chatted idly, laughed and told jokes, and they gave us news of the outside world, but at some point Rasputin always found a way of reminding us of the reality of our situation.

'You will never get out of here,' he would say to us, 'don't delude yourselves.'

Naively, we were counting on a royal pardon on Throne Day or on Hassan II's birthday. But Rasputin insisted on shattering our dreams in the name of sanity.

My mother, who never participated in these discussions, tried to comfort us.

'Can't you see this man is crazy? Don't let him upset you, children, he doesn't know what he's talking about.'

Rasputin did look every inch the madman, but he would go to any extremes to help us. During the two months that followed his last visit, we lived in hope while waiting for the changing of the guard. He had his allies among the relief guards who were to bring us replies to our letters, a radio and more books, for the ones our grandfather sent us were never sufficient.

On the appointed day, Raouf, who was as agile as a mountain goat, clambered up to the top of the ramparts and settled down to watch through a tiny loophole. I joined him. We saw the trucks arriving and the others preparing to leave. The police officers were pleased to see their friends, greeting and embracing.

We were very excited at the sight of the cases in the trucks. They promised days of reading, music and happiness.

Raouf elbowed me. There was anxiety in his voice.

'Kika, look. There's something going on. They're all rushing around in a frenzy.'

I followed his outstretched finger and saw there was some sort of commotion. Rasputin was running. Someone had betrayed him . . . The nurse was caught. They searched his belongings, found the money, the radio, the books and the hi-fi system. Everything he had brought us was confiscated, except the letters, which he had kept well hidden.

Forty-eight hours after the dismantling of our network, Yousfi, a senior intelligence officer, arrived flanked by three henchmen. We already knew him: he had interrogated my mother when my father died.

After searching everywhere, he set up a little table and began a heavy interrogation that lasted all day. We were treated to the whole works: the typewriter, the written statement. After beating about the bush for ages, they told us that the nurse had informed them that we were plotting something. They wanted to know what it was.

Rasputin had been sharp enough to denounce all the guards, so that no-one in particular would be punished. He claimed that they had helped us for reasons that were both political and humane.

'We acted as family men with children,' he had argued. 'Anybody would have done the same.'

So all our guards were arrested, only to be released again immediately. At the fort, it was us who were to suffer the consequences.

The new team of *mouhazzin* drafted in to guard us kept us under much closer surveillance. There were friskings and searches, the guard was doubled, and that was the end of the letters, books and contact with our family.

We were given less and less food. Luckily, we had built up reserves, enough to feed a regiment, and that was how we managed to survive.

RESISTANCE

These new conditions appalled us. But what could we do? We were so powerless and alone, so entirely dependent on the monarch's whims.

One night when I felt utterly desperate, like so many others, I went out into the courtyard to gaze at the sky. For the first time in ages I began to cry. I sought a response to my tears in the beauty of the starry dome. The night was pure, and calm. And hopelessly silent. God was not answering our cries for help. We were being buried alive and we were going to die here, cut off from the world, without anyone to help us. I had an urge to scream, but the proximity of the children stopped me, as it did each time cries of rage or pain rose to my lips.

On the morning of my twenty-third birthday, I woke up very early and sat on a chair, all alone, facing our pigeon house. The others were still asleep. During those few hours' respite, I thought about my life, about the years going by and my vanishing youth.

I was painfully conscious of time taking its toll on my face and body. I wore my hair very long, down to my hips, and when I walked past the big mirror we still had, or when I caught the guards looking at me, even though they were very paternal towards us, I knew I was beautiful. With a sense of hopelessness I admired my firm, sculptured body and youthful face, telling myself that this ripeness would be lost for ever. No man would love me and enjoy the bloom of my twenties.

I suffered for Mother, who had seldom been so beautiful as she was now. I would sometimes stop what I was doing to stare at her. I suffered for my sisters who were becoming women without having been children, for Raouf, deprived of a father figure, and for Abdel-latif, deprived of everything, and I felt remorse for Achoura and Halima, imprisoned alongside us out of loyalty.

I suffered for us all, robbed of freedom and hope. I had mourned my father. Now I was mourning my own life.

In all this wretchedness, there was one thing of which I was certain: we were the only ones who could do anything for our cause. That was what gave me strength when my morale plummeted.

We sent the King a petition signed in our blood. We gave it to the camp commander, who passed it on to his superiors. This naive, almost childlike letter appealed to the monarch's magnanimity. We wrote that it was unworthy of him to permit the persecution of a woman and children.

My mother, Raouf, Mimi and I then went on hunger strike. It was the middle of winter, and the ground and the walls were frozen. We stayed in our beds, curled up under our thin blankets, trying to preserve a tiny bit of warmth.

At first, although we were weak, we were determined and full of enthusiasm. Then our instinct for self-preservation took over and we started eating again, out of sight of the guards. In one of my mother's trunks, kept in the cubby hole where we had stored our luggage, we had saved around thirty French loaves, which we put out in the morning sun to soften them. We called that the 'sunbathing' session.

I cleaned the bread with a shoe brush to remove the mould, and passed it round from bed to bed. We had also saved a store of chick peas, for us the hunger strikers' sole food, which we ate in secret:

chick pea *tagine*, chick pea soup, chick pea nibbles. These measly rations kept us going and we sent back the scant food provided by our captors untouched.

But we were still corruptible. The promise of a kilo of butter put an end to our strike. We could almost smell the aroma of pancakes and cakes . . .

In any case, our strike had led nowhere. Nobody was interested in our fate.

But we had to do something. We decided to escape.

Shortly before our hunger strike, Raouf, who was in the habit of poking his nose into everything, had noticed that the window in the little luggage store had probably been bricked up. He was desperate to see outside, and we set to work removing a few of the blocks. We discovered a wrought-iron window, with shutters that we pushed open.

The landscape was a revelation. It was no longer dark, the sky was ours at last. The window looked out onto an oasis below. We heard crows cawing, turtledoves cooing, shepherds calling their flocks, and even the splashing of water.

We fought for our turn to enjoy the view. Looking into the distance, drawing a deep breath of fresh air . . . You take these things for granted when you can do them.

We closed the window, making sure we could open it again when we pleased. From time to time, when one of us was feeling low, we would sit in the store room and watch the dawn, or the sunset, spring starting at the oasis, evidence that nature and the seasons still existed.

Maria and Soukaina went there more often than the rest of us, feasting their eyes on the slightest details. It was heart-rending to find them there and catch the mournful expression on their little faces pressed up against the bars. Like hunger, depression in a young child is an unbearable sight.

When we decided to escape, our initial idea was to enlarge this window. But the guards heard us prising out the bricks and throwing them in the five-metre-deep latrine pit. It made a terrible din. They came in and searched everywhere. Luckily, we were able to conceal the evidence of our crime before they arrived and they didn't notice it. This alert reminded us that the utmost secrecy was needed.

We had to attack on a different front. The kitchen, with its hard-packed mud surfaces, seemed the perfect place. All Raouf and I had in the way of tools was a small spoon each. We began to dig into the wall to make a tunnel, at a height of twenty centimetres from the floor. In less than ten minutes we had already removed a lot of earth, but we had to take care not to cause the whole wall to collapse.

In one afternoon, we had dug a hole big enough to crawl through. I slid inside and made my way along the tunnel behind it, and found myself confronted by a blocked opening.

I felt something brush against my thigh and began to scream.

'I'm not going any further, Raouf, it's infested with rats.'

'Kika, do you want us to get out of this wretched place? It's our only chance. You'll just have to get used to it. Come on, be strong.'

Raouf was so insistent that I ended up obeying him. We pressed on.

We began to clear away the rubble. It was a dangerous, exhausting job. We had to carry very heavy loads without dropping them, for fear of alerting the guards. But our persistence was rewarded. The door was finally clear and we emerged among awe-inspiring ruins, which gave us a wonderful feeling of freedom.

We were intoxicated, dazzled by the sky and the fresh air. We walked in silence, communicating with our eyes and expressing ourselves with our hands. We had been living in silence for nearly three years. But this first walk was very nearly our last. A column of stones collapsed at our feet with an infernal noise. We just had time to jump out of the way.

It took us a few moments to recover from this scare. The column could have crushed the pair of us. Raouf looked at me; we were both thinking the same thing. Who, up there, was protecting us like this?

My brother and I didn't need to say much to understand each other. Our escape had to be prepared in minute detail, like a commando operation. The two of us would be the ones to go. Any more would be too dangerous.

We stayed outside for nearly two hours, analysing, weighing up, calculating. We climbed up to the highest level of the fort, wary of the rocks that could roll on top of us at any moment.

Below, in the oasis, a few guards were out enjoying a stroll. We could even hear their laughter. Hidden behind the rocks, we gazed at the almond trees, the lush grass and the red earth.

Then Raouf told me to look beyond a little path.

'You see, there's water, there's a river that flows around the fort. We'll follow it to Ouarzazate.'

We returned reluctantly, but we had to get back to our family and convince them of the viability of our plan. The little ones were keen; they drank in our words, ready to set off at once. Mother, who was more sceptical, listened in silence.

To convince her, we knotted together two lengths of the sturdy fabric that covered our mattresses and explained that we were going to descend the ramparts with this makeshift rope.

The spot we had chosen was twenty metres high. When we showed it to her, my mother was adamant: she wouldn't allow us to take such a risk. Nothing would make her change her mind.

'OK to the escape plan,' she said, 'but find another solution that's less risky. I don't want to lose you.'

She thought for a moment, and her face lit up. The fort was bound to have a gate that opened onto the oasis. We just had to find it and clear away the rocks blocking it, and then we would be able to leave. We looked for the gate among the ruined columns and the heaps of boulders. In my haste I nearly fell over the edge of a sheer drop, and I owe it to my presence of mind and probably that of my guardian angel that I didn't plunge to my death. I turned round. Mother was ashen.

Now, when we say that someone has 'the ruins look', it means that they're staring glassy-eyed and horror-stricken, like Mother when she thought I was going to fall.

Prompted by an inspired guess, my mother asked us to help her move a huge rock. The gate we were looking for was behind it, and it did indeed open onto the oasis. We wouldn't need to risk our lives to escape.

But before the big day, we had to train. Build up our stamina. Three times a week Raouf and I went out at midday, when the sun was at its most cruel, each carrying a very heavy rucksack, and marched around the courtyard for four hours.

We built castles in the air. We had a little of our grandfather's money left. After crossing the oasis, we would take the bus to Ouarzazate. We also needed to pack some food. We had no identity documents, but I had found among my papers the vaccination record of a male Moroccan friend whom I had met in Paris. I gave these to Raouf and I memorized his sister's name, in case we were stopped. We were still such children . . .

Among all our books, there was one we had always scoffed at because it was about magic, witchcraft and the occult sciences. My mother picked it up at random and having flicked through it, decided to use it to invoke spells for the success of our venture.

She made a wax doll and stuck needles into it, uttering mysterious incantations that were supposed to help us escape. We were all creased up with laughter as Mother, who had never in her life believed in all that twaddle, struck up an attitude of intense concentration. We called her a witch.

On the appointed day, Raouf and I found ourselves outside for the final run-through.

One of the girls came rushing out in a panic to fetch us.

'Come in quick. They're here. They want to see Mother.'

We arrived breathless and dusty. The police told us that we were leaving Tamattaght. We redoubled our teasing of Mother—her witchcraft had backfired.

'You wanted to move?' she retorted, mortified. 'Well, we're moving.'

The children were glad to leave. We had been locked up for four and a half years, and had spent more than three years imprisoned in this ruined fort. Abdellatif, whose birthday was in February, was about to turn eight, the girls were thirteen and just fifteen, Raouf nineteen, Myriam twenty-two. I was twenty-three and Mother had just turned forty. While the little ones were excited, I was wary and anxious, fearing the worst.

Of course, we weren't told where we were going, but we were led to believe that our living conditions were likely to change for the better. It was probably in response to our petition . . . Yes, the King had taken pity on us. Our treatment would be gentler. Tomorrow, maybe we would be free . . . Hadn't they asked us to sort out our possessions, taking only our own things and leaving the mattresses, blankets and everything that belonged to the state? Perhaps the situation was going to be resolved . . .

All this was implied, but nothing was confirmed. Why this ambiguity? Probably to ensure our cooperation during our transfer. We were torn between hope and dread. I instinctively concealed my little radio about my person. Subsequent events proved me right, and I later congratulated myself on my intuition.

I thought there were limits to human suffering. At Bir-Jdid, I was to discover that there were none.

6

BIR-JDID PRISON

26 February 1977–19 April 1987

A BAD START

Our baggage was in the courtyard, the place was in chaos. We didn't want to leave Tamattaght without our beloved pigeons, but they didn't understand that we were leaving and were flapping around above our heads, beating their wings and cooing indignantly.

The children were darting around and each time they succeeded in catching one, they shut the pigeon up in a wicker basket. Maria, Soukaina and Abdellatif laughed their heads off. This departure was almost a game for them. We adults were more anxious—worried sick, to be honest.

One incident sent a chill of fear through us: the police wanted to split us up into pairs in separate armoured trucks with blacked-out windows. They were rough, brutally shoving us forward with their bayonets. Mother refused to allow us to be split up in this way. She screamed, begged and cried. They gave in, probably to avoid a big fuss. Mother was to travel with the two boys, Myriam with Achoura and Halima, and I with the two girls.

It was completely dark inside the vehicles. We stumbled as they made us sit down quickly. We placed the baskets containing our precious pigeons at our feet. We hadn't been able to catch them all. Two *mouhazzin* armed with bayonets came and sat facing us.

Even the children were quiet now. The atmosphere had changed. Borro, the new commander of Tamattaght camp, was not softhearted. He had replaced the former commander a few months earlier, when the number of *mouhazzin* guarding us had been tripled. This change had been due to the fear that we would escape, aided and abetted by a mysterious commando from Algeria. At least that was what we understood. That was perhaps why we were being made to leave Tamattaght.

In any case, no explanation was forthcoming, as usual. We only hoped that Borro would not be coming with us, wherever we were going.

The journey lasted twenty-four hours, becoming increasingly exhausting as we drove. We were under constant surveillance. We could not even find a discreet spot when we got out to relieve ourselves; the police came with us and watched us until we had finished.

It was February. The vehicle slowed down briefly and I took advantage to press my face up against a crack in the armoured truck. The trees were hung with streamers. People were busily preparing for the Throne Day celebrations, evidence that the King was more powerful than ever. I wallowed in my memories for a few moments. At the Palace this festival was always a happy time, a time when we were spoiled. But then I came back down to earth and frantically tried to fathom out where we were, but it was so dark outside it was impossible.

Tired, worn out from the journey and numb with cold, I inhaled deeply. The air smelled damp; I could hear frogs croaking. I concluded that we had left the desert and were near the coast. I was not mistaken. The Bir-Jdid barracks, where we were being taken, were forty-five kilometres from Casablanca. This we discovered much later.

The road was flooded, making it impossible for the armoured trucks to get through. We had to get out and continue in Land Rovers, still split up into three groups. They blindfolded us, but we had time to catch a fleeting glimpse of the countryside. We were in an agricultural area with fields as far as the eye could see. In the distance we could make out a farmhouse. Was that where we were being taken? The building was surrounded by wire fencing and watch-towers.

I was shivering and my teeth were chattering with cold. From the depths of the darkness, like in a play, I heard a man's voice, a distinguished, well-educated, profoundly humane voice, in marked contrast to the coarse yelling of Borro and the *mouhazzin*.

The man stepped out from the shadows. He was Colonel Benani, responsible for our transfer from one prison to the other. He wrapped me in his burnous, offered me cigarettes and, when I accepted, went to fetch two packets for me. I was moved to tears by this thoughtful gesture, the first for so long. Then we drove another five hundred metres. When the convoy finally came to a halt, I could make out the nightmarish throbbing of an electricity generator.

The King had answered our petition.

We were shown into a house, our eyes still blindfolded. Someone closed a door and removed the scarves. Then we saw we were in a little colonial-style residence built of cement, in the shape of an L.

We entered through a wooden door that led to a long avenue bordering a little courtyard where five old fig trees stood guard like sentries. Four doors opened onto this courtyard, and these were our four cells, the first, which was to be Mother's, at right angles to the other three.

In a tiny recess by the first cell, two huge palm trees formed a canopy of foliage. The walls enclosing us, so high and thick that they shut out the sky, separated us from a barracks with watchtowers at frequent intervals. Soldiers at arms stood in sentry boxes all around the house. Our every move was being watched.

We were told right away that we would be separated at night. We would be allowed to see each other during the day and to eat together, but at night each person would have to go back to their own cell. Mother shared hers with Abdellatif, my sisters and I were in another one, Achoura and Halima were together and Raouf was all alone.

This news made us all sob. Mother cried and pleaded, saying they didn't have the right to separate her from her children.

'I can bear anything except that . . .'

'Madame, please understand that I am ashamed of what I am doing,' replied Colonel Benani, terribly embarrassed. 'This mission will plague me for the rest of my life. But I have been given orders, and unfortunately I must obey.'

Our respective cells did not bode well for the way we would be treated. Even though we were already accustomed to discomfort, filth and very basic amenities, this was downright squalid. The walls and reinforced doors had been hastily repainted squirrel grey and the cells were so damp that rivulets of moisture ran from the ceiling down to the floor. The wan electric light came from the generator that operated only for an hour or two at night. The mattresses were just thin layers of foam with covers of dubious cleanliness.

Each of our cells comprised several little rooms and a tiny open-roofed recess, with thick bars over the opening. That would soon be our sole source of fresh air. There were three steps up to Mother's cell. The main cell had a toilet and a cupboard one and a half metres high, placed halfway up the wall and accessible with the help of a stepladder. We put our remaining belongings in there.

Once there had been a window, but it had been sealed up and covered with opaque Perspex. While he was still little enough to stand up in there, Abdellatif made it his observation post. He managed to pierce the plastic with the tip of a skewer and he would glue his eye to the hole to try to see out.

Their cell, like the others, was closed by a newly fitted reinforced door. In the corner of the courtyard, another door led to the cell I shared with my sisters. In addition to the recess covered with a metal grating, we had a cell in which we installed our four beds, dimly lit by a skylight covered with Perspex, a toilet, a cupboard where we stored our suitcases, another pompously named 'the gym', and 'the bathroom', an alcove where we 'showered' with buckets of water. It was adjacent to Mother's cell.

The water they brought us was for washing and drinking. When we poured it away, it drained across the sloping floor into a little gutter which ran under the wall separating us from Mother's cell. Our first instinct was to remove the iron bars from the bed frames and dig away at the earth. We followed the course of the water. When we were no longer allowed out of our cells, this gutter would act as our mirror.

Mother would lie on her stomach on the ground, and we did likewise on our side. The only way we could catch a glimpse of one another was via our reflections in the water. For years that was our only means of contact, other than with our voices. These were highly emotional moments. We wanted to touch and kiss, and we weren't able to do so.

Achoura and Halima's cell was next to ours. The two women slept in a tiny cell and cooked in a recess with a double grating over it. Next door was Raouf's cell, whose 'toilet', a pit dug into the ground, looked out onto the fig trees in the courtyard. Security was tightest around my brother; you had to go through three doors to get to his cell.

The first search took place at the beginning of April, two months after our arrival at Bir-Jdid. The aim was to intimidate us. As we had dreaded, Borro was in charge of the new camp. He was a sinister character, utterly sure of himself and without an ounce of compassion. He received his orders from Rabat and carried them out to the letter, confiscating our records, books and hi-fi player. Luckily, we were always on the alert and had developed fast reflexes and a healthy mistrust.

While some of us distracted the *mouhazzin*, as quick as a flash the others dismantled the hi-fi and divided the parts between us, concealing them between our thighs. We hid the little radio in the same way, as well as a few textbooks and electric wires. During the ten-year nightmare, the radio enabled us to link up to the world. Without it, we wouldn't have survived.

A few days after searching our rooms, they came with pickaxes and removed everything that still gave the place the aspect of a home—the parapets, flowers and trees.

Each year, for the King's birthday, we sent him a letter begging him to pardon us. In July 1977, we enclosed with our letter a few portraits that I had drawn and which bore a fair likeness—one of him, one of his son, Sidi Muhammad, and one of Muhammad V.

His expression of thanks was not long in coming. Shortly after we sent the letter, Borro and his henchmen locked us up in Raouf's cell until nightfall. We could hear dull thuds, the sound of hammering. When we were finally allowed out, the damage was impressive. They had taken all that remained of our meagre belongings, our trinkets, the last textbooks, Abdellatif's toys, our food reserves, nearly all our clothes, Mother's jewellery and my photo album.

Then they lit a huge bonfire with everything that was combustible. We were invited to watch the show. The children were all the more traumatized when the hated Borro forcibly searched Soukaina, who was only thirteen, and discovered the radio batteries on her. Afterwards, she was in a terrible state of shock. She ran a high temperature for ten days and had to stay in bed.

The next morning they came back again. They made us go out into the courtyard where Borro was pacing up and down.

He told us that he was aware how fond the children were of the pigeons. It was true that for several years those little creatures had boosted our morale.

'But pigeons,' he added, 'aren't meant to be kept as pets. They're meant to be eaten. So we're going to kill two every day.'

Despite our tearful entreaties, they carried out their threat. For a few days, they came back each day with two dead pigeons. We decided to spare Abdellatif this sight. The child, who had turned eight on 27 February, the day after our arrival at Bir-Jdid, was at the end of his tether.

Shortly after our arrival, he tried to kill himself. He still had his little bicycle and was cycling along the path round the courtyard with the fig trees. I was chatting to Mother, while watching him out of the corner of my eye. Suddenly I saw him wobble and fall off. We rushed over. Abdellatif had a glazed look and couldn't stand up. Soon he fell into a deep sleep. Raouf held him under his arms to support him, and I tried to get him to drink a henna infusion.

There was total panic. Achoura and Halima wailed and tore their hair, and the three girls were dazed. As for Mother, she went into a state of shock. She was deathly pale and gazed at us helplessly, too overwhelmed to cry.

I managed to make him bring up most of the pills he had swallowed, all the Valium and all the Mogadon for Mimi's fits that Mother had hidden in a little pillbox which she always kept on her. Goodness knows how he managed to steal it.

Informed of the incident, Borro came up to the bed, saw that the child was asleep and shrugged. He couldn't do anything except refer it to Rabat.

'What if he dies?' sobbed Mother.

Another shrug was our only reply.

Abdellatif was a robust child. He woke up with no ill effects. His explanation devastated us. Since being imprisoned with us at Bir-Jdid, he had overheard all our conversations, all our outpourings of grief, anxiety, fear and anger.

Somehow he'd imagined, in his little mind that was too mature for his years, that killing himself would be the best way to get us all out of this mess. He didn't want to see us suffer any more.

From that day on, we vowed to spare him. We wouldn't talk in front of him any more, we'd hide our grief from him, we'd invent a fantasy life for him and we'd get him to believe in it.

HELL

The first circle of Hell belonged to the past. During the next ten years, we were gradually to enter the others. Until then, we had managed to preserve a family life, a cocoon where we protected each other.

At Bir-Jdid, family life was out of the question, and so was privacy. Everything was out of the question.

At first, we were all allowed out into the courtyard together. From eight o'clock in the morning the cell doors were open and we could go in and out of one another's cells. Generally we all gathered in mine. This freedom of movement lasted a few months, but Mother,

Raouf and I knew that sooner or later we would be in solitary confinement and that we had to prepare for it.

The dreaded moment arrived at the beginning of 1978.

On 30 January, Raouf's twentieth birthday, my brother was locked up alone in his cell. He would no longer be allowed out or to see us. A few days later our turn came, on the pretext that we had dared to ask for extra butane because we were freezing to death. Halima and Achoura were spared being totally locked up. They were allowed out into the courtyard once a day to gather twigs for the charcoal brazier.

In the early days of our permanent separation, we were allowed to go out into the courtyard for a breath of air at different times. Mother went out in the morning until ten, then it was our turn.

I would stand under Raouf's window and he would cling to the bars of his 'toilet', and we'd chat about this and that. He monopolized the conversation, he was so desperate to express himself. He suffered cruelly from his isolation.

He would often talk about our father and his longing to avenge him. He was obsessed with the idea. And then we were no longer allowed out of our cells.

Now we were locked up twenty-four hours a day, separated and ill-treated. All the links with our former life had been severed. We had become mere statistics. We had to learn to come to terms with our cells, that tiny space that was to become our life, our world, our time, punctuated only by the seasons.

Mother, Raouf and I were their main targets. They were determined to break us—Mother, because she was the wife of the hated General, me because they were aware of my influence over the rest of the family, and Raouf because he was his father's son and it was natural that he would want to avenge him. In their minds, he had to be stopped at all costs. Of us all, it was Raouf who suffered the most physically, and who took the most knocks.

The guards, all *mouhazzin* now, were forbidden to speak to us kindly, or to show any interest in us. On the contrary, they were to humiliate us in every little way possible. I lived with a permanent fear in the pit of my stomach: fear of being killed, beaten or raped, fear of constant humiliation. And I was ashamed of being afraid.

We were never seriously beaten, apart from Raouf. Only once was I punched in the face because I had dared to defy an officer. I fell backwards and my head hit the wall of the corridor with a violent thud. The girls came out of the cell, ashen. I got to my feet to reassure them and told them I'd lost my balance. Later, I told them I'd been hit, but I implored them not to say anything to Mother. I felt humiliated, but I was angry at myself too.

The man who embodied this fear even more than Borro was Colonel Benaich, the King's officer who, back in the days of Tamattaght, had been the instigator of our new regime. He contrived to make our lives impossible. It was he who had given the order to kill the pigeons, and to deprive us of food. We rarely saw him. We guessed his arrival from the sound of a helicopter in the sky, or from the attitude of the *mouhazzin* who were suddenly standing to attention.

But at the same time, a particular relationship was developing between prisoners and torturers. We were victims, but we were also able to manipulate our gaolers within our limited scope. We would seize any opportunity to reverse the balance of power without their noticing.

With Benaich it was impossible; with Borro, difficult. The brute was disciplined to the very core of his soldier's being. Had he received orders to stab us to death, he would have done so without hesitation. He was trained to obey orders. The *mouhazzin*, on the other hand, for all their fierce bravado, were actually very stupid. It took only a little cunning to throw them off balance.

We put up a struggle.

We were allowed a wheelbarrow-load of firewood once a month for cooking. The *mouhazzin* opened the reinforced door and called me. Their tone of voice alone was enough to fill me with dread. When I came out, I was not allowed to venture beyond the threshold. I was dazzled by the light. They threw the logs onto the ground and ordered me to pick them up.

The first time, they brought big branches about one-and-a-half metres long. I took my time casually sorting through them, and gave the longest ones to the girls. Raouf had suggested we hide them in a little cavity high up in the wall of our cell, in preparation for a possible escape. The branches could serve as girders to shore up a tunnel.

The third month, the guards started bringing us nothing but tiny logs. They had realized what was in the back of our minds.

Our chief means of resistance was what we called the 'system', the only means we had of communicating with each other. It probably saved our lives.

Using a spoon and knife, Raouf had managed to prise up a paving slab under his bed. Under it he hid our precious radio, wrapped in old rags to protect it from the damp. At night he took it out and listened to it and felt less lonely. Then he had the brainwave of using the five or six amplifiers and the electric wire we had salvaged from the hi-fi speakers to make a transmission network from cell to cell.

The metal bars from our beds made good conductors. Each night the girls and I removed them from our beds and joined them, pushing the ends together. They had to stretch to Raouf's cell, through Achoura and Halima's, via holes in the wall at floor level. But, even placed end to end, they reached only halfway.

Raouf had the idea of adding the electric wire from the speakers and connecting it to the amplifier he had. I did likewise. The connections were thin steel wires, taken from the double grating above the reinforced door to our cell. We twisted them round the positive and negative terminals of our amplifiers. During transmission we often had to replace the wires, which kept snapping, but the sound came through quite well.

When Raouf was interested in a radio programme, he broadcast it to us by connecting up the amplifiers. I did the same for Mother and Abdellatif. To communicate with them directly, I used a length of hosepipe that I had stolen from the courtyard, seizing the opportunity when the guards' attention wandered for a moment. I had made a 'telephone line' through the wall separating our cells. During the day I hid it in Mimi's bed. The guards didn't dare search her because of her epileptic fits, which terrified them. They were simple souls at heart and were convinced she was possessed by jinns.

With these crude but effective means, we were able to communicate all night. The effect was magic when the voice of José Artur or of Gonzague Saint-Bris came through the walls to keep us company. It was as if they were in the cell with us. We were enthralled. Later, I would tell a story every night using the same system.

I subsequently refined the invention. I got rid of the bed bars, which were too heavy and awkward to manipulate, and substituted cut-up springs which we kept in our suitcases. But the principle remained the same.

At night, the minute the guards switched on the generator, we assembled our 'system' under cover of the din it made. Removing the bars from the beds and passing them from cell to cell made a terrible racket. But to our immense satisfaction, the only one we had in that nightmare world, they never discovered our communication system. Our amplifiers were always concealed between our legs.

Eventually, there was only one left that had not succumbed to the damp, and I kept it on me. That one was sacred. It was for Raouf's survival, the only means we had of keeping in contact.

Barefoot and dressed in rags, we shivered in winter and suffocated in summer. We no longer had a nurse, or medicines, or watches, books, paper, pencils, records or toys for the children. We had to plead, beg and wheedle the occasional favour out of the gaolers: a precious pen that we used sparingly, or batteries for the radio that we eked out for months. We managed to get these from a little old man who had known one of my uncles, his regional governor.

Our routine was regulated by the guards. They came into our cells three times a day, morning and evening to bring us meal trays, and at midday to give us bread. At around eight thirty, they brought us breakfast, prepared by Achoura on her patio. It was coffee mixed with chick-pea purée, so diluted that it was little more than hot water. First of all we would hear their shoes pounding the ground outside, then the hateful jangling of their keys. Their arrival terrified us, for we always had something to hide: the radio, the batteries, the system or the holes in the walls.

As our cells were at right angles to each other, whenever they opened my door at the same time as they opened Mother's, we would each position ourselves so as to catch a fleeting glimpse of the other. We were constantly thinking up schemes like this. Around midday we heard their whistles announcing the arrival of the bread van, then around seven thirty they came back again, opened the doors and deposited our trays.

They never allowed us any respite; we were never able to forget that we were locked up in those wretched cells. We were watched around the clock, day in and day out. When we clung to the gratings to glimpse a patch of sky, we would see them watching us from the towers; they spied on us all the time, even through the walls.

For the first few months, we clung to a semblance of a timetable. In the morning I would play volleyball with my sisters in the 'sports hall'; we had made a ball with scraps of fabric. Depending on our mood, we might then have a 'bums and tums' workout, and afterwards, sweaty and exhausted, we'd have a 'shower'. Soukaina had developed a tendency to put on weight. I rationed her food and made her exercise to stop her letting herself go.

Later, we gave up physical exercise. Our bodies no longer responded. We lost interest in everything.

The days dragged on interminably. Our main enemy was time. We saw it, we felt it, it was tangible, monstrous, threatening. The hardest thing was to master it. During the day, all it took was a gentle breeze wafting in through the window to mock us and remind us that we were prisoners.

In the summer, dusk brought back memories of the sweetness of the old days, the end of a day at the beach, time for an apéritif, the laughter of friends, the smell of the sea, the tang of salt on my bronzed skin. I relived the little I had experienced.

We didn't do much. We'd follow the progress of a cockroach from one hole in the wall to another. Doze. Empty our minds. The sky changed colour and the day drew to a close. The weeks dragged by, and we lost all notion of time. A week felt like a day, the months like weeks, a year meant nothing. And I was wasting away. I learned to die inwardly. I often had the feeling I was living in a black hole, surrounded by darkness. As if I were a ball falling down a bottomless well and bouncing off the walls, *boing, boing, boing*.

We were becoming progressively immured in a silence broken only by the *mouhazzin*'s footsteps, their whistles, the jangling of their keys, the singing of the birds, the braying of a donkey we called Cornelius, at around 4 a.m., or the rustling of the palm trees in the wind. The rest of the day we didn't hear a sound.

We gradually forgot the hubbub of the city, the murmur of conversation in the cafés, the ringing phone, car horns, all those familiar sounds that are part of everyday life and which we had so sorely missed.

Mimi was the one who had an infallible sense of time. She calculated it from the sun's rays that filtered through our tiny window. Whenever we asked her the time, at any point in the day, she would poke her head out from under her covers and say:

'Ten past three,' or 'A quarter past four.'

She was never wrong.

We were allowed a small packet of Tide each month, with which we had to wash ourselves, our clothes and the pots and pans. We used salt to clean our teeth. At one point we had the bright idea of cleaning them with earth, as we sometimes did with the plates. But one morning Abdellatif woke up with his mouth purple and swollen and his tongue covered in white spots, so we stopped.

When the guards opened my cell, I would rush over to the cold-water tap on the wall opposite to wash my hair with Tide. There was foam everywhere. The *mouhazzin* thought that it was thanks to this treatment that we had such straight hair.

They talked about it among themselves:

'She's got lovely hair. I tried washing powder on mine, but it didn't make any difference.'

Using washing powder as shampoo mainly made our hair fall out and gave us eczema.

We always wore the same clothes, which we called our combat gear. Mother salvaged the fabric from our old clothes and the covers of the foam mattresses. She made us trousers with elasticated waists.

As if by deliberate coincidence, all seven of us had our periods at the same time. We had no cotton wool or sanitary towels, so we cut hand towels into strips and used them over and over again until they were worn out. We had to wash these rags, pass them to Halima to dry by the fire, and wait with our legs apart until they were ready so we could re-use them.

This lack of privacy was torture. We lived in full view of each other all the time—washing, going to the toilet and moaning in pain or with a fever were all shared. Only at night could we cry our hearts out under the covers without anyone hearing us.

Despite everything we got along well. There were no arguments apart from the occasional quarrel between the girls, but I always kept my eye on them. As we didn't have Mummy with us, I became their mother. It was I who raised them and taught them good manners and respect for others.

I wouldn't allow the slightest breach of manners, not even in prison, not even at Bir-Jdid. We behaved properly at the table, we chewed delicately, we said 'please' and 'thank you', and 'excuse me'. We washed our hands before meals. We washed ourselves scrupulously every day, especially when we had our periods, despite the freezing salt water we were given every day in the middle of winter that turned our skin bright red and made us shriek.

I was unable to divest myself of my Palace upbringing. When Raouf wanted to make fun of me, he put on a German accent and mimicked the governess, Rieffel. I didn't care. Of course, the mind had to triumph over the body, and that's what made it possible for us to bear anything, or nearly anything, but I insisted we take a pride in ourselves so as not to lose our humanity.

Sometimes I would indulge in a fit of vanity. I wanted to stop my face ageing. Mother had told me the beauty secret of the Berber women: they made a face mask of steamed, puréed dates and applied it all over their complexion. We were allowed a few dates only during Ramadan. I grabbed them all and made a paste, which I kept on all night. Result: the mice feasted to their hearts' content on my face, and my skin did not seem any the better for it.

We cut our hair with the little nail scissors that Mother had been allowed to keep to make our clothes. Raouf didn't have a beard, and that made him anxious, especially as we used to tease him about the three hairs on his chin.

Towards the end, however, he grew a goatee; he claimed that the day he shaved would signal the end of our incarceration.

This prediction, made up on the spur of the moment, came true. One morning he asked our gaolers to shave him, invoking the pretext of virility which was their soft spot.

'I'm a man,' he pleaded, 'I can't stay like this.'

They took him out into the courtyard and shaved off his goatee.

A month later, we escaped.

STARVATION

Hunger humiliates, hunger debases. Hunger makes you betray your family, your friends and your values. Hunger turns you into a monster.

We were always hungry.

Every two weeks, the *mouhazzin* delivered provisions to Achoura's cell, and she cooked for us all. She had to contrive to feed nine people with what they gave her until the next consignment. And that was very little.

We never had any milk, butter or fruit, except a few shrivelled dates and mouldy oranges from time to time. Rotting vegetables, two bowlfuls of flour, a bowl of chick peas and one of lentils, twelve bad eggs, a piece of spoilt meat, a few lumps of sugar, a litre of oil per month and a little tub of Tide—that was all we were usually given. There was no question of throwing anything away. But . . .

I had never seen vegetables in such a state, and, above all, I could never have imagined that anyone could eat them. The carrots were long, thick and green. Achoura would use the mouldy green aubergines to prepare a dish that the children nicknamed 'Japanese *tagine*'. The lentils were full of creepy-crawlies that floated in the water.

By cooking and recooking each ingredient, we managed to soften the food's consistency and forget the way it tasted and looked. Worse, we actually fought for second helpings. Our digestive problems seemed small compared with the other ills that permanently dogged us. Our bodies had become used to the lack of hygiene. We had unlimited water to drink, but it tasted salty and didn't quench our thirst.

I suspected that Achoura and Halima had organized a mini black market with the food, swapping sugar or bread with the other cells. No matter how often I counted, down to the last chick pea, something was always missing. They would say:

'It's the rats, it's the mice, it went off . . .' but I didn't trust them.

So I decided to take charge of the food stocks. As soon as the provisions arrived, I made an inventory and confiscated them. I forced Achoura to pass each item to me one by one through a tiny hole we had made between our two cells. I put everything they gave us in the little cell next to ours, in a makeshift larder under the paving slabs. The bread was hidden in a suitcase. I wanted to save as much as possible, to make sure we would be able to last out until the next delivery.

Every day we needed a little sugar for our coffee, a snack around eleven o'clock for the boys, especially for Abdellatif, who was growing fast and was the most obsessed with food. We girls ate little: after the coffee in the morning, we ate nothing more until supper time, when we had vegetables. In summer we didn't suffer too badly from hunger; it was too hot, and we were used to this starvation regime. In winter, however, our stomachs protested violently but we pretended not to hear them.

In the evening I gave Achoura the ingredients to cook a *tagine*, which she prepared over the brazier and then shared between the nine of us. Invariably, the same scene would take place. The Oufkir household's cordon-bleu chef would sob against the wall:

'But, Kika, how am I supposed to feed everybody with so little?'

Her tears left me unmoved. I was merciless. If we were to hold out for the whole fortnight, we had to be thrifty.

In spring we ate a wild plant, a weed, a sort of dandelion that Halima gathered in the courtyard and that I boiled up. I would add garlic and a dribble of olive oil, and use it in sandwiches.

I invented recipes to make our supplies go further. In winter I would mix a small glass of flour, a small glass of semolina and a small glass of powdered chick peas which I put in a saucepan with a litre of water, sugar and three spoonfuls of oil. Then I poured the mixture into tumblers. We reused the disgusting coffee grounds from our morning coffee over and over again. A sprig of mint spent days and days being passed from one cup of hot water to another to give us the illusion of mint tea.

Every two days, the guards brought us bread in cardboard boxes. I would tip the loaves out onto the floor and Soukaina and I would quickly lift up the flaps on the boxes and remove the thin layer of paper that lined them. We used it to write down the stories I told. This paper was as precious to us as food.

One day, while I was busy pulling off the paper, I saw the three girls licking the floor for crumbs that had dropped from the box. From that moment, I established a rule. Instead of fighting like stray dogs, they would each have their day, their turn at the crumbs.

At Bir-Jdid we were never once given a normal egg. The shells were green, and inside was a vile black liquid, the smell of which made us feel ill. I broke them, left them to aerate over night, and in the morning I whisked them with sugar. I soaked chunks of bread in this mixture and fried them in oil.

As soon as the smell rose up, a thrill ran from cell to cell. It was party time. The French toast warded off our hunger, it was substantial, it filled our stomachs and it wasn't so disgusting.

We had become experts in the art of salvaging everything. We even ate bread soaked in the urine and faeces of the mice that overran the cell. I can still picture Mimi, sitting up in bed, picking off the little black droppings sprinkled all over the bread with the delicacy of a duchess, before raising the morsels to her lips. All our rations were fouled by rodents.

To improve our everyday fare, we gathered the figs that fell from the trees in the courtyard. The first year, when we were still allowed out, we crammed in as many as possible. Achoura made fruit salads, which satisfied us a little. When we were all in solitary confinement, Halima gathered them on her own.

Once the guards saw that we liked these figs, they would shake them down from the trees before entering our cells, and then stand and eat them in front of us. We had to make do with the rotten fruits, or dried ones, and we were only too happy to have those.

Hunger sometimes drove us to the limit. It was so violent that we would cast envious glances at one of the others who hadn't yet finished their meagre share. Only the strict rules of behaviour that I had instilled in everyone stopped us from fighting.

We fantasized about a piece of meat, we salivated when the smell of the guards' *tagine* wafted in on the wind. Then we were as excited as hounds scenting their quarry.

Day and night we dreamed of eating and we felt ashamed to have sunk so low.

Mimi, the most fragile of us all, had no scruples about secretly stealing a few dried beans which she'd chew all day long, her head under the covers. We nicknamed her 'Mimi the baker' because she loved flour and bread. When we played our favourite game, 'you have forty-eight hours' freedom, you can do what you like', she would invariably reply:

'I stop outside a baker's shop, I stuff myself with bread and I bring back tons of cakes.'

Raouf planned to screw every woman he met. I wanted to raid a bookshop and buy as many books as I could carry away with me. I added with a sigh:

'And make love with a passing stranger, just to find out what it's like.'

The children dreamed of toys.

In our family, Christmas had always been sacred. Even at the Palace, where Islam was dominant, Christmas was still Christmas. Rationing didn't stop us celebrating it in style, and the same went for birthdays. We planned for them months ahead, saving up to make a cake. We cut down on everyone's portions, and put aside eggs and sugar, depriving ourselves of everything. But on the festive day, we had our big cake, which the guards unwittingly took from cell to cell, for we hid it under heaps of rags.

A few days before Christmas Eve, Achoura and Halima slid their gas pipe through the hole in our partition wall. I connected it to my little butane gas stove. That was how we made huge Yule logs, with fried chick peas, flour, eggs, oil, coffee and sugar. We were very well organized: we divided the work, and passed our various preparations—shortbread biscuits, custard, chocolate or vanilla substitute—from Achoura and Halima's cell to ours. We didn't need a fridge: it was so cold that I put the Yule logs outside to freeze. We enjoyed them so much that we squabbled over the last crumbs.

Christmas wouldn't have been complete without toys. We made some for little Abdellatif with pieces of cardboard that we salvaged whenever we could. One year we built him an aircraft carrier with fighter planes, tanks, Mercedes trucks and saffron yellow Volkswagen cars with wheels of silver foil. Then, I could have made anything out of a piece of cardboard. Now, I wouldn't know where to begin.

Every year I wrote him a letter in forged handwriting. We pretended that Father Christmas had left it specially for him. He believed it until the age of fourteen.

Halima collected some mud from the courtyard and Mother used it to draw footprints on the floor of her cell.

Then, Abdellatif was the happiest child in the world, and his happiness made our hearts glow.

SCHEHERAZADE

As we had no textbooks, exercise books or paper, I had stopped giving lessons. But the girls were curious to learn about life. They asked me if I had already had a boyfriend, how you kissed a boy on the mouth, what it felt like to have your breasts caressed. I answered as best I could, drawing on my own limited experience and on what I'd learned from books.

Abdellatif was avid to learn; Mother needed to talk. Raouf, the most isolated of us all, used the 'system' to give vent to his feelings. Achoura and Halima suffered from depression.

I listened, I comforted, I advised, I taught, I told stories, I mothered. I was a real chatterbox. At the end of the day, I felt exhausted from having given them all my energy. But how could I refuse, given that they were my entire *raison d'être*?

Then I had a brainwave. I was going to tell them a Story. In this way, I could talk to them of life, of love. I would give the younger ones the benefit of my experience; I would take them on journeys, make them dream, laugh and cry. I would teach them history and geography, science and literature. I would give them everything I knew, and for the rest, well, I'd improvise . . .

It was no small undertaking. I had to take into account their different ages to try to sustain everyone's interest. At twenty, Raouf had very different concerns and fantasies from the three girls, or little Abdellatif. Not to mention Mother, Achoura and Halima who all had their own preoccupations. But they all liked the idea so much that we immediately put it into practice.

As soon as the generator started up, we passed the 'system' from cell to cell. An hour later, the infernal noise stopped and, in the dark, I was able to start my Story.

I went on telling it night after night, for ten years, just like Scheherazade.

At first I'd go on until three o'clock in the morning, and then until four. Towards the end, I'd stop around eight o'clock, when the guards came to wake us up. I had reinvented the radio serial. The minute I picked up my microphone, I would get comfortable and I was off.

I simply needed to sketch an outline or say the characters' names for them to take shape in my mind. There were a hundred and fifty characters altogether, all different, all fascinating. Their appearance would reveal itself first, then their personality, their paths and their destinies. Then I would invent a past for them, a genealogy and a family, for the children craved to know everything about them.

The Story was set in nineteenth-century Russia, although I didn't really know why. I hadn't seen any films or read any books about it, apart from *Doctor Zhivago*, which takes place a little later. I described the palace at St Petersburg as if I had lived there. I told them of the raids of the Cossacks, the sleigh rides on the frozen Volga, the aristocrats and the muzhiks. I was at the same time novelist, screenwriter, director and actress. In creating all these roles, I explored my own emotions, fantasies, desires and nightmares to the full.

Thus I vicariously experienced adultery, homosexuality, betrayal and passionate love. I was perverse, shy, generous, cruel and deadly. I took turns being the hero, the heroine and the traitor.

I was disturbed to realize the extent of my power over the others. The Story was so real to them that I could manipulate and influence them at will. When I sensed they were unhappy, I would restore things with a few phrases. The Story was part of our everyday life, to the point that it caused arguments and passions to flare. One faction was for this character, another was against. They discussed it among themselves during the day.

'Do you think Natasha will be all right?' asked Soukaina.

'No,' explained Raouf, 'I don't think Russia will declare war.'

The Story was called 'The Black Flakes'. The protagonist was a young prince, Andrei Ulianov, who lived in Tsarist Russia. Handsome and very wealthy, he was also perverse and evil, and thought only of spreading wickedness around him. He had lost his parents when he was a baby; his mother died in childbirth and his father had committed suicide. The only family he had left was his grandmother, whose stunning looks he had inherited.

Ulianov lived in a vast palace, surrounded by thousands of acres of land. He owned a thousand muzhiks. His only passion was horse-riding. His grandmother wanted to present him at court, but he vehemently refused. He preferred to gallop across his estate at sunset. On hearing him coming, everyone would hide. He was so evil that he thought up thousands of nasty tricks, just for the pleasure of seeing others suffer.

One evening he fell from his horse. His initial reflex was to look around him to make sure nobody had witnessed his humiliation. Wasn't he one of the best horsemen in the kingdom? As he scrambled to his feet, he noticed an object glinting in the dust. He groped around and found some amulets. He picked them up and remounted his horse.

On his return home, he demanded to know the identity of the

owner of the amulets, otherwise he would massacre all the muzhiks. His steward went to visit the elderly Ivan, a patriarch with a long, white beard, and implored his help. Old Ivan turned pale. The amulets belonged to his fourteen-year-old granddaughter, Natasha. The steward asked Ivan to bring her to him, but the girl had fled.

Out riding the next day, Andrei Ulianov was intrigued by the sound of laughter. He hid behind some bushes and saw Natasha and her betrothed, Nikita, bathing naked in the pond. Natasha was stunningly beautiful, as dark as Nikita was fair. She was dancing for him. When they saw Andrei, they took fright and ran away. Ulianov pursued them on horseback. He shot at Nikita, who vanished into the marshes. He caught little Natasha, raped her and carried her off to his palace by force.

Two days later, Nicolas Barinsky, the son of the governor of Moscow, came to see him. He told Andrei that he was going to have to leave for the army. Barinsky was accompanied by some friends, including one Brezhinsky, who had to flee the country. Leaflets had been found at his home. Andrei agreed to help Brezhinsky. He lent him a horse and guided him through the marshes. For the first time in his life, he was involved in an act of rebellion against the ruling powers, but he was not yet aware of all the repercussions it would have.

That was the opening chapter. Each night I added more characters, honing the descriptions of people and making their paths cross. I created suspense, alternating new developments and dramatic turns of events. I managed to keep them all on tenterhooks.

Nowadays, I would be incapable of telling a story so rich in graphic detail. I don't know how my imagination managed to produce something like that and keep it going for those ten years without my ever tiring or boring my audience.

Frequently one of the wires would snap in the middle of the night. To inform us that the sound wasn't working, Raouf would whistle non-stop. Carried away by my story, I didn't hear a thing, but one of the girls would come and tell me. Then we'd all repair the wire on our side, and Raouf's whistling would stop only when he could hear me again. This could happen several times in one night, as it did when the guards came and asked Raouf why he was whistling.

Obliged to answer, my brother explained that it was the only way to frighten away the rats and mice that infested the prison. The guards looked at him in amazement. Raouf replied haughtily:

'What, you didn't know that? But it's common knowledge. It's the only way to scare them off,' he replied.

The guards were often amazed at our resourcefulness and intelligence. They may have ill-treated us, but they still admired us. They respected us for the clever way we grasped opportunities and turned them to advantage. They believed my brother immediately.

From then on, when Raouf whistled, we heard them whistling back. We were torn between the urge to laugh at their stupidity, which we never let slip an opportunity to do, and the wretchedness of being watched so closely that not the slightest movement escaped them.

Then, carried away by the spirit of the game, I told other stories. Our imaginations roamed from Tsarist Russia to Poland, Sweden, Switzerland, the Austro-Hungarian Empire, Germany, the American Civil War and the Bavaria of 'Mad' King Ludwig II or Empress 'Sissi'. I even wrote a novel, a series of letters between a grandmother and her granddaughter, based on *Les Liaisons dangereuses*. Soukaina noted it all down, and even designed the cover.

I did actually consign the Story to paper. I scribbled it down during the day on the thin sheets of salvaged paper. Unfortunately, during our escape, all my scrapbooks were destroyed by the friend I had entrusted them to, because he was afraid of being compromised.

These days, when we're together, we rarely speak of our time in prison, but the Story has lost nothing of its magic. When one of us mentions one of the characters, faces light up. It remains our best memory of this horrendous period.

I truly, humbly believe that this Story saved us all. It helped give a pattern to our lives. The radio permitted us to keep track of the date, but we had no markers, no milestones in our lives, other than those of Christmas and birthdays. So our characters had them for us: they got engaged, married, had babies, fell ill, died.

We would say to each other:

'Oh yes, don't you remember, it was so hot the day Natasha met the Prince . . .'

Or:

'No, you're wrong, I didn't have a fever when Andrei's grandson was born, but when he became Tsar . . .'

Thanks to the Story, thanks to the characters, we didn't succumb to madness. When I described the ball gowns in intricate detail, the beaded dresses, the lace, taffeta and jewellery, the carriages, the dashing officers and the beautiful countesses waltzing to the strains of the Tsar's orchestras, we forgot the fleas, the sanitary towels, the cold, hunger, filth, the salty water, typhoid and dysentery.

ILLNESSES AND SCOURGES

We could all have died twenty times over, but every time we emerged again unscathed from the numerous illnesses we contracted in prison. We were protected by a mysterious god whose main design was to keep us alive, although he didn't spare us the most horrific ordeals.

Some of the illnesses we suffered were very serious: violent fevers, infections, diarrhoea and mysterious viruses. Others were less virulent: sore throats and bronchitis, headaches or toothaches, haemorrhoids, rheumatism. But they were just as painful, for we had no medicines at all. I treated everything with olive oil.

Maria became severely anorexic. She suffered fevers and violent sweats that were so bad, she stayed in bed all the time. I had to wash and dry her four or five times a day. Then I would apply scalding hot water to her chest from a powdered-milk tin heated up by Achoura. It was the supreme remedy for all our anxiety attacks.

Mimi was the sickest of us all. Her epileptic fits left her exhausted and bedridden. She suffered a severe depression after the brutal sudden withdrawal of her tranquillizers. She stayed in bed almost without moving for eight years. I had to force her to wash.

Poor Mimi also had so many large haemorrhoids that she daily lost pints of blood from the open wounds. Every day I cleaned them with soap and water to stop them festering, which made her flinch with pain. It was impossible for her, in this condition, to go to the toilet. Anyway, she no longer ate anything.

Towards the end, Mimi's health deteriorated completely. Her life hung by a thread. The lack of food and loss of blood made her anaemic. But she remained stalwart. She never complained. In vain I pleaded with Borro to send her a doctor. Her gums were white, her complexion sallow, and she had no nails left. She was dying before our eyes and we couldn't do anything to prevent it.

On top of the illnesses, we had to deal with unwelcome guests, often carrying diseases. During the torrential rains, thousands of tree frogs fell to the ground. We collected them by the bucketful and gave them to Abdellatif to play with. They kept him occupied for quite some time.

Then there were the cockroaches. Fat, black and shiny. At night I couldn't sleep, my joints were constantly painful. Lying in the dark, I could feel them crawling over me, freezing cold, their long antennae brushing my skin.

Our cells were situated below a water tower; the walls oozed, even in summer. The mosquitoes loved it. The ceiling was covered with them, and at night they attacked, dive bombing us with a noise that sounded like jet engines. We organized competitions: an egg for the person who killed the most mosquitoes by the end of the week. Maria was the champion mosquito slayer.

Each spring swallows nested on the little wall facing our cell. At first we were thrilled; they distracted us from the usual monotony. For two weeks we watched them going about their lives. The same couple came back every year, for ten years. They built their nest, mated and then the female laid her eggs.

Each stage was accompanied by a running commentary from us, especially when they were mating. They were not content to do it just once. All day we heard *tit, tit, tit*, which meant that the male was at it.

But the swallows also brought fleas, which bit us mercilessly. They attacked our armpits and our groins. We scratched ourselves until we bled, and the pain was unbearable.

After a few days, our genitals were so swollen that they hung down our thighs. As usual, we made a joke of our misfortune. We told the neighbouring cells:

'The four girls have got balls now!'

The mice made more agreeable cellmates. Tiny and quick, they were everywhere. At night they emerged from their big holes and ran over our beds. We coped with them better than with the rats that invaded us, despite the traps and poison we put down during the great drought. We adopted one mouse, which we nicknamed Bénévent, giving it the princely title of the French statesman Talleyrand because, like him, it had a club foot. It died from overeating, which is ironic given that we were starving.

As I said, those mice merrily devoured our food reserves. They gnawed everything they found and left their droppings as a bonus. I had a heavy woollen plum-coloured jellabah that I hung on a nail behind the door when the dry season came. At the start of one winter, I went to fetch it as usual. All that was left was the embroidery around the neck, the front and the hemline. The mice had eaten up the rest of it, in the same way that they nibbled away at anything else they could get their teeth into.

For a few months there was a nauseating smell in the cell. No matter how often I washed myself and my clothes, I couldn't find the source. I hunted everywhere. Finally the girls helped me search inside my mattress. A mouse and her babies had nested in it to keep warm. I had crushed them in my sleep. We removed their withered corpses. The stench was unbearable.

I must also mention the crickets; they got in everywhere as soon as the hot weather came, and our ears hummed with their chirring. Not forgetting those delightful visitors, the scorpions that scuttled everywhere.

Of all our undesirable guests, the rats inspired the greatest fear and loathing in us. At night they waited until the generator shut down to come and visit us. We lay curled up in our beds, rigid with terror, listening anxiously, but that didn't mean we didn't still manage to joke about them. They arrived in hordes, thud, thud, thud, and squeezed under the reinforced door, jostling for first place, which made them even more aggressive. Their scrabbling broke the silence. They clambered onto the beds without biting, but ran over our bodies as we lay numb with fear.

They turned really belligerent when the guards started putting down traps. They were starving because of the drought. At that point they started coming into our cell during the day, looking for food.

One fat female was always followed by two young rats that were said to be crawling with plague-carrying fleas. I wanted to find out if it was true. With the help of the girls, I pushed one of the baby rats up against the wall and pinned it there with a short stick. Millions of red fleas invaded the cell. The floor was suddenly covered with them, which sickened me to the stomach.

I decided to go on the attack. I cornered one rat, closed the door on the others, and chased it with my stick. Fear and rage had made it swell to three times its size, with its ruffled fur making it look like a wild beast. It stared at me menacingly, ready to pounce. I could see nothing except its front fangs.

I told myself:

'It's only a rat.'

Sensing that I was bent on attacking it, the rat shot up the wall into a corner and launched itself from on high, landing on my head. I screamed blue murder. The girls rushed over to rescue me from its claws. I battered it, but its death made me feel uneasy. I felt as though I'd killed a human being, its screeches were so heart-rending.

The rats' visits became rarer, then after a week they were back. We had grown used to their presence. Later, they even became a standing joke.

We would ask Mimi the time:

'It's nearly time for the rats,' she'd reply.

HUMOUR

One day at Tamattaght one of the captains of the gendarmes, Chafiq, banged his foot against a table. Thinking he was expressing himself in the polished French he had heard us use, he turned to Mother, his face crimson, and said:

'*Mi suis cougné*—I beng m'sef.'

We adopted the expression and it became part of the special language of the Beavers, for that was what we had called ourselves—a reference to our desire to go and live in Canada.

A sergeant who called himself 'chief Brahim' we nicknamed Cappaccico, the name of one of our cooks whom he resembled. He always strutted around with his hands in his pockets, jiggling his male attributes from one side of his trousers to the other.

One day, in conversation, he said to us, pointing to his head:

'I've got it all up here. Electronics come from in here.'

After that, whenever we spoke about someone who was clever, we had only to look at one another and make that gesture to burst out laughing.

Humour allowed us to survive even—and most of all—at the worst moments. From the time of my father's death, that was how we functioned among ourselves, laughing at the most painful things, mocking other people and especially ourselves. We spoke our own coded language full of allusions understood only by us.

This permanent banter helped create a barrier between us and the guards, and strengthened our bond as a family. Our favourite sayings were often utter nonsense.

If we said, for example, 'The Beavers entered Sydney brandishing wooden spears,' it meant that we had succeeded in what we had set out to do.

Mouthing 'ra.t.t.t' meant that something was an out-and-out victory. When one of us was trying to tell a story and got mixed up, we'd say they had 'done a Malaga', because the flight to Malaga was fraught with air pockets. We still use these codes today when we don't want strangers to understand what we're talking about.

Princess Nehza, the King's sister, was killed in a car crash in September 1977. We heard the news on the radio and it saddened us, for we had all been very fond of the Princess. But our sense of humour got the better of us.

'If only they'd let us out for the wake, we'd hide among the *talba*,' we said.

For these paid mourners dressed in white who kept vigil over the body, reciting verses from the Koran, it was an opportunity to be fed well in the great bourgeois or royal households that employed them for the occasion. Then we pictured ourselves, disguised, concealing as much food as we could in our jellabahs to bring back to prison.

Each of us had one or more nicknames, depending on the circumstances. Maria was 'Haile Selassie' or 'the Negus' because she was so skinny. Raouf was 'Bobino the Chip King', or 'Mounch', or even 'Jiji Machakil'—Jiji after a little dog my father once had which used to run round in circles, like Raouf, and Machakil which means 'with problems' in Arabic. We called him this because he was always trying to square the circle.

Mimi was 'Petit Pôle', a Disney polar bear cub, because she was always cold, or 'Mimi the baker' because she loved bread. We also referred to her as 'Bert the atom'. This nickname had come about one day when Mother had lost her temper with her for the hundredth time over her clumsiness.

'She's a muddler, she can't do anything properly,' said Mother, beside herself when Mimi once again accidentally knocked over a bowl of food or the precious dish of embers which we used to warm our hands.

'Mummy, you're wrong,' I said, 'she's going to be a genius. When Albert Einstein began his research into the atom, he was also very clumsy and was always burning himself.'

So whenever Mimi knocked something over, we laughingly called her 'Bert the atom'.

Soukaina wasn't very keen on being teased. Her official nickname was 'Charlie', but in secret we called her 'Bob is too fat to run fast', a veiled reference to her plumpness, in memory of the English lessons I gave them in Tamattaght. I was called 'Hitler', 'Mazarin', 'Stalin' or 'Mussolini' because of my bossiness.

Mother and Abdellatif were nicknamed 'Wassila' and 'Bourguiba', an allusion to that inseparable couple Habib Bourguiba, the President of Túnisia, and his second wife, Wassila Ben Ammar. Mother was also known as 'Sigmund', pronounced with a German accent, when we wanted to poke fun at her tendency to analyse everything, or 'Old Scrooge', to tease her about her wild extravagance now that she was deprived of everything. Achoura was 'Barnaby' or 'Baby'.

Obsessed with her frizzy hair, Halima treated it as best she could with plants she gathered in the courtyard. She tried to conceal it under a little headscarf, but there was nothing to be done: two stiff strands of hair escaped from the scarf, like 'Dingo' ears. This nickname suited her very well.

And lastly, we nicknamed my father 'the Big, Bad Wolf', or 'Moby Dick, king of the sea', an allusion to the day at the beach, just before the coup d'état, when he had put on huge lifebelts to go waterskiing. The only times we ever complained about the actions that were the cause of our incarceration, we did it jokingly.

'Moby Dick would have done better to have drowned himself that day. We wouldn't be here now . . . He would have enjoyed a state funeral.'

TWENTY YEARS OUTSIDE TIME

Thanks to our little radio, we knew what was going on outside. Raouf, who listened to it all day, gave us news of the world. He spent hours explaining it all to us.

With the 'system' we were able to tune into all the book programmes, as well as the Moroccan and French current affairs programmes. We listened to RF1, France Inter and Europe 1.

I wouldn't miss Jacques Chancel's *Radioscopie* or José Artur's *Pop Club* for anything. I listened to the stories that Jean-Pierre Chabrol told in his rich, husky voice, and Alain Decaux's history broadcasts. Mother's favourite programme was *L'Oreille en coin*. We also had other favourite broadcasters. Not having seen their photos, we imagined what they looked like so we could picture them when we listened to their voices. They were our friends, our only companions. We owe them a lot.

They helped us survive. Thanks to them, we were able to maintain a link to life, like castaways on an island. At midnight, we listened to Gonzague Saint-Bris and his *Ligne ouverte*—a phone-in programme covering every subject under the sun. When the first bars of the theme tune composed by Eric Satie rang out in the half-dark, the cells went quiet. We felt as though he were speaking only to us. The presenter's voice had become so familiar that I was convinced he would end up mentioning us, as if we too were his friends.

One evening his guest was Michel Jobert, the French Minister of Foreign Affairs. He was talking about Morocco, and Gonzague Saint-Bris asked him about the Berbers. I listened with thudding heart and bated breath, my mouth dry. I just knew he was going to utter our name.

'Michel Jobert, isn't the symbol of this proud, desert people General Oufkir?' asked Gonzague Saint-Bris.

The minister agreed, and quickly changed the subject. But in the darkness enveloping us, I was overwhelmed with an indescribable feeling of joy. I had heard my name. I existed. We all existed. We could be reborn some day.

The wall between ourselves and the outside world was so thick that when food was brought to us, the guards hurriedly tore up the newspaper in which the meat and vegetables were wrapped so that we wouldn't even learn the date, or find out what was happening.

Despite all their precautions, Achoura and Halima sometimes managed to filch a fragment of newsprint. Raouf thus came by a half-torn page with a photo of a divine, half-naked blonde. That scrap of paper, which he hid as carefully as the radio and the microphones, became his bible, the basis for all his fantasies.

We teased him, we'd ask him how his beloved fiancée was . . . Until the day when a second fragment of paper arrived, via the same route. This time the photo was of a paunchy, moustachioed trade union official. Raouf got his own back by saying he was Mother's and my dreamboat, and it was his turn to tease us.

Another time, I got hold of a small photo of a footballer who played for Lens, a splendid athlete whom I could admire to my heart's content.

We were all football fans, especially me. During the World Cup tournaments we often had to stuff rags into our mouths to stop ourselves from screaming, especially when France was playing.

I still remember the famous France–Germany match of 1982, and our enthusiasm and disappointment when France lost in the penalty shoot-out. Mother had made a football out of rags so that Abdellatif could train in his cell, shooting against the walls. We had explained the rules to him, and he had become an ardent supporter.

The radio made me aware of feminism and sexual liberation. Had I been free, I would have followed those women. I would probably have been an activist like them. I was fascinated by Benoîte and Flora Groult, Muriel Cerf and by the success of Régine Deforges with *The Blue Bicycle*, her Second World War novel based on *Gone with the Wind*. I envied her a little for having succeeded in doing what I tried to do with my own stories: retelling works of universal literature in my own way.

Over the years, the radio also became a source of misery for me. When a film came out, I said to myself that I could have been in it. When Robert Hossein set up his theatre company, I spent entire nights dreaming about being part of it.

When I heard the presenters talking about technical advances and new inventions, colour television, videos, computers, Concorde and high-speed trains, I shut out the information because it served only to highlight the gulf that separated me from the world, and I couldn't bear it. Then I really felt outside time, cut off from everything.

We comforted each other by imagining that when we came out, the planet would resemble the bravest of all new worlds. A universe created so that we could spend our lives sitting or lying down. We would order breakfast and dinner and carry out all the most routine daily tasks by remote control. Those fantasies were a tremendous source of entertainment.

But when the programme was over, when the dream ended, we found ourselves back between our four dreary walls. Nothing had changed.

NIGHT

That was all there was to do. Think, ponder, cogitate, reflect and wonder. All day our brains were working. At night it was even worse; my past life came back to me in waves, my present was just this void and my future was non-existent.

When my sisters fell asleep at last, I would often get up and sit beneath the fanlight to glimpse a patch of sky. I railed against God. I constantly asked Mother how she could believe in him when unutterable horrors were perpetrated on earth. I wasn't thinking only of us. I had been deeply affected by the Jewish Holocaust.

'If there was a God,' I'd say to her, 'do you think he'd tolerate such massacres?'

I turned to God only to rebuke him and to confess that I questioned his existence. However, I did sometimes lose my nerve. I was so terrified at the thought that I might be cursed as a punishment for my disloyalty that I would say to him:

'I take back what I said and we'll go back to square one. But I warn you, I'm waiting for a sign.'

I gazed at the sky. But nothing happened. The night was black. Like our life. Like our thoughts.

I waited impatiently for nightfall, for the peace it brought me. During the day I wore a mask, I was Malika the strong one, the authoritarian, the person who breathed life into the others. As soon as dusk fell, I dropped my defences. At last I felt close to other human beings: in sleep, we were all the same.

But I was also at the mercy of my demons, my ghosts.

I thought about my father a lot. In the early years, I felt guilty for not having been able to prevent his death. I had not been up to the task, I had not been able to utter the necessary words. Each time I pictured him, I imagined the moment of his execution. That terrible moment when he realized that he was going to be massacred like a dog. I swung between humiliation, pain and rage.

I had made him a gift of my resistance to the King. The name that the monarch wanted to exterminate had to be upheld as an example of courage. The Palace received reports of our dignified behaviour. Our haughty attitude meant that we were standing up to the King and that we refused to accept the punishment he was inflicting on us.

It was a deliberate choice. There was no question of submitting. I tried to accept my fate. It depended neither on the King nor on anyone else, it was mine and there was no alternative.

I often wondered why Hassan II had imposed this long-drawn-out death instead of killing us right away. Our disappearance would have made matters much simpler. After turning the question over in my mind, and discussing it often with Mother and Raouf, I had come to the instinctive conclusion that at the beginning of our incarceration he did not have the means to eliminate us. The two successive coups d'état had shaken his power. He was being challenged, he the leader of the faithful, God's representative on earth. Politically, he was isolated. He no longer had a strong man at his side, as my father had been, to help him re-establish his authority and restore order. He had been betrayed, and was going through a difficult time.

Later, the Green March into Western Sahara had enabled him to assert his power at home and to give Morocco an international role. He had played his cards well, attracting enormous media coverage with excellent results. After the march, our situation changed. We were forgotten. What would have been the point of killing us then? He had inflicted the worst possible sentence on us.

I also felt—but that was no doubt an over-sentimental image of him—that he was torn between the hatred he now felt for us and the affection we had shared. The more he suffered, the more he had to persecute us. Us, the offspring, the descendants, and also this woman, my mother, the only person to stand up to him and defy him.

She had to be reduced to silence.

In fact, our incarceration was very much in keeping with the Palace's ancestral tradition of punishment. Opponents would be made to 'disappear' and their names would be proscribed. Anyone mentioning them would suffer serious consequences for daring to flout the unwritten law. But they were not killed. They were left to die.

We survived, but even so, we crossed over to the other side. We were gradually moving away from the world of the living towards the realm of shadows. Stripped of everything that had made up our former lives, each day we drew closer to the grave. This detachment was difficult. Because of our youth, we were vibrant with passions, impulses and rebellion. But we had to stifle them, and learn to live without them, in order to stop suffering. Paradoxically, this anguish was intoxicating. The darkness enabled me to converse with death, to venture dangerously close to it, until I seemed to fuse with it. It was an extreme sensation and I have never experienced anything like it.

Night was conducive to dreams, and dreaming helped us escape and see into the future. I dreamed that the King was in Ifrane, and that he had decreed a movement of national union: something that actually happened a few years later, in 1983, as we learned from the radio.

I also dreamed about a great celebration at the Palace, to mark the marriage of Prince Moulay Abdallah. He died a few weeks later, in 1984. I could still see the King in the Western Sahara surrounded by a crowd of black men dressed in white. He was escorted by a cloud of turtledoves. We watched this journey closely, hoping its outcome would be beneficial for us. It took place some time after my dream, but while it was a political success for the King, to us it brought nothing.

A short time before we decided to dig the tunnel, Halima dreamed about my father. We were all in a room of baked clay, with an open roof, and she was the only person who was able to communicate with him. He gave her a rope and told her to give it to us: we were to use it for our escape.

None of this surprised us. We were seeking symbols, omens, and our dreams provided them. I had a recurring nightmare that had begun when I was five years old. I would find myself dressed in rags in the garden of the Villa Yasmina. I'd run upstairs, but when I opened the door I was still in the dark. In vain I tried to switch on the lights, but everything stayed black. The house was in ruins.

Eventually, my nocturnal respite became a torture. Solitude was no longer a joy. I was afraid of it now. I was exhausted by the Story, which I would tell for four or five hours without stopping. I suffered from rheumatism. My muscles were wasting away through lack of exercise. I often lay awake, rigid in the darkness, for the slightest movement would make me howl with pain. In vain I sought relief.

LOVE AND SEX

Each of my birthdays was like a dagger piercing my heart. At the age of thirty-three I became resigned. I would never experience a great love; I would never have my own family; no man would ever take me in his arms and whisper sweet nothings or words of burning passion in my ear; I would never know the physical and mental thrill of being in love.

I was condemned to wither like a wrinkled fruit. At night, I dreamed I was making love. I would awaken with an acute feeling of frustration.

I quickly learned to get a grip on myself. I forced myself not to think about it. I could not burden myself with these little troubles when I had so many others. I tried to remain in control of my body, to suppress everything to do with human appetite, desire, hunger, cold, thirst. To suppress my impulses and my desires.

To anaesthetize myself.

When I told the Story, I dwelled on true love rather than physical pleasure, so as not to frustrate my audience.

Raouf suffered a lot more than we did from this enforced abstinence. Unlike his sisters, he had had some sexual experiences before being imprisoned. As an outlet for his frustrations, he would tell us about his visits to prostitutes, which was how all young men from bourgeois families lost their innocence. His comic accounts had us doubled up with laughter.

The *mouhazzin* did not, as a rule, take advantage of our vulnerable situation. One of them, however, did come close to raping me. Our radio had been confiscated and I desperately wanted to replace it. But it had become very difficult to bribe the guards to bring us the small things we needed to preserve our sanity, such as radios or pens.

I singled out the man who had the keys to our cell, Staff Sergeant Cappaccico. Week after week I pleaded with him, promising him money via my grandfather if we were able to get in touch with him.

He didn't say no. For us, that meant yes, and we waited eagerly for that radio.

But Cappaccico dragged his heels and shilly-shallied.

One afternoon, the door opened at an unaccustomed hour, and Cappaccico entered. He was accompanied by another soldier whom he asked to stay outside the door. I ordered the girls not to get out of bed; I wanted to negotiate with him alone. He shoved me up against the wall. I could feel he was aroused.

He pressed himself against me, and began to grope my breasts and bite my mouth. He lifted up my blouse. I could hear him panting like a rutting animal, he smelt bad, his breath was offensive, his body was crushing me, but I was incapable of fighting back.

I was powerless: I couldn't scream or defend myself in any way without frightening the others. Raouf would probably have tried to kill him and would doubtless have come off worst.

I endured his assault for a few minutes without him obtaining what he wanted, then I pushed him away as calmly as I could. I was shaking and my heart was thumping, but I was determined not to let it show.

'You asked me for a radio, didn't you?' he said.

'Yes.'

'So why put up a fight? You're going to die soon, your body's no longer any use. Even if you once had a fiancé, he's not there any more. Everybody's abandoned you.'

His tirade was like a slap in the face, but I didn't flinch.

'OK,' I said at length. 'You will get what you want. But not straight away. I too want to see proof. Bring me the radio and you'll have the rest.'

I was prepared to do anything to get that radio. As far as I was concerned, this resignation was worse than rape. The incident was soon forgotten. Cappaccico had got cold feet.

Over the years, the barriers of natural modesty between parent and offspring had been eroded. We told each other everything that was on our minds, there were no taboos. After ten years in prison, we had become monsters, ready to do anything. We were no longer a mother, children, brothers or sisters. Only our moral values prevented us from acting out our desires. Our fantasies were not only sexual. We had even sunk so low that we could envisage killing. 'For food,' we said, 'we would be capable of disembowelling and slaughtering like savages.'

We were like drug addicts, so far gone that we were permanently scarred.

Towards the end, we were like caged beasts. We were no longer even capable of feelings. We were tired and enraged, aggressive and cruel. None of us wanted to go on wearing a mask. We no longer believed in anything.

MY FAMILY

My mother was an example. Our example. For twenty years, she always held her head high, without expressing the slightest complaint. And yet she suffered even more than we did, if that were possible. She could not bear being separated from her children; she cried in secret because we were starving, because we were lacking in everything, because this prison was robbing us of our youth.

Through her dignity she inspired us with courage. She was the kamikaze pilot; the escape was her idea. She knew the risks involved, knew that she could lose us in this attempt, but her conviction remained unwavering.

During those terrible years when we communicated without seeing each other, I came to realize the importance of the voice. Through the wall, I was able to perceive the tiniest changes in tone that told me more than the lengthiest discussion about Mother's current state. She could do the same with me. She was a spectator of my life, powerless to change it.

Our relationship had always been very close: we were allies even in suffering. Since the day I was born, my relations with her had never been less than passionate and heartbreaking. The thought that I would not be able to have children distressed her. It was part of the curse she believed had plagued me from the beginning.

Our ears were alert for the tiniest sound, we sought the slightest opportunity to catch a glimpse of each other, either in the water of the gutter or, more rarely, through the open doorways. I could tell that Mother was awake in the morning from the movements coming from her cell. She was bustling around looking after Abdellatif, and now they were having breakfast. Then they paced up and down, she inside the cell and he on their patio, when it wasn't raining, from nine o'clock in the morning until seven o'clock at night.

We owe a lot to Abdellatif. He had known nothing but prison all his life, and, of all of us, he had adapted to it most readily. Things that seemed aberrant to us had been his normal daily routine since his earliest childhood. As a result, he had a way of thinking that was often sharper than ours. As he paced up and down, he used what knowledge he had to invent the things we lacked. We called him 'Géo Trouvetout'—the fixer—because he always found a solution.

He had discovered, for example, that it was possible to recharge fading batteries by warming them in the sun, or soaking them in boiling water. This was very valuable to us, even if their extra lifespan was limited.

From the minute we arrived at Bir-Jdid, Abdellatif had thought of nothing but escaping. He scraped the walls to remove the distemper and analyse it. After a few experiments, he managed to make an imitation plaster from Tide and flour, and he invented a cement made up of ash, ebonite (from the batteries) and earth. We were later to use this for our escape.

There was, however, an ambiguity in the relationship between Mother and me. Unwittingly, and against my will, I had usurped her role. I had become the mother of Raouf and the girls.

I can still picture Maria and Soukaina snuggling up to me on my bed, questioning me about the meaning of life or much more trivial things. They told me all the secrets they would never have told Mother, first of all because at that age you don't confide in your mother, and secondly because they were separated from her by a solid concrete wall.

I looked after them, I brought them up, I tried to keep their spirits up, I was their big sister, their mother, father, confidante, their guide and support. It came naturally to me. I had developed for all of them a profound feeling that was well beyond mere sisterly affection. I loved them more than anything else and, like Mother, I suffered a lot more for them than I did for myself. I remember instigating dancing lessons in the cell because Maria was crying over her shattered dream of being a ballet student at the Paris Opéra, the diets I made up for Soukaina, the way I nursed Mimi, the toys and drawings I made for Abdellatif. I can still hear the long conversations I had with Raouf, thanks to our 'system'.

I had a duty not only to love them but even more to protect them as best I could, to help them survive without too much damage, until the day—if it ever dawned—when we would be released.

For we thought of nothing else but our release. We discussed endlessly what we would do afterwards. Mimi wanted to get married and have a child. Soukaina, Maria and I wanted to live together in a château outside Paris. Maria would learn to type and become my secretary, and Soukaina would cook for our guests. I would become a famous film director. They would remain in my shadow.

At other times we would buy a farm in Canada and live there all together with our respective partners. Raouf and I wanted to study medicine in Montreal. We would live in the student hall of residence. Once we graduated, we would go and practise in Cameroon. In this way, we went on to consider every profession on earth. If we held out for so long, in such abysmal conditions, it was because we were together and we loved each other. Even when we were kept apart, we formed a unit, supporting and encouraging each other.

Together, we were a force, and that was something that nobody and nothing could take away from us. When one of us became dispirited, there was always someone to make them laugh or remind them of the words of the blind seer from Assa: *Zouain, zouain bezef*; it will be miraculous, very miraculous.

THE NIGHT OF THE LONG KNIVES

Despite her courage and dignity, and even though she was accustomed to the intrigues of the Palace, Mother was still very naive. She firmly believed that we would be pardoned on 3 March 1986, for the King's Silver Jubilee.

I was more sceptical, and subsequent events proved me right.

That morning, around ten o'clock, the guards came into our cells. They didn't utter a word. They merely exchanged glances, their gaze focused on the gratings over the reinforced door and our patio. Then they left, still without saying a word, and we mused over their strange behaviour, each of us coming up with a different theory.

At eight thirty the following morning they opened all the doors and shoved us outside. We staggered, not knowing how to walk any more, and the light hurt our eyes.

We were wild with joy to be together again for the first time in so many years. We had all changed so much and each one of us had grown taller or older. Mother didn't recognize her little girls. She had last seen Soukaina and Maria when they were fourteen and fifteen years old, and now they were young women of twenty-two and just twenty-four. Raouf was a man, resembling my father in build. Abdellatif was now a youth of seventeen.

Mother was as beautiful as ever, but the hardship and grief had taken a terrible toll. Achoura and Halima had grey faces and hair, the colour of the ash that filled their kitchen.

We must have looked like walking corpses—we were gaunt and pale, with dark rings round our eyes and bloodless lips, a glazed expression in our eyes, sparse hair and legs that were barely able to carry us . . . Halima, who had kept a fragment of mirror, had cried one day on looking at her reflection. She wouldn't believe that the ghost staring back was indeed herself.

But we were so thrilled to see each other again that we didn't want to say anything that might spoil our immediate happiness. And yet we were torn between the natural urge to touch each other and kiss, and the determination not to show our tormentors how cruelly we had missed this contact. We restrained ourselves. Astonished by our attitude, Borro encouraged us to approach one another, then he added that, to celebrate Throne Day, we were now allowed to get together from eight thirty in the morning until eight o'clock at night. We were being granted this concession after fourteen years of prison.

In the mornings we would gather in my cell. They had reinforced the bars over the roofless recess. The doors were left open, we were able to go out into the courtyard. After lunch we were locked up together until evening, and then we were separated again.

At first, the elation of being reunited eclipsed the grimness of our situation. Mother gazed at us for hours. She never tired of looking at us, but cried in secret to see us so emaciated, so starved. Nevertheless we had decided to relish every joyous moment of being together again.

These happy times lasted from March until November. To entertain ourselves, we put on shows. After lunch, we made a sort of stage using military blankets. Mother imitated Poulidor on his bicycle and I was a radio presenter. Abdellatif and Maria dressed up as *mouhazzin* and took the mickey out of the way they spoke.

We organized circus shows. We announced the start with drum rolls and music, then Raouf cracked a whip made from scraps of fabric and the elephants made their entrance. The elephants were Mimi on four legs, wearing a pair of red and black tights. She was painfully thin. Raouf cracked his whip on the ground and Mimi had to raise her legs in the air. We shrieked with laughter. We never tired of joking, touching each other and embracing.

Around two o'clock in the afternoon, Raouf would go off for his nap. Having lived in solitary confinement for so long, he needed time on his own even more than the rest of us. To get some peace and quiet, he would plug his ears with little balls made from crumbs of bread which he rolled for hours. From time to time, we heard him growl angrily at the mice going berserk as they tried to get hold of the bread. In the evening, I carried on with the Story with renewed energy. Abdellatif stood with his eye glued to the little hole in the wall of the toilet of our cell. He had spotted a military truck and never tired of admiring it. He tried to scrape away a bit more to see it better. But the opening remained tiny, barely the size of a coin.

One morning when he was at his post, the guards stormed into the cell without warning. He didn't have time to move. The alert was given. Borro came to examine the hole. 'I knew you were trying to escape,' he said.

It was a Friday. According to his authoritative calculations, the hole would be finished by Sunday.

At the time I found his stupidity a relief. The hole was tiny, and halfway up the wall, which, as everyone knows, is the ideal place to make a tunnel. It didn't occur to me for one moment that he could believe his own story.

That evening, they split us up without any explanation. The next morning they told Mother that we would be locked up as before. She decided to go on hunger strike immediately, until we were allowed to be together again. We heard the conversation through the wall. I passed the news on to Achoura, who told Raouf. That day the authorities began to build a second wall to reinforce the first. The construction job lasted a week. We had no idea what they were hatching. The din drove us mad. We were too accustomed to silence.

Mother was even more resolute in her decision to stop eating. But she didn't want us to follow her example. She had decided to die alone. Her sacrifice might result in our freedom.

I tried to convince her not to do it, but she wouldn't listen. During an urgent family council, all the children chose to copy her, except me. Somebody had to be available to talk to Borro. It was easiest for me to take on this role because my body couldn't cope with fasting. The others went to bed, spoke little and refused all nourishment except water.

For an entire day Soukaina refused even to drink, but this nearly drove her out of her mind. The survival instinct prevailed, and I made her drink a little liquid. During this hunger strike they brought us copious provisions. The vegetables were fresh, the meat wasn't rotten and the fruit wasn't overripe. It was torture, but I didn't touch it. Although I had decided not to fast, when it came to the point I found I couldn't bring myself to eat when the others were not eating. In the evening, I drank a large glass of hot water with a mint leaf floating in it, so as not to become too ill.

After twenty days, Borro came to see me and launched into a long hypocritical speech to get me to persuade the others to stop. He told me that we would end up burying the first one to die. Nobody would lift a finger to save our lives. But I turned a deaf ear.

When the guards realized that the food was beginning to pile up, they forced their way in. We were on our forty-fifth day of hunger strike, and we were nothing but skin and bone.

And nothing happened. Nobody would listen to us.

Faced with the hopelessness of our struggle, we gave in to despair. Shattered by our failure, we were so despondent that we wanted to die. We weren't even proper prisoners because our demands barely counted. Our hunger strike wasn't going to get us anywhere.

Everyone was terribly feeble and unable to start eating again. Our bodies could no longer take the tiniest morsel of food. We felt as though we were poisoning ourselves the minute we swallowed a tiny mouthful.

We were at the end of our strength, at the end of hope, at the end of life. Death was our only refuge. For the first time in fourteen years, we yearned for it with all our hearts. We had to put an end to it all.

I remember the night of 26 November 1986. It was a magnificent, star-studded, peaceful night. A full moon shone in a pure, cloudless sky. During the night, with her little nail scissors, Mother slit her veins.

Just before committing this act of despair, she repeated to me that she loved me, and that she was entrusting my brothers and sisters to my care. At first I did not react. If she wanted to die, it was her absolute right. But gradually I started to become frantic.

Around four o'clock in the morning, I called Abdellatif and I asked him to see whether Mother was dead or alive.

'Her heart is beating very feebly,' he replied through the wall.

I grabbed the handle of the reinforced door and clung to the grating screaming:

'Help! My mother is dying, we are all going to die!'

I shouted for all I was worth, but they did not reply. I heard the sound of my voice like an echo in the darkness, and I was humiliated that I had to beg them to save my mother's life. I ran out of arguments and threatened to blow us all up with the butane cylinder if they didn't do anything.

Alarmed, they marched into Mother's cell. I heard Borro yell. Then they came out again without having done anything to treat her.

I explained to Abdellatif how to make a tourniquet with strips of sheet. Mother was breathing, although she had lost a lot of blood.

She would be saved, but we were all going to die. We were all out of our minds. The despair accumulated during those fourteen terrible years, exacerbated by our physical and mental decline, turned into collective hysteria. Until then we had always managed to avoid open revolt. That night, we suddenly went crazy, the whole situation became a psychodrama brought to life. In all the cells, the despair was tangible. Abdellatif watched over Mother, while Achoura and Halima wailed and tore out their hair. As for us, we had completely lost our bearings and all notions of reality.

That 'night of the long knives' as we called it was the worst night of our entire lives.

It was the Apocalypse.

Anything was possible: murdering a sibling, suicide, or blowing up the prison with our butane cylinders.

We all wanted to be the first to take the plunge. We drew straws, and Soukaina won. She lay down on her bed and made herself as comfortable as possible. Sitting opposite her, I started to slash her wrists with a piece of metal from a sardine can and a knitting needle.

I drove the point in as hard as I could, sobbing as I lacerated her flesh. I felt as if I were wounding myself. She winced and smiled at me at the same time.

At last I managed to puncture a vein. The blood spurted out. Soukaina bore the pain with an ecstatic expression. It hurt me as much as it did her. She fainted.

Maria, Mimi and I looked at her, thinking she was dead. From time to time our eyes met, brimming with tears that did not flow. We were desperate but relieved to think that she was no longer suffering.

Soukaina regained consciousness after a quarter of an hour. She was trembling all over; when she realized she was still alive, she turned on me.

'You don't want to kill me, you don't want to see me die . . .'

'Of course I want you to die, Soukaina, I tried everything but it won't work . . . look at all the blood you've lost.'

We held a brief consultation. Should we make her a tourniquet or not? Then sleep overtook us. We sank onto our beds, half asleep and half unconscious.

We were exhausted.

These abortive attempts scarred us all deeply. Such a close brush with death was not unlike dying.

That night, we had all crossed over to the other side. I don't know what strength, what instinct, what energy, impelled us to survive.

The nightmare went on. The next morning, I heard the guards' footsteps heading for Raouf's cell. Harsh voices were shouting.

Peeping under the reinforced door, I could see their feet running in the opposite direction. That night, Raouf too had chosen to put an end to things by slitting his veins. And he had come closest to succeeding: they thought he was dead. I told Mother the news, and she too was in a bad state after her aborted suicide.

We waited all day, but nobody condescended to give us any news. That evening they dumped his body in the courtyard; it was freezing cold. They were to leave him there, without medical attention, for four days.

Raouf was in a coma. He did not have long to live, or so they thought.

But that was without taking into account his incredible faculty for recovery. My brother gradually came round. The fourth night, he was still lying in the courtyard, but if his body was extremely weak, his spirit was more or less intact.

Feigning unconsciousness, he overheard Captain Chafiq speaking to his men.

Then Chafiq turned to Borro.

'This situation has ruined my life,' he said. 'I'm ashamed to look my family in the eyes. I am haunted by what we are doing. Murdering children is beyond me. I can't carry on. What do they want?'

'Don't you understand?' replied Borro. 'It is clear enough. They are going to die. All of them. And they will be buried here. We'll just wait as long as we have to. Those are our orders.'

Our persecutors' words had the effect of an electric shock on my brother. With a superhuman effort, he returned to his cell and closed the door.

He spent all night prising up stone slabs and enlarging the hole in his wall. Achoura and Halima did the same on their side. Thus I was able to get close to him and communicate with him: a single wall separated us.

He lay down on his side and I on mine. We couldn't see each other, only touch by poking our fingers through a tiny hole. He twisted mine rather than gripped them.

I closed my eyes and listened to his voice, trying to picture him. His voice had the same intonation as my father's.

His despair was unbearable. On searching his cell, the guards had found his precious radio and confiscated it. All our links with the outside world had been severed. Raouf blamed himself.

'Kika,' he sobbed, 'we're going to die here, that's what they want. I heard them. They said they were going to kill us. The first one to die will be buried in the courtyard.'

For hours and hours I attempted to console, reassure and convince him, casting around for the right words when I myself was so bereft. I begged him not to give in.

'But no, Raouf, you'll see, we'll always have the upper hand. They won't kill us. We're going to stand up to them.'

We stayed there holding hands until morning. My eyes were dry, belying the anguish I felt inside.

But that 'night of the long knives' and Borro's words especially, had changed our attitude. We would no longer allow them to play with our lives. We would no longer be passive. The escape plan had begun to hatch in our minds; now all we had to do was make it real.

THE TUNNEL

Borro had received orders to step up surveillance. All sharp objects were taken away from us and the remaining window panes replaced by board. The shutter over our skylight was removed and our knives and forks were confiscated. Even our beakers were plastic oil bottles cut in half, and we had fits of giggles watching them crumple up when we poured in boiling water.

From now on, on Mondays, Wednesdays and Fridays, at eight o'clock in the morning, the guards searched the cells for the slightest hint of a tunnel or a hole. This latest gem came from Colonel Benaich, who was never at a loss for new ways of making our lives a misery.

These searches were not so ridiculous. Our resolve had hardened; we were all agreed that we would escape. Since the night of the long knives, we had reached rock bottom.

From listening to the soldiers' footsteps when the guards came on and off duty, Raouf knew every millimetre of ground intimately, its resonance, its dryness. We asked Achoura and Halima to dig up some earth from their cell and send it to us for analysis. We all did likewise.

After endless discussions, and even a few trials in Achoura and Halima's cell, we decided to excavate our tunnel in the blind cell next to ours where we kept the suitcases and food stores. The stone slabs were in good condition, it would be easier to touch them up to conceal our efforts.

There was another argument in favour of this spot: I knew, from raising my blindfold on our arrival at Bir-Jdid, that our cell overlooked a field, and we had every reason to believe that it wasn't cultivated. No sound, no life, not even the braying of a donkey ever reached our ears. Our gaolers must have asked the farmer to leave it fallow.

Mother and Raouf, the two engineers of the group, endorsed our choice. This blind cell was the best place to prise up the stone slabs. Raouf analysed the colour of the earth I sent him and explained to me how to identify each stratum of soil. Clay meant that I had reached the foundations, and then it was time to start digging horizontally.

I listened to his advice carefully, for it irked him not to be part of the action. He paced up and down his cell like a caged lion. On the afternoon of 27 January 1987, we smashed the concrete and eased up the stone slabs with a spoon, a knife handle, the lid of a sardine tin and an iron bar from one of our beds.

By we, I mean Maria, Soukaina and myself. Mimi was in no condition to help us, but she encouraged us and was very efficient when it came to clearing away the earth.

After barely two hours, despite our fear of discovery, we had already made good progress. We had removed eight stone slabs. For two weeks we practised removing them and replacing them with the cement mixture that Abdellatif had invented, a combination of earth, ash and ebonite.

As this was not good enough, we came up with a way of getting hold of real cement. Using the heavy iron bar that we still kept hidden in our beds, we enlarged the holes in the walls made by rats and mice. The guards would come and fill them with cement, which we would then retrieve. To stop it from hardening, we kept it soaking in a bucket of water.

It wasn't easy to replace the stone slabs. We had to be careful not to damage them as we lifted them up, and then file away the cement clinging to the edges with an old vegetable grater. So as not to alert the gaolers, we waited for the cries of the swallows: that infernal din we so hated turned out to be a blessing in disguise.

The day we finally managed to put the stone slabs back in the right order, we embarked on the next phase—digging a hole down to the foundations of the building.

After the layer of cement that we smashed with the iron bars, we encountered gravel and then larger stones. On the first day, I struck a rock as big as a menhir. It was impossible to go any further.

I conveyed the bad news to Raouf.

'Try to pull it out,' he ordered.

'But where will I put it?'

'Find somewhere. Do you want to escape or not?'

In Mother and Abdellatif's cell, there was a high storage area where they kept their belongings. They needed a wooden stepladder to reach it. After the 'night of the long knives', the guards had removed the stepladder and bricked up the opening.

The minute their backs were turned, Mother had the presence of mind to put Abdellatif on her shoulders so that he could remove one of the bricks, in anticipation of the day when we would need that room. The cement was still wet. They managed never to let it dry out so they would be able to remove that brick and others if necessary.

We dug a huge hole under my bed, between Mother's cell and ours. After a great deal of heaving we got the 'menhir' out, and Mother and Abdellatif removed the other bricks in the little storeroom and hid it there. It was no simple matter passing each subsequent 'menhir' to them in the same way. We had to enlarge the hole. Abdellatif climbed into the little room and Mother passed up the huge stones. Heaving and panting, they managed to lay them on thick layers of clothing to stifle the heavy thumps.

To avoid attracting attention, we passed the 'menhirs' along under cover of the noise made by the generator starting up.

Then we passed them the surplus stones as we removed them from the tunnel. When they arrived higgledy-piggledy in Mother's cell, she placed them on a sheet which she fastened like a bundle, then Abdellatif stood on her shoulders and threw them through the opening into the little room.

The guards checked the damp patches on the walls, but they did not detect the ingenious system that Abdellatif 'Géo Trouvetout'—the fixer—had contrived, which consisted of filling the cracks between the bricks with a mixture of Tide and flour that looked like plaster.

He used red-hot embers prepared by Halima and Achoura to dry it faster. Still sitting on Mother's shoulders, the boy moved the dish back and forth over the wall, until there were no traces of damp.

After a while we had made such good progress that we could no longer throw the earth into the little room next door as we had done with the stones. Also, we couldn't risk the stone slabs sounding hollow if the guards had the bright idea of testing them. So Mother made rectangular cushions of various sizes out of old trousers. We stuffed them with the earth we dug out and shaped them into balls, and called them 'Chinese lanterns' and 'elephants'.

It was like a production line; we worked like robots. Down in the hole, I filled an empty five-litre oil can with earth. Then I pulled on the rope from which it was dangling, and the girls hauled up the load. They threw the earth onto a heap in the centre of our cell.

Myriam filled buckets with water which she poured over the earth and then kneaded it like dough. She was helped by Achoura and Halima, the bread experts, who slipped into our cell via the enlarged hole in the wall between our cells. Abdellatif squeezed through the narrow hole we had made between his cell and ours, and he too joined in.

The three women made mud balls the size of a fist, which we passed through to Mother's cell one at a time. She filled the cushions with them and sewed them up. Abdellatif passed them back through the hole and we put them back in our tunnel. The elephants replaced the big 'menhirs', and the Chinese lanterns, as we called them, replaced the smaller stones.

When we reached the foundations and the red earth gave way to clay, we began to burrow horizontally, still following Raouf's advice. He had calculated that the tunnel should be about five metres long for us to surface beyond the two walls.

We found a supernatural strength, never suffering from fatigue or feeling the weight or the effort. We had become silent beasts, intent on our task, with nothing human about us. There was no need to speak: we understood one another from a gesture, a glance.

I had no nails left, my skin was covered with eczema, and my fingers were bleeding sores. But it didn't bother me. We used improvised candles for light. Mother plaited little wicks as she had learned to do as a child in the countryside. We dipped the wicks in oil and lit them at night.

When I emerged from my hole, I often wondered whether I was dreaming. Those pale faces framed by dusty hair, the emaciated bodies barely lit by the makeshift candles that cast a wan light onto the walls full of cavities and the floor strewn with stones and earth. Ghouls . . . the living dead . . .

Demolishing and digging was easy for us Beavers. The hard part was reconstruction. At four o'clock in the morning, when we heard the donkey Cornelius braying, we knew we had to stop and put everything back in order, carefully seal up the tunnel and fill in the holes between our cells.

The first time we opened up the tunnel, we weren't able to close it. But we soon got the hang of things. First of all we put back the elephants and the Chinese lanterns which we wedged with little stones and a few larger ones, having numbered them to make it easier to replace them in the right order, otherwise the stone slabs could sound hollow once they were back in position.

Then we spread a layer of red earth on top, moistened and smoothed with the palms of our hands, adding on top of that a layer of cement into which we sank the stone slabs. To finish off, we filled the cracks with plaster. This job was given to Soukaina, the artist, who then smeared them with mud to conceal all traces of our enterprise.

By dawn, nobody could have imagined that a tunnel was being dug in this little room. I had two hours before the arrival of the guards to wash the cell and get rid of the earth and the dust. Sometimes I didn't have time to get dressed before they were already opening Mother's door. She detained them as long as possible, asking them ridiculous questions and requesting used tyres to make soles for our shoes, or some other nonsense.

We had some terrible scares. Occasionally we dried the last layer of plaster and then realized, in the morning, that the earth underneath was still damp, which gave the stone slabs a yellowish tinge. We quickly repaired the damage, and sent a message to Mother to waylay the guards. They didn't notice anything.

Another time, while I was digging quietly, I heard a guard sneeze so close to me that I could hear him breathing. I froze and rushed back up. When I came out, I saw my sisters' anxious faces leaning over me. A heavy silence fell over the room. We waited for the guards to appear, but the door didn't open.

And I dived back into my hole.

During the searches, we would stay in our beds without budging, pretending to be ill. The guards carried out a painstaking inspection, even in the little room where the tunnel was. They beamed their torches into corners, they looked everywhere, under the beds, on the ceiling, in the cavities. They tapped the floor with their feet listening for a different sound, the faintest echo.

Mother and Raouf were like cats on a hot tin roof when they heard the guards' heavy tread and their banging on the walls. But the panic was mingled with exhilaration. We were staking our lives, double or quits, and the feeling was intoxicating. At last we were shaking off our lethargy. I forgot my suffering, my hunger and my wounded hands. I no longer felt the breastbone I'd cracked during the digging, which was agony when I breathed or bent down.

No guard ever set foot on our stone slabs. They walked round them, stopped just in front of them, and that was all. We were convinced the Virgin was protecting us: the first time we opened up the hole, the irregularity of the ground formed the shape of a cross, the length of the stone slabs. We made another cross out of cardboard, which we placed on top of the last layer of stone before sealing it up. We called the passage 'Mary's tunnel'.

We believed this so fervently that we prayed on our knees when we opened it up every evening and when we closed it every morning. We had rejected Islam, which had brought us nothing good, and opted for Catholicism instead. Mother, who had spent her childhood in a convent, knew all the prayers by heart and at our insistence taught them to us, although with reluctance. She herself had remained a good Muslim.

Maria, whose real name was Mouna-Inan, changed her name in homage to the Virgin. Abdellatif and Soukaina followed her example. All three had been named by King Hassan II. They didn't want to be beholden to him in any way. Soukaina decided that from now on she would be called Yasmina, and Abdellatif, Abdallah. Of the three, Maria was the only one to stick to her guns. She would not answer to any other name. The other two gave up fairly quickly, finding it too complicated to have a dual identity.

During the day, I continued to tell the Story. We were addicted to it. We barely ate or slept any more; we were living on our nerves. We communicated with Raouf thanks to the 'system', keeping him up to date with our progress at every stage. But he was so furious at not being able to participate that he started digging from his side too.

One evening, to our great delight, he surprised us by joining us, but he didn't do it again. It was too risky, and besides, he suffered like me from water retention as a result of malnutrition. We were both bloated, enormous. He had great difficulty in squeezing his blown-up one-metre-eighty-five frame through the hole.

But from his cell, he was our consultant engineer. He insisted we should shore up the tunnel for added safety. When we had finished digging, he asked me to retrieve my stash of wood, the long branches I had collected on our arrival. I had put them in a little storage alcove over our bathroom a long time before they bricked it up.

This recess was about three metres from the floor. To reach it was a real acrobatic feat. We had to stand on each other's shoulders, which we did one evening, shouting with laughter. We were certainly in need of it.

Maria, who weighed only thirty kilos, was as agile as a monkey. After slipping down countless times, she managed to reach the alcove and retrieve the pieces of wood. The hardest part was closing it up again. At that height it was almost impossible, but we did it. We sealed up the hole with Abdellatif's preparation, but it wouldn't dry, despite all our efforts.

The next day, I forestalled the guards' questions by informing them that there was a leak in the wall that needed repairing. I could relax: the minute we asked them for something, we could be certain we wouldn't get it.

By 18 April I had tunnelled the agreed five metres, and I stopped excavating. I had worked tirelessly, without complaining, despite my tendency to claustrophobia. I had almost turned into a cockroach or a reptile. On several occasions I felt I was on the verge of madness.

Sometimes I would suddenly stop my work and bang my head and stop up my ears because I thought I heard the sound of keys, or footsteps. I would drop whatever I was holding and fling myself to the ground, my heart racing, to see who was coming after me, but nobody came in.

Those sounds haunted me. I was constantly asking the girls if everything was all right. I lived in fear of suddenly going mad.

We had all agreed that the escape should be in December. We wanted to make our getaway on a moonless winter night when the guards, who were sensitive to the cold like all Moroccans, would be ensconced in the snuggest corner of their watchtowers, their faces muffled by the hoods of their jellabahs. A night when we could slip away unnoticed. So we sealed the tunnel and disguised the stone slabs. Two weeks before the escape, we would start digging the shaft to the surface. Before that it would be too risky.

We held countless family consultations to decide who would go, and what to do once outside. We had no money, but we still had the solid gold nameplate from my father's identity bracelet that my mother had managed to hide from the guards all these years. We had carefully filed off his name.

Abdellatif made a revolver from cardboard, ebonite and flour-and-water paste that looked more convincing than the real thing. He had been ably advised by Raouf, who had been a firearms enthusiast in his youth, to the point of taking shooting lessons. This toy was to get us out of difficult situations.

The first task was to find out exactly where we were. By listening carefully to the sound of long-haul aircraft overhead, my mother had concluded that we were somewhere between Casablanca and Marrakesh, probably closer to Casablanca.

The second task was to devise a way of putting ourselves out of range of the guards as quickly as possible. We had thought up several scenarios, some reasonable, others crazy.

Once we reached the road, we would wait for a taxi to come past. To attract the attention of the driver and allay suspicion, I had decided to pass myself off as a prostitute, much to Mother and Raouf's horror. After leading the driver on, I would brandish the revolver, call the others and we would all get into the car.

'Supposing he's not alone?' someone objected.

Nothing easier . . . we would knock his companion unconscious with a window bar that Abdellatif had managed to remove.

If the driver turned out to be sympathetic, we had an alternative scenario less violent than the first. We were emigrants, living in

Belgium. We had come back to Morocco to visit our family. Our car, a Volvo, had broken down and we absolutely had to find a mechanic.

Our goal was the French embassy, where we intended to request political asylum. But we needed time. On the morning of our escape, my mother was to waylay the guards as long as possible, to stop them raising the alarm immediately.

We thought of everything, planning the whole business down to the minutest detail. We had a stock of pepper to fend off any stray dogs. Mother had cut out and sewn black escape outfits for us and balaclavas with openings for our eyes, mouths and noses. She had made us shoes from the leather of our Vuitton suitcases, with soles cut from rubber tyres. They looked bizarre and resembled moon-boots rather than fashionable court shoes.

We envisaged the worst: if we were recaptured, we didn't want to survive. Mother planned to cause an explosion with the little butane stove. Raouf, the perfectionist, had honed every last detail to pre-empt the tiniest unforeseen hiccup.

That wasn't my style. I was burning to rush headlong into the venture. We would just improvise as we went along.

On tiny sheets of paper that had once wrapped saffron, and which we had painstakingly salvaged, Raouf had written about ten pamphlets that we wanted to hand in to the French embassy. They were addressed to various well-known politicians and leading arts personalities. Each of us added a few poignant lines.

The thorniest question was still to be resolved. Which of us would escape? Raouf wanted to go alone, he was so afraid for us all. But it was obvious that I would go with him. Maria had declared outright that if we didn't take her, she would kill herself. I knew my sister, and she was perfectly capable of carrying out her threat. We would also take Abdellatif who had seen nothing of life, who had no past and no bearings—he needed to be part of this adventure. Mother wanted to come with us, but she was physically unable to do so. Her body was bloated like the rest of us, and she couldn't even squeeze through the hole between our cell and hers. Only Abdellatif could wriggle through like an eel. We couldn't enlarge it for fear of breaking the slate tiles supporting the wall.

Soukaina agreed to stay behind too, demonstrating her generosity and courage. We needed her to seal up the tunnel after us. That would enable us to gain more precious time.

Mimi too would stay: she was simply too weak to come with us.

THE ESCAPE

On Sunday 19 April 1987, the day after we had closed the tunnel, I was sitting on the floor of the cell, my face turned towards the spring sunshine. We could hear the birds chirping. Nature, like us, was awakening from a long sleep. We felt strangely well, despite the prospect of several months' wait. We had emerged from the tomb. At last we had reason to hope.

Mimi lay in bed, the other two were cuddling up to me and we were chatting light-heartedly.

I heard the warning signal coming from my mother's cell.

'Listen, Kika,' she whispered, 'I overheard them. They have been given orders to build a lookout post and a watchtower on the roof of the tunnel cell. The lookout post will be exactly in line with the exit, and there'll be floodlights.'

'What will we do?'

'There is no choice,' she decided. 'They will have finished in forty-eight hours. And then it's goodbye to our escape plan. You must dig the escape shaft straight away and leave tonight.'

I had any number of objections. Dig a three-metre shaft in a few hours? It wasn't possible. We expected it to take a week.

But she wouldn't listen.

'It's that or nothing,' she repeated. 'If you don't leave tonight, you will never get out. Tell Raouf.'

Raouf agreed with my mother, we had no choice.

I started digging around midday. By six o'clock, I had finished the shaft. All we had to do was clear away the earth. I filled the oil can, pulled on the rope and the girls hauled it up. They emptied the contents on the ground and sent it back down to me.

I worked furiously. The spoon wasn't enough. If I could have ripped out the earth with my teeth, I would have done. I dug, I scooped out the earth, I no longer thought, I no longer existed, I had become a machine. Digging, scooping, digging, scooping . . .

At one point I came across some deeply rooted ivy. I pulled with all my strength. For hours I battled against those roots, straining to pull them out. It was an impossible task, but I put every ounce of energy I had into it, and more.

I had to succeed.

And suddenly my field of vision turned blue. It was the late afternoon sky, swept by a warm spring breeze that gently caressed my cheek.

I stood stock still for a while just clutching the ivy and looking out with one eye. I was jubilant.

'My God, how wonderful. Life is there, so close.'

I resumed digging and ripping everything out as best I could. And then, weeping, I poked my head through. It was too beautiful. I was afraid of what I could see. Freedom was so close that it frightened me.

I returned to the cell announcing triumphantly that I had won.

'The Beavers have entered Sydney brandishing wooden spears.'

The shaft was finished. Soukaina and Maria also tried it and managed to get through. We sent Abdellatif ahead as a scout to locate where we were going to surface. We wanted to know whether there were guards on the other side of the wall.

He came back, his heart pounding. When he had poked his head through the opening, he had found two eyes staring into his. He closed his eyelids. We were done for. To fail so near to the end, he could have wept . . .

When, after an eternity, he finally dared open his eyes again, he nearly burst out laughing. It was only a cat watching him. Then, no doubt bored with this uninteresting sight, it turned its back and left him there. Abdellatif was very proud of his adventure.

Mother passed us the outfits, the balaclavas, the provisions, the sandwiches, the pepper and the iron bar. I insisted on taking the notebooks containing the Story in my bundle, despite Mother's protests. She was afraid they would be destroyed. Her intuition would prove correct.

Shortly afterwards Raouf turned up in our cell.

At nightfall it was time to say goodbye. I lay on my stomach and Mother did the same on her side. She was distraught, wondering whether she really ought to let us go. It was the only time I saw her waver. We conveyed all our love through our clasped hands. Her voice was trembling slightly.

'I'm entrusting my flesh and blood to you,' she said to me. 'I know that you are also their mother. Promise me you'll bring them back alive.' Soukaina shivered. Her teeth were chattering and her eyes were shining, but she didn't shed a tear. She carried an enormous responsibility. She had to cover all our tracks to delay the guards' discovery of our escape for as long as possible.

Mimi tenderly clasped me to her and whispered in my ear:

'I'm sure you'll make it.'

Halima and Achoura were more hysterical, wailing their anguished fear and sorrow at seeing us go. But we were in a state of great elation, which I will never forget. I don't know if it can be called courage. It was rather a determination to survive that gave us each the strength of ten.

We dressed in silence, picked up our bundles and one by one we lowered ourselves down into the tunnel. Abdellatif and Maria got through the exit without any difficulty. They were so thin, so light . . . Raouf made the earth shudder. We held our breath, but he managed to push through and free himself without any damage.

When it was my turn, I managed to get my upper body through the exit hole, but my hips became wedged. I couldn't go any further. I was stuck. My bloated body was much too wide for the narrow opening.

Raouf encouraged me, whispering gently to calm me down, but I couldn't. I was unable to budge. I strained, I cried, I was drenched in perspiration. Then I heard Soukaina behind me.

'Kika, come back,' she said. 'Too bad, don't go. You're making too much noise, they'll hear you.'

If I persisted, I might get us all caught. But no way was I going to stay behind. Once again I summoned all my strength. It was like labour, a second birth. Malika was re-entering the world.

At last I was expelled from the tunnel. I'd scraped off all the skin on my thighs, but at the time I didn't even notice.

We had come out on the other side of the outer wall. Raouf's calculations had been right.

We kept close to the wall. Ahead of us was a wire fence covered with ivy, around four metres high. Maria stood on Raouf's shoulders and climbed up. He held her up and then pushed her over the top. She landed in the field.

We waited a little and then, as the guards didn't stir, I followed her over. Abdellatif and then Raouf came after. We huddled together, clutching one another, our hands trembling, loath to tear ourselves apart. We held our breath, keeping very still. Those few minutes seemed to go on for ever.

But they were crucial in establishing that the coast was clear.

And to get our breath back before the great adventure.

7

ESCAPED PRISONERS

19 April–24 April 1987

WANDERING

We had been living in the shadows for so long that our eyes had grown accustomed to the dark. We stood rooted to the spot, clutching one another, gazing at the night without any sense of fear. On the contrary, we were thrilled, exhilarated, convinced that the divine protection we had enjoyed so far would continue to safeguard us.

There was no sign of life from the guards' quarters, and we began to crawl across the damp field.

We could hear the barking of stray dogs. They were racing towards us, making straight for us, aggressive, starving and more ferocious than watchdogs. There must have been about ten of them, bounding through the dark behind the leader of the pack. They were getting closer and closer. We could feel their panting breath. Once again we huddled together for protection. Their leader came forward baring his fangs, growled and looked poised to attack. We froze, like statues, and held our breath, waiting for a miracle. Which, improbable as it seemed, was what occurred. The dog gave an unfathomable whine and slunk away, followed by the rest of the pack.

But the reprieve did not last long. Alerted by the dogs, the guards beamed their torches and floodlights onto the field. We froze again, praying that we would melt into the shadows. Certain of discovery this time, we stood there shivering, waiting for their shots to ring out.

The guards in the watchtowers exchanged a few words. At last the lights went off.

We stood there, unable to move for two or three minutes that felt like hours, then we set off again, crawling towards the right instead of going straight ahead. We were trying to move out of sight of the camp.

We found ourselves in a field of beans, closer to the barracks side. We needed a short rest, so we rolled over onto our backs and looked at the camp facing us for the first time. The full moon clearly picked out the top of the fence, the watchtowers and the walls. The rest was engulfed in a whitish halo of fog. It was a grim sight.

So this was the place where we had spent ten years of our life, where we had lost our best years, our hopes, our illusions, our health and our youth. In this death camp—there are no other words to describe our prison—we had been pariahs, cast out by the world, waiting for the end that was so slow in coming. Locked up inside, we had tried to forget where we were. But now, in that field, contemplating the place where we had suffered so much, the reality suddenly came home to us. And we were devastated.

I couldn't stop myself from sobbing at the thought and I wept even more when I thought of those we had left behind. I was so afraid for them. My heart contracted and a shudder ran through me. I heard the others crying softly; they all felt the same way.

We lay there for a moment, then we pulled ourselves together. The field was planted with broad beans, which we ate raw. Fresh, sweet and delicious, they tasted of freedom. Crawling, we set off again, and then, when we judged that we were far enough away from the barracks, we stood up and walked on in silence. The fields were so wet that we were soaked from head to foot.

In the pitch dark, with no landmarks and no signposts, we quickly realized that we were going round in circles. It was as distressing as being lost at sea or in the desert.

There was nothing to give us any clue where the road was, and none of us had a good sense of direction. Mother had taught me to read the stars, but I must have been a very bad student as I couldn't find the Great Bear, or Cassiopeia, or the Evening Star.

We continued to wander aimlessly.

A cough sent a chill down our spines. It came from overhead. Looking up, we saw a watchtower: we were back at the camp.

We didn't hang around, we turned on our heels and ran. We began to feel desperate. Tired, with dread in the pit of our stomachs, we stopped and lit a precious cigarette that we had carefully saved for this occasion. We smoked in silence, our hearts heavy, still thinking about Mother and the others.

We weren't on safe ground yet. We didn't know which way to turn. Then I asked Abdellatif to guide us.

'We are adults,' I said to him. 'We may have committed sins, but not you, you are so pure . . . if there is a God, he'll take pity on you. You will lead us to freedom.'

We followed him without a word. Our bodies were aching and our clothes soaked through, but we had to keep going.

'Kika, come and see, there's something hard. I don't know what it is.'

Abdellatif had never walked on asphalt. We rolled on it and kissed it. We felt like cosmonauts venturing their first steps on the moon.

We went back into a field to change into our 'civilian' clothes. I put on a long dress that Mother had worn in the Seventies, a cashmere print in autumnal shades. The others slipped on plain trousers and sweaters. They were a bit outmoded but were supposed to make them look 'normal'. We wore our Vuitton boots and we dumped our combat gear in the fields.

We set off again. As leader of the band, I accelerated the pace, exhorting the others to keep up. They trailed behind dragging their feet, they were so tired. Raouf laughed at my manic speed. He put on a German accent and urged me on, saying, 'Go, Jeanne, go,' a subtle allusion to my Alsatian governess.

Eventually we came to a large building, a dairy cooperative. We conferred and decided to try out our first scenario. Maria and Abdellatif hid. Supported by Raouf, I launched into a Moroccan-style screaming fit, invoking Allah and the Prophets.

This brought out a guard, armed with a stick. He wore a jellabah with a hood. I crumpled into his arms without waiting for his permission. He had no option but to support me.

He looked at Raouf suspiciously and asked him what was going on.

'My wife had a miscarriage last week. She can't get over it.'

The man was doubly suspicious.

'I didn't hear any noise. Where have you come from out of the blue, in the middle of the night?'

Without giving him time to ask any more questions, I fell to the ground again, pretending to writhe in pain. With many polite phrases, Raouf asked him for a glass of water. He explained that we had come from Belgium and hadn't been back to Morocco for fifteen years.

'Our car has broken down,' he added.

The guard was suspicious, like all Moroccans who have learned to survive under a regime of terror. He did not believe Raouf and questioned him closely, trying to catch him out. But he did fetch me some water.

During the conversation, I managed to slip in the fact that we were related to Driss Basri, the Minister of the Interior, which had the desired effect of intimidating the guard: the man calmed down a little. We tried to get him to talk, we wanted to know where we were. He suggested we wait for the dairy truck that was going to Bir-Jdid, the nearest town. At last we had the information we so badly needed.

We waited forty-five minutes for the truck, terrified that the man might raise the alarm, but he had no telephone. The dairy gates opened, the truck came out . . . and drove off without stopping to pick us up.

We were frantic. It was already four o'clock in the morning, we had been going round in circles since eleven o'clock at night and we had just wasted another three-quarters of an hour waiting for the truck. The only positive thing was that at last we knew where we were going.

* * *

We set off down the road again, our spirits at a low ebb. We must have formed a strange procession in the dawn glow, two boys and two girls walking like robots, with halting steps, and staring straight ahead. But we didn't have time to think about our appearance; we had to keep moving.

After a few kilometres, we came across one of those local buses that stop in all the villages. The farmers thronging around the bus stop carried bulky sacks, and there were chickens and sheep milling about.

We joined the fray. We felt awkward, convinced that everybody was staring at as. Until then we had been protected by the dark, but now it was daybreak and the dawn light made us feel exposed.

Raouf offered to pay the driver with the nameplate from my father's identity bracelet. The other passengers paid for their tickets with eggs or hens, bartering as hard as they could. The driver was wary, and refused. He wanted cash and nothing else. We gave up the idea of the bus and set off again on foot.

A truck drove past and I stuck out my thumb. The driver, a friendly hippie type, gave all four of us a lift without any questions. He simply warned us that at the entrance to Bir-Jdid we were likely to encounter a police roadblock but that we could avoid it by following a little path where he set us down.

Luckily, he was wrong and we reached Bir-Jdid without seeing anything resembling a roadblock.

The town was tiny and extremely poor. The road was lined with a few neglected houses, cafés and butchers' shops, and that was all. It was half-past six. The cafés were just opening, and through their doors radios blared out deafening music. The waiters bustled about and customers ordered coffee or mint tea. Life was there, unchanging, resuming its course as it had done each morning that we had been excluded from it.

The street felt strange to me, and it took me a few minutes to realize why. I was no longer accustomed to noise. The shouts, the voices, the hooting, the oriental songs, the tyres screeching on the road . . . all those sounds grated on my ears. Raouf and the others were in a similar state. The light hurt our eyes, and our heads throbbed.

Frightened by so much commotion, we stared eagerly about us and people stared back. But, even though we cut a wretched figure, we did not look out of place in these surroundings, especially Raouf, who was as toothless as the peasant farmers, as a result of abscesses and beatings.

At the end of the village was a collective taxi stand where a dense crowd was milling around. Raouf went ahead as a scout and when he came back, he told me that the taxis were headed for Casablanca. He went off again to negotiate with one of the drivers, and their discussion lasted a good twenty minutes. I was anxious, I was sure his plan would never work; and so when I saw him waving excitedly, I didn't realize straight away that he wanted us to join him. But another miracle had happened: the driver had agreed to take us in exchange for the gold nameplate.

Two men were sitting in front next to the driver. The four of us got in the back, and the taxi roared off. We were silent and pensive. I thought of Mother and my sisters with a heavy heart.

My gaze rested on Abdellatif. For the first time in ages, I realized just what a terrible state he was in. He had been incarcerated since the age of three and a half. He was outside for the first time in his life, at the age of eighteen. My little brother sat open-mouthed, watching the road fly past, a glazed look in his eyes. Bewildered by so many new sights, he was like a zombie who had just climbed out of the tomb.

He had been in a car only two or three times in his life, and then only to be shunted from one prison to another.

My sister Maria weighed barely thirty kilos. Her huge dark eyes devoured her tiny, gaunt face. Raouf was as thin as she was, but bloated from water retention. He was pale, feverish and toothless.

Nearly fifteen years had gone by, fifteen years of torture that had scarred us terribly. But, when I studied the three of them closely, I would catch an expression, mannerism or smile that reminded me of the children they had once been.

I felt responsible for their condition. I cursed prison for what it had done to them, what it had done to each one of us.

CASABLANCA

I will never forget my shock on our arrival in Casablanca, as we drove through the working-class district. I had completely forgotten what the city was like. The crowds walked hurriedly, jostling, filling the pavements and rushing across the road without looking. It made my head swim, the screech of brakes, the cries of the street vendors, a horse-drawn barouche, two women arguing, a policeman blowing his whistle at a speeding car. I inhaled the smell of petrol and the aroma of food coming from restaurants and stalls.

It was the first time in fifteen years that I had seen so many people at once, that my ears had heard so many sounds, and my senses had been assailed in this way. It seemed to me that the population of Morocco had tripled. Everything was bigger, newer, more modern. There were more women in the street, dressing in European-style clothes and make-up; they were well groomed.

This continual procession of people walking with their heads down, not seeing where they were going, reminded me of Chaplin's *Modern Times*. I felt curiously sorry for them. All in all, they were more to be pitied than I was. Perplexed, I mused: 'So is this life, is this freedom? They are just as much prisoners as I was . . .'

Myriad details that I had never been aware of in my previous life jumped out at me: the apartment blocks like rabbit hutches, the vacant stares, poverty, exhaustion, needless stress.

My companions were probably not thinking along those lines at all, or at least not in so many words. Abdellatif's jaw dropped in amazement, Raouf and Maria were silent. The taxi was driving too fast. I was afraid every time it suddenly braked. After all the trouble we had gone to, this was not the moment to die in an accident.

The driver began to complain. He was suspicious of us and wanted to go to the police.

'I'm not allowed to take you into the centre of town . . .'

Raouf managed to sweet-talk him into it. After all, we had given him a little piece of solid gold, the equivalent of two thousand five hundred dirhams, for a journey that was barely worth fifty.

Raouf gave him the address of Jamila, his teenage sweetheart, in the residential district of Anfa. While the driver was looking for the street, I stared out without recognizing anything. I felt as though I had landed on another planet. We were like the Lilliputians arriving in the Land of the Giants in *Gulliver's Travels*. Anfa had always been like a miniature Beverly Hills with its neat rows of immense villas. Some looked like palaces. They had swimming pools, tennis courts, golf courses, striped lawns and flower beds that were a riot of colour. In the garages stood dozens of gleaming cars. Armies of chauffeurs, gardeners, butlers and maids attended to their masters' comfort.

But fifteen years later, the houses looked even more luxurious to me, the gardens even more impressive and the display of wealth even more ostentatious. And, indeed, this was probably true. There was no possible comparison between all this luxury and the sordid prison we had escaped from.

The taxi dropped us off and left without waiting. Jamila had moved. We felt marooned but I didn't want to dwell on this painful feeling. I told the others to wait outside while I went up to one of the villas. A gardener in a white apron was watering the lawn.

I greeted him haughtily and asked him to call the mistress of the house, claiming I had an appointment with her. He looked me up and down and then brandished his hosepipe and threatened me with it, ordering me to leave.

'Get a move on or I'll call the police. We don't want your sort around here.'

Without waiting to hear any more I ran to join the others. I was mortified, humiliated. In the days of the old Malika, that man wouldn't even have dared talk to me. And now he was chasing me away as if I were a poor beggar . . .

We continued walking, at a loss as to what to do. At random I chose a villa with a beautiful wrought-iron gate and rang the buzzer. A woman's voice replied. I asked her for a glass of water. Moroccan custom demands that you never refuse a beggar a glass of water.

A stunningly pretty maid in a pink apron and a little cap perched jauntily on her neat hair came out of the house. I stared at her, envious of her appearance, before starting to talk to her. My demented expression must have frightened her because she recoiled.

Then I launched into my story: Belgium, fifteen years away, the miscarriage, and asked her if I could make a telephone call. She began to warm to me but replied that she would have to ask her employer's permission.

She closed the door. I signalled to the others to stay hidden behind the bougainvillaea hedge.

A few minutes later the door opened again, revealing a tall, handsome man of about fifty with salt-and-pepper hair. He was wearing a towelling bathrobe. I had probably disturbed him while he was dressing, for he was holding an electric shaver. He smelt nice and was well groomed; this man was on a different planet from me. He winced at my poverty-stricken appearance.

My eloquence saved the situation. I immediately spoke to him in my most elegant French, with judiciously chosen phrases. My language no doubt reassured him and he began to address me as '*chère madame*'.

'My maid tells me that you've had a miscarriage. I hope you're not haemorrhaging? I'm a doctor, I can take you to hospital.'

I stammered a vague explanation, repeated my Belgium patter, and then, before he had a chance to think, I asked him if I could use the telephone. He said yes and invited me in.

His house seemed like a palace to me, and yet there was nothing luxurious about it. But it exuded order, cleanliness and middle-class comfort with its white walls, red hexagonal floor tiles, and plants in the windows. The telephone was on a pretty little table next to the phone directories.

I hadn't forgotten how to use the phone, but my heart started thumping as I picked up the receiver. I felt as though I were in *Hibernatus*, that film with Louis de Funès, where the hero comes back to life after being asleep for many years and mustn't give himself away. Like Hibernatus, I couldn't help making blunders.

My grandfather's phone was continually engaged. Dr Arfi—for

that was how the owner of the house introduced himself—pointed out that you had to dial six numbers whereas I kept dialling five, as in the old days.

'Oh yes,' I said casually, my heart pounding as if it would burst at nearly having given the game away, 'I know. But it's always like this, even when we call them from Brussels. They're always on the phone . . .'

He offered me a coffee. At that point I told him that I was accompanied by my husband, my sister and my brother-in-law. He seemed unfazed, so I signalled to the others to come in while he went to get dressed.

The maid arrived, carrying a tray covered with delicious food: exquisite-smelling coffee, cakes, bread and jams. We looked at one another in silence. We were so hungry we couldn't touch a thing, otherwise in a few minutes we would have devoured the lot—the food, the carpet, the furniture and even the dog. Abdellatif was fascinated by the animal, for he had never seen a pet dog before. It was a playful little cocker spaniel that licked him and stood on its hind legs in its excitement. My brother was torn between delight and fear.

We sat in the lounge, holding ourselves bolt upright, careful not to dirty the white carpet with our pitiful shoes that were covered in mud and wet from the dew. After an eternity, the doctor joined us. He wore a suit, a clean shirt and a tie, which for us was the epitome of elegance.

He began to converse in an urbane manner while offering us coffee. I told him that we had friends in Casablanca, I mentioned the B— J—s and the B—s, two bourgeois families. His face lit up. He was on familiar territory.

'Incredible,' he said, 'they are friends of mine too.'

Reassured to discover we had mutual acquaintances, he offered to drive us over to the B— J—s.

They belonged to a family of Casablanca bankers. One of the sons, Kamil, had been considered the handsomest boy of his generation. His younger brother, Laarbi, had been one of my close friends. During my last holiday in Kabila, just before the coup d'état, I had organized a birthday party for him at our house. I used to see them every day and I was very fond of them.

When the doctor dropped us off outside the house, I told the children to hide again and I walked straight in without ringing the bell. I just pushed open the door. Suddenly it was as if those fifteen years had melted away. I recognized everything, the furniture, the paintings and the familiar smells. My head swam.

The house seemed empty. I stroked the dog who was overjoyed to see me, then I walked through the house to the kitchen. I saw a telephone. Without thinking, I dialled a number, my grandfather's. Each time, a stranger picked up the phone and answered 'hello' in a gruff voice. I was terrified, but I kept trying.

Eventually I realized that it was an internal line and then I recognized the voice. It was Laarbi's. I asked him to come downstairs without telling him who I was. He did so, grumbling.

When he walked into the room, I was taken aback by his appearance and it took me a few moments to recognize him. I had known him as a slim twenty-five-year-old, and now before me stood a portly, greying forty-year-old. We greeted each other. He didn't seem to know who I was.

'I am Malika,' I said.

'Malika who?'

'Hadji's daughter.'

Hadji is an honorary title for someone who has made the pilgrimage to Mecca, like my father.

I was unable to utter my surname. I was afraid of stating my identity, a fear that stayed with me for many years.

'I don't see . . .'

Not without effort, I finally managed to stammer my name:

'Oufkir, Malika Oufkir.'

He was rooted to the spot.

'What do you want?' he asked me in a tone that was both brusque and haughty.

I told him that we had been released and that I was with Raouf, Maria and Abdellatif. I was shaking with fear, and worst of all I didn't know where I stood. During all those years in gaol, we had thought of ourselves as innocent parties, convinced we were in the right. We were victims, not culprits, as Laarbi's reception implied. Never could I have imagined that our own friends could display such total amnesia.

Laarbi had just given me my first slap in the face.

I swallowed my pride and forced myself to think of the others who were waiting for me, and of everything that lay ahead of us.

'I need money,' I said dryly. 'And I would like you to drive us to the station.'

I had learned of the existence of this new railway line from the taxi driver. In my day there was no train from Casablanca to Rabat.

Without saying a word, he left the kitchen and came back a few seconds later holding out three hundred dirhams—about twenty pounds. That seemed plenty, a royal sum even. I was unaware that the dirham of 1987 no longer had the same purchasing power as before.

Laarbi gave me a little moralizing lecture forbidding me to go near his elder brother who had been suffering from depression since the death of their uncle. Kamil, I was certain, would never have treated us as Laarbi did. He had always been kind, humane and sensitive. And loyal. But I didn't have time to check this out. Laarbi took the car out of the garage. He eyed the others with a mixture of contempt and fear, without a trace of pity for their wretched condition, then he motioned us to get in. He dropped us like bundles of dirty washing outside the station.

This encounter had shaken me but I didn't want to brood over unpleasantness. With my dirhams in my pocket, I felt rich, and my first purchase was for Abdellatif. I bought him *l'Equipe*, a sports paper. He had discovered football thanks to the radio, and he could recite the names of all the players in the French and Moroccan teams as well as the results of all the matches.

We stocked up on cigarettes, thinking of Soukaina. She loved smoking so much that in Bir-Jdid she would dry the grass and leaves gathered by Halima in the courtyard, and then roll them in paper salvaged from the bread boxes or in saffron wrappers.

Buying tickets was more of a challenge for us. We were afraid of the crowds, and especially of the uniformed inspectors. The giant portrait of the King hanging on one of the walls induced a fresh panic attack that sent us rushing outside, panting and trembling, as if Big Brother himself were after us.

Of course it was stupid, but we couldn't help it.

We finally boarded the train, conscious of our bizarre appearance and aware that people were staring at us. We settled down in the compartment, ordered coffee and lit our cigarettes, experiencing, for the first time in hours, a sense of freedom. But when the inspector came in to check our tickets, we began to shake from head to foot again.

Next to us, a French couple was berating the corruption of the regime, the excesses of Throne Day, the expense involved and the fact that tourists had been turned away from La Mamounia, the famous luxury hotel in Marrakesh, even though they had reservations, because the government had requisitioned the rooms for the occasion. The conversation reassured us that we were not the only ones to criticize the authorities.

From time to time the French pair glanced over at us, intrigued. We had a desperate urge to talk to them, to tell them about our fate. They seemed friendly and open, but how did we know they wouldn't inform on us despite their fine words?

We had become too suspicious.

We swallowed our appeals for help.

Abdellatif was in a state of shock that intensified with each new discovery. He had never seen a newspaper in his life. He stared, gaping, at the photos of the players with their footballs. The only football he had ever seen was the one we had made for him in prison.

His amazement grew when the train pulled out of the station and began to go faster and faster. His mouth fell open and he gazed wild-eyed at the landscape. Raouf tried to relax him but to no avail. To our dismay, Abdellatif was an *enfant sauvage*, a wild child, bewildered by the avalanche of new experiences and sensations.

During our five days on the run, he continued to feel that he was riding on a moving train. Later, in Tangier, in the bar of the Hotel Ahlan, which we made our headquarters, he asked if the train was ever going to stop.

RABAT

With a feeling of dread in the pit of our stomachs, we walked through Rabat central station. Had the alarm been raised? Would we be arrested on the platform? Or outside? But no, nothing seemed out of the ordinary, there wasn't a policeman in sight. We hesitantly made our way towards the taxi rank. This station was much too big, much too new and much too busy. The crowd jostled us, people seemed to be in a hurry. They knew where they were going. But nobody was waiting for us.

Raouf and Maria got into the first taxi and I took another one with my little brother. It was nine o'clock in the morning. We were to meet up at the French embassy. A Moroccan policeman was guarding the entrance. I faltered for a moment then I went up to him.

'I want to go in,' I said.

'The embassy is closed,' he replied, as if it were obvious.

It took a few minutes for it to dawn on me. It was Monday 20 April, in other words, Easter Monday. Despite our carefully laid plans, we had overlooked this important detail. Who knows what would have happened if we had escaped one day later?

Raouf came over and tried to engage the policeman in conversation, but he looked at us suspiciously. It didn't take him long to realize there was something odd about us. He bombarded us with questions, and even asked us if we were on the run. His eyes swept over us with contempt, from the top of our balding heads to our muddy shoes.

Without giving him time to question us further, we climbed back into the taxis. The driver also glanced at me suspiciously when I asked him to drop us outside the American embassy.

It was our only back-up plan in the event that our request for political asylum at the French embassy was refused.

'Why do you look as if there's someone after you?' he asked me. 'Where are you from? There's something odd about you. You look like a European, but no, there's definitely something strange about you . . .'

We didn't answer. He asked more questions as he drove, but we held our tongues. We pulled up in front of the American embassy, and I decided to try my luck alone. Another Moroccan policeman stopped me at the entrance and asked me to put down my bundle. It contained the revolver that Abdellatif had made that looked so authentic it could be mistaken for a real one. I was afraid of being taken for a terrorist.

I stammered that it contained my brother's toys. But the man snatched the bag from me, flung it into a corner of his sentry box and told me to pick it up on the way out.

I was despondent. We had been so confident of success at the French embassy that it had not occurred to us that we would have to improvise in the event of failure. Nor did we have the moral strength. In our agitated, bedraggled condition, executing a finely honed plan that we had been preparing for weeks and learned by heart was still feasible. Coping with the unforeseen required an effort that was beyond us.

I was disoriented.

Trembling, I walked down a ramp to the embassy offices. On the right, there were two uniformed GIs in a glass-walled office, watching the comings and goings on their surveillance monitors. Facing them, on the left, a Moroccan in a suit and tie stood guard in front of the chain barring the entrance to the offices.

I requested immigration forms from the Moroccan and asked him how to fill them in. As he replied, my mind was racing. All I had to do was thrust aside the chain and I would be on American territory. On the other side, the officials went about their business. I tried to attract their attention, imploring them with my eyes, but in vain.

A man came over to the Moroccan orderly. He showed him his badge and the orderly raised the chain. I dithered again as to what I should do. Should I rush after him, jump over the chain and yell that I wanted political asylum? But if they accepted me, what would become of the other three? Would they be turned away? Denounced? Arrested?

If the Moroccan had been American, I would have stepped over the chain without any qualms. He would have represented deliverance, America, the Rights of Man. But could I trust a fellow Moroccan? Supposing he barred my way?

When I finally decided to act, it was too late. The GIs in their glass office had become suspicious. They spoke to each other in English, pointing at me, then barked into their PA system, telling the Moroccan that there was something odd about me. One of them came out and walked towards me.

I panicked. I gathered up the forms, retrieved my bundle and ran away, my heart pounding as if it would burst. I rejoined the rest of the little group in the taxis. It was a disaster. Our only hope now was the British embassy or the Spanish embassy. But they were closed too. We were utterly at a loss.

There was someone else who could help us, a friend of my grandfather's, a fellow Berber. One of his daughters had been at school with me at the Palace. We asked the taxis to take us to the Agdal district, where he lived with his family—his wife Lalla Mina and his daughters, Latifa and Malika. In the old days, the Agdal consisted entirely of charming little villas. But all the houses had been pulled down and replaced by apartment blocks.

We didn't recognize anything. The taxis drove round in circles, and we were increasingly disoriented. Then I remembered that their house was next to the post office. Luckily, it was the only one that had not been demolished.

The concierge asked me who he should announce. I told him I wished to speak to Lalla Mina, that I was Malika, Hadji Fatima's daughter.

He came back and told me with an air of distrust:

'She doesn't know anybody of that name. If you don't get out of here straight away she'll call the police.'

I pleaded with him.

'Tell her I'm Malika, Oufkir's daughter.'

He stopped in his tracks, surprised, almost frightened.

'Don't insist,' he said at length, 'there's no point. She doesn't want to know.'

But he gently shut the door between the living room and the hall, and threw me a curious look. I asked him where Latifa lived.

'She lives in Agadir.'

Malika, her sister, lived on the other side of the street. I had known her well; she had been a teacher when she was younger. In the days when my father was still head of national security, she used to come to the house and give private lessons to the children. Now she was married to an entrepreneur and had children of her own.

Without much hope, I decided to try my luck. We stood outside the building and waited for her. Around half-past twelve, we watched a car draw up. A plump woman got out followed by four children in single file, like a mother hen with her chicks. Malika must have put on ten kilos with each pregnancy.

I approached her. She stared at me, and her expression froze. The closer I got to her the more flustered she became.

In the end, she grimaced, stepped back and began to cry.

'But why me?' she screamed. 'Why do this to me? You don't have the right . . . Children, go inside quickly,' she went on, on the verge of hysteria.

She continued to distance herself, shooing me away as if I were a leper.

We went back to the city centre to send our letters from the main post office. We had written about twenty, to politicians and personalities from the entertainment world, including Alain Delon, Simone Signoret, the former President of the European Parliament Simone Veil, Robert Badinter the former lawyer now President of the French Constitutional Council, and José Artur. We also wanted to make some phone calls. We shut ourselves in a telephone booth but we couldn't work out how to operate the phone.

Each time somebody approached, we rushed out of the booth as if we were going to be pursued. Although we were afraid, we had a good laugh, which allowed us briefly to forget that we were fugitives. But we didn't manage to dial a single number.

The hours were ticking by. We had to find shelter somewhere. The only people we could turn to were our childhood friends, and one of them was Reda, a close friend of Raouf's. In the old days he used to live nearby, in the Allée des Princesses. To reach Reda's house, we had to go past our own old house. I had always promised Abdellatif that I would show it to him one day. He had no recollection of it, but he loved to listen to us wistfully talking about it.

It was now or never.

I arranged to meet up with the others outside Reda's house, and Abdellatif and I turned off towards ours.

I dreaded what I might find, what changes might have been made by the new tenants. Would they have kept it the same? Was my room still there, between the swimming pool and the sauna? And what about the garden? Would it still be full of the flowers I so loved?

When we arrived at the gate, I thought I'd come to the wrong address. Instead of the majestic red ochre villa surrounded by a lush green lawn, there was nothing but a wasteland. After our departure, the house had been looted. Our former hangers-on had helped themselves to the furniture, the paintings, the carpets, my mother's jewellery, the photo albums, trinkets, clothes, mementoes . . .

Then Hassan II had ordered the house to be razed to the ground. It no longer existed, just as we no longer existed. Through this brutal act, he had obliterated us.

I reeled under the blow. That house had been terribly important to me. When I lived at the Palace, it had always been at the centre of my thoughts, the symbol of a normal, happy home, the haven of peace I craved.

During all those years in prison, I had clung to it. I could visualize it clearly. At night, before falling asleep, I would wander through all the rooms, drinking in every detail. It was my umbilical cord, my last link with my father and the long-lost days of happiness.

With its disappearance, I had lost my anchor. I felt sullied, violated, crushed. Alone in the world, once again. Nothing made sense any more. I didn't want to upset Abdellatif, so I pretended that I was lost and couldn't remember where the house was. He meekly swallowed my lie.

We got back into the taxi and set off for Reda's house. A gardener was standing outside the door.

'Reda?' he said as if talking to an idiot. 'Reda got married. He doesn't live here any more . . . His parents? But they're in France . . .'

When pressed, he grudgingly told me that Reda now lived in the Zawha apartment building. We clambered back into the taxi, more downhearted than ever. At the entrance to the building, the concierge stopped us. He was suspicious, nosy and probably an informer, like most concierges in Morocco.

I affected a casual tone and asked him where Reda's apartment was. I picked my way there with great caution, as if crossing a war zone. I felt as though I were passing a dangerous frontier, and might be stopped in my tracks by a bullet at any moment.

I rang the bell. A maid opened the door. Reda had just left, and she wouldn't tell me where he was having lunch. I asked her for a glass of water, and begged her to let me use the phone.

I wanted to call José Artur at France Inter. His programme had comforted us so often during our captivity that I was certain he would help us . . . but she refused my request and showed me the door.

I was about to start pleading when I heard the familiar drone of a helicopter in the sky. I took Abdellatif's hand and rushed down the stairs. Maria and Raouf, who were waiting for me at the entrance, also began to run.

The craft was flying so low that we could clearly see the soldiers sitting inside, cradling their machine guns. The four of us kept running until we found a hiding place behind some cypress trees. We huddled together, quaking. We had no idea that our grandfather also lived in this apartment building and that this was the first place the police had searched.

Then Raouf had a brainwave, another one, but at this stage we weren't going to argue. Next to the Zawha residence was the villa of some other childhood friends, Patrick and Philippe Barère, a Moroccan French family. We had always been on good terms with them and we were fond of their parents, especially their mother, who was a real mother hen, always fussing over her offspring.

After a few minutes' walk, we came across their enchanting little house set among trees and lawns.

A maid opened the door.

'We would like to see Mme Barère. Please tell her Malika and Raouf Oufkir are here.'

She shut the door again. We were prepared for anything: to be driven away like thieves, insulted, despised and denounced. We were exhausted, hungry, numb and desperate. Incapable of taking another step.

Then we heard running footsteps in the hall and the door flew open. Michèle Barère stood before us, weeping.

She was crying so hard she was incapable of speech.

She flung open her arms and embraced us, murmuring:

'My children, my darling children, how wonderful.'

She showed us in. We felt safe for the first time since our escape.

She was having coffee with her husband, and invited the four of us to follow her. Luc Barère owned a timber plant. I knew that in the old days he had been well thought of at the Palace. He rose and embraced us. He seemed very surprised to see us. I told him that we had been released.

'But how? There was nothing about it on the radio or on the television . . .'

'You know, that's how things are. When we disappeared, there weren't any explanations either . . .'

My reply was plausible. So many people who had disappeared had simply 'reappeared' one day, without any rhyme or reason. I got into my stride: my mother and the others would be out soon, there was going to be a second convoy. We had been given a little money for the journey.

I didn't feel comfortable telling these lies. I could sense he was sceptical.

It was a huge effort for me to pretend we had been released, that everything was normal, and keep back all the things that were bubbling inside my head. I wanted to scream, there, in that neat living room full of pretty little knick-knacks arranged lovingly on every polished surface, that we were wanted, that the entire Moroccan police force was after us; and that for fifteen years we had been paying for a crime we had not committed; that Mother, Soukaina and Myriam were still locked up, perhaps, as I spoke, being tortured to make them reveal our whereabouts . . .

I was churning with fear, anxiety, rebellion, guilt and anger. Life had gone on without us . . . our reappearance was disrupting the smooth workings of the world and frightening even those who once loved us. For fifteen years we had been ghosts—people avoided mentioning our name, or spoke it in a whisper, for fear of reprisals.

But I couldn't say anything. I had to be content to smile, pretend and utter platitudes to cover up the drama of our situation.

Luc Barère announced that he had to go off to work, which was a relief. We wouldn't have to keep up the pretence. His wife believed our story. She bustled around in the kitchen, preparing food and drinks, repeating:

'My poor darlings, I'm so happy . . .'

We spent a few hours relaxing, eating and drinking, but we remained on the alert. Nevertheless, the respite was welcome. Michèle Barère gave us news of our old friends. She told us how our house had been demolished, and which of the hangers-on had participated in the scramble to loot it. I fought back my tears.

She also told me about the death, some ten years earlier, of Mamma Khadija, my courageous grandmother who had acted as messenger on her moped, delivering letters and parcels to the police at Tamattaght. My grandfather had remarried shortly afterwards. His new wife was very young.

She also told us that one of her sons, Philippe, who now lived in France, was on holiday in Morocco with his wife, Janine, an old schoolfriend. He would be so thrilled to see us again. I was terrified that one of us would give the game away, and I was petrified when she switched on the television. We had never seen colour pictures other than at the cinema. Cartoons appeared on the giant screen, and

Abdellatif sat glued to the TV set. He was mesmerized and ignored us completely. He had become a little boy of three again, laughing at the silliest gags. I was anxious that he was having to cope with too many new experiences, too quickly. And I didn't want Michèle Barère to have any inkling of the conditions we had suffered in prison so had decided to disclose as little as possible.

While we sat chatting idly, and the hours ticked by, I became increasingly convinced that we had failed. I tried to imagine death, for we were adamant in our resolve to kill ourselves if we were caught. It had been easy to make that decision in the isolation of our prison, but it was much harder now we were back in the world.

Luc Barère came home late that afternoon. He wouldn't leave us alone. He didn't believe a word of our little story, and asked us the same questions a hundred times, dissatisfied with our replies. His wife tried to reason with him, and kept telling him to leave us in peace.

'You can see that these children have been through hell, Luc . . . When I think of all those people who didn't care what happened to them . . .'

We tried to change the subject, asking for news of different people, but he kept returning to the attack. He finally declared that our release was something to celebrate. He offered to telephone our grandfather who deserved to share the good news. How were we to dissuade him without making too much of a fuss and deepening his suspicions?

'He's elderly,' I said, 'it would be a shock for him to see us in this dreadful state. We'd rather get our strength back before calling him. He's all the family we have left. We don't want to kill him.'

This was a long way from the truth, of course. We were in no doubt by now that the police were tapping his phone and watching his house. We would be arrested immediately.

Michèle Barère came to our rescue.

'Give them a chance to recuperate,' she said to him. 'They'll go and see him tomorrow. We'll warn him first,' she added, to reassure us. 'I'll phone him myself.'

We were about to sit down to eat when the front door opened. We heard a man sobbing in the hall. Philippe Barère had heard that we were back and had come to see us with his wife and son. He embraced us tearfully.

He kept saying the same thing over and over again.

'It's not true, what a nightmare, why did they do that to you?'

Then he calmed down, looked at us, and said that seeing us again was the best thing that life could have given him.

That dinner was one of the strangest, most painful meals of my entire life. Philippe alternated between laughing or gazing at us with a blissful smile, and sobbing. We tried to maintain a semblance of normality, but we were terribly bewildered, and in any case we were utterly exhausted.

After dinner, Michèle Barère showed me to our rooms upstairs. I politely declined the one she offered me, on the pretext that I wanted to sleep alone. She immediately said that I could sleep where I pleased, in other words in a room where there was a telephone. Then Luc Barère came out and gave me some sleeping pills, to ensure that we all had a good night. I took the pills and thanked him and, the minute he turned his back, I hurriedly flushed them down the toilet.

My paranoia was increasing by the hour.

We took it in turns to wash. Abdellatif experienced his first bath. I was the last to use the bathroom. When I tried to remove my dress, I found I couldn't. I tugged it off violently and with it came the skin from my legs that was stuck to the fabric with congealed blood.

Without realizing it, I had scraped myself badly in my attempt to squeeze out of the tunnel. The pain was already excruciating, but worse was to come. My shoes were stuck to my feet and I couldn't get them off.

I closed my eyes, counted to three and pulled hard. I had to bite my lip to stop myself from screaming. I had pulled off my toenails, and my feet were bleeding. The blood ran onto the fitted carpet.

Alarmed, I looked around for something to clean the carpet with, and then the door opened and I dived into the bath. Michèle Barère saw the blood on the floor.

'What's happened to you?'

'It's nothing, I caught my nail in the door.'

She began to panic. The situation was getting out of hand. She went out, and I washed and did my best to clean up the mess. She had lent me a tunic to sleep in, but my feet were bleeding so badly that I sat up all night so as not to get blood all over the tunic or the sheets.

I spent the night writing. A letter to Jean Daniel, editor-in-chief of *Le Nouvel Observateur*, poems and SOS messages. Around four o'clock in the morning, I gently picked up the telephone.

On the other end of the line, Luc's voice asked me if I needed anything.

'No, I heard the phone ringing.'

'You were dreaming . . .'

Around six thirty that Tuesday morning, I got up and put my clothes on, then I went to join the others. They were already awake. I asked them to get dressed quickly and I went down into the kitchen.

Michèle Barère was humming as she prepared breakfast. The table was laid and the room was filled with the aroma of toast and coffee. Everything seemed so normal. And we were so utterly excluded from that normality.

I kissed her. She asked me affectionately if I had slept well. I fought back my tears, disarmed by her trusting kindness. Then I commented on Luc's absence.

'Impossible to stop him . . . you know what he's like . . . he drove off to tell your grandfather.'

I went up to tell Raouf the disastrous news. Then Philippe arrived to have breakfast with us. Raouf drew him to one side and asked him if he could give us a lift.

'No problem. Where do you want to go?'

'We'll tell you when we get there.'

I told Michèle Barère that Raouf and I were going for a drive with Philippe.

The previous day we had noticed the Swedish embassy a short distance from the Barères' house. It seemed our last chance to seek political asylum, but we no longer had much faith in this solution. We gave Philippe directions, then we told him to park.

He gazed at us wordlessly for a long time. Our faces, like our silence, spoke volumes. We finally explained our situation to him. He banged his head against the steering wheel and howled with grief.

'Why, oh why, won't this nightmare stop?' It was impossible to calm him down. And yet we continued to talk to him steadily, as if comforting a child.

'Listen,' said Raouf, 'we're going into the embassy to ask for political asylum. If in a quarter of an hour we're still inside, it will mean our plan has worked. In that case, please bring Abdellatif and Maria over here at once. If we come out again, all we ask of you is to drop us at the station.'

He agreed, still crying. He would have agreed to anything.

We had to queue to enter the embassy, and our turn was slow in coming. After ten minutes, Raouf became impatient. He took a sheet of paper, and wrote in large letters:

'General Oufkir's children ask Sweden for political asylum.'

We slipped the sheet of paper under the glass door behind which a huge blond woman was sitting. She grabbed the paper, read it and rose to her feet. Standing up, she seemed even more colossal. She looked daggers at us and slowly mouthed the words:

'GET OUT.'

Terrified, we fled as fast as we could. Sweden, the country of human rights . . .

Philippe was waiting for us in the car. We had to go back to his house to pick up Abdellatif and Maria. His mother opened the door. She didn't understand why he was sobbing. She probably didn't want to understand.

Then Luc Barère came in, followed by my young uncle Wahid, his face puffy and his eyes brimming with tears. Barère had been to my grandfather's house, where he had found Wahid and told him that we had been released. My uncle had collapsed in his arms.

'They have escaped.'

He had been informed of this news by the secret services. The police had come looking for him the day before and all night they had beaten the soles of his feet to force him to reveal our whereabouts.

They had dumped him back at home half an hour before Barère arrived. Wahid had not seen us since our departure for Assa. He hadn't received any news since Tamattaght, except, from time to time, the announcement of the death of one or the other of us.

Thus he had been informed that Myriam was dead, then Raouf, then me. He made me swear that Mother and the others were still alive. He was howling, crying, gesticulating and kissing us each in turn.

I was overwhelmed at seeing him again. I loved him like a brother, but I steeled myself to remain impassive. It wasn't the moment to give in to emotion. I wasn't in a state to cope with his grief. I wanted to toughen him up, shake him and make him understand that our lives were at stake. Above all I was terrified that he had been followed.

'It's all very well crying now, but for fifteen years you all abandoned us,' I said coldly. 'If you want to redeem yourself, there is only one thing for you to do: tell our whole story to the international press, because they won't catch us alive. And find us some money.'

Luc Barère began to shout.

'Why do this to me? I trusted you. I welcomed you into my house! I'm not going to be able to work in this country any more! I'll be thrown out . . .'

'I didn't intend to lie to you or use you,' I replied. 'We are alone in the world, we didn't know where to go, and if we didn't tell you the truth it was to protect you. You can tell the authorities that you didn't know and that we deceived you all.'

His wife tried to calm him down. Philippe for his part grew angry, berating his father for never having tried to do anything for us.

'We are all guilty, we all share this shame,' he repeated.

Wahid didn't have any money on him. He asked Barère for a loan and Luc gave us three thousand dirhams. I gave the manuscript of my Story to Philippe, making him swear to bury it somewhere and give it back to me one day. He promised to do so. But he was so frightened that he rushed to destroy it all the minute we were out of sight.

Michèle Barère gave us clean clothes. I inherited a sort of lavender-coloured tunic and high-heeled sandals with uppers made of netting. I looked odd to say the least. But the younger ones and Raouf were properly attired.

We took a taxi and asked to be dropped off at Agdal station. Leaving from Rabat station, in the city centre, was too risky. We wanted to go to Tangier.

TANGIER

Why Tangier? First because we no longer knew where to go and the city seemed to mark the ultimate stage of our adventure. We were deprived of sleep, tired, depressed, and crushed by the shocks and disappointments that had come crashing down on us over the last two days. The other slightly more concrete reason was that the Barères had told me that one of my former suitors, Salah Balafrèj, was the owner of a hotel in Tangier. Maybe he would be able to help us?

In any case, Casablanca and Rabat had become too dangerous for us and we needed a goal. So why not Tangier?

While we were waiting for the train, we sheltered in a car park, hiding under the cars to avoid detection. We had two and a half hours to kill. Raouf went off to buy tickets and then came back and hid with us. We started imagining the wildest runaway scenarios, each one crazier than the last.

Our sense of humour kept us going; it was the best—the only—remedy against despair. We tried to alleviate the tension with the most childish jokes.

We imagined escaping from Morocco by swimming the Straits of Gibraltar. But Maria was afraid of sharks.

'Listen, Negus, no sharks would want your bones,' retorted Raouf with a smile, alluding to her skinniness.

Abdellatif, who took everything literally, grew anxious because he couldn't swim.

Raouf decided that in Tangier we would buy diving suits worthy of Captain Cousteau. We would rub seal blubber all over our bodies to protect us from the cold. We would also obtain shark repellent lozenges to reassure Maria, and distress flares to signal our whereabouts to passing ships.

These silly notions kept our spirits up. No doubt swimming the Straits of Gibraltar was just another crazy idea, but in comparison with the tunnel we had dug with our bare hands, and our fantastic and surreal escape, it seemed feasible. We let our imaginations run riot, dreaming up lots more crazy scenarios inspired by the world of cartoons.

We needed a place to stay on our arrival in Tangier until we contacted Balafrèj. Going to a hotel was risky—we would be asked to produce our identity cards—and we didn't want to deplete our money. Should we go knocking on doors? We didn't know many people and, given our reception in Rabat, we were afraid of getting our fingers burnt again.

Besides, the police had been looking for us for two days and they were probably already in Tangier. Descriptions of us had been circulated, and our friends were under surveillance. We had to be careful.

We decided to make some new friends on the train. Raouf and I would set out to charm them. We drew up a profile of the sort of people we were looking for: a working-class man and woman, naive enough to swallow our lies. That way we would have somewhere to sleep.

We went from one compartment to another, and miraculously found a man and a woman who just about fitted that description. The woman was sitting to the left of the window and the man opposite her. He was around thirty years old, with a kindly air and a modest appearance, but I didn't waste time staring at him.

Chatting him up was not intended to be a game, but a way of ensuring our survival. I sat down opposite him, while Raouf sat facing the woman, a plump Moroccan aged about fifty, spilling out of her clothes. She was dressed from head to foot in a delightful combination of pinks, and her face was heavily painted.

I looked at Raouf and whispered, giggling:

'Poor darling, look what's in store for you.'

I was cold and tired, and shivering in my flimsy tunic. The man offered me his sweater. I thanked him in French with an Italian accent. This time, we weren't from Belgium but from Italy, and we had even chosen a *nom de guerre*: Albertini. It was just as well because it turned out the man came from Belgium. He was a cook and was going to see his family in Tangier.

The plump woman joined in our conversation. They asked us where we had come from, and I came out with my Italian saga. From the south, I added, when she pointed out that I was olive-skinned like the Moroccans.

I changed places to sit next to the cook. After a moment, I feigned sleepiness and let my head fall on his shoulder. I avoided Raouf's eye. I guessed that my brother was furious to see me flirting with a man to ensure a roof over our heads. I felt pretty bad about it too. But did we have any choice?

The railway followed the coast with its white sand beaches. Abdellatif watched the scenery hurtle past with that wild look in his eyes again. He had never seen the sea, or at least he didn't remember it. The woman asked him, somewhat surprised, whether it was the first time he had seen it.

We changed the subject, not wanting to give too many details about our supposed life in Italy. The woman was a little too suspicious. As for the cook, he was in seventh heaven. He was convinced he would soon have me, and he was already drooling.

The four-hour journey was a real ordeal. Our stomachs were churning with fear. But concentrating on playing the Albertinis helped us to relax and allowed us to forget everything else for a while.

The train finally drew into Tangier. We each looked at the others before going into action. We understood one another without the need for words. I entwined myself with the cook; Raouf glued himself to the plump woman's side. Maria and Abdellatif fell back together. On the platform, the police were watching the passengers alight from the train, although without particular zeal. The country was in a state of alert, with the police looking for us in public places, but the government was in a quandary. They had to be careful that public opinion, outraged at the fate we had suffered for fifteen years, didn't turn against the country's rulers. We were to find that out later.

Passengers descended from the train, jostling one another, and soon formed a dense throng into which we dived. Once again, we managed to leave the station without hindrance. The reason was simple. The police were looking for four runaways skulking in corners, not a lovesick girl affectionately cuddling her fiancé, nor a tall skinny youth on the arm of his podgy girlfriend, and not even a sweet young couple walking arm in arm.

Most importantly, they didn't know what we looked like. They had no recent photo of us, we were later told by the director of the secret services. Since 1972, we had all had plenty of time to grow and change enormously.

The cook didn't understand why I suddenly turned pale and anxious. He thought it must be because of the police.

'Yes, that's the way things are here,' he said. 'I'm sorry. In my country there are cops everywhere.'

The fat woman, who worked as a secretary in Rabat, said goodbye. On parting, she gave me her address. I clung to the cook's arm. He asked me irritably why I didn't get rid of the others.

'I can't ditch my family. They wouldn't understand . . .'

I tried to find out where he lived but he didn't answer. There was something unreal about our walk through Tangier as the lights went on at dusk. The sea breeze caressed our faces, our nostrils were filled with a salty tang, and the ships' sirens gave us a sense of vast spaces and open frontiers. Freedom was there, within our grasp; we were so close to enjoying it again. We were intoxicated by the beat of the Tangier nightlife that echoed that of its neighbour, Spain, so close at hand. But Tangier the city of fun had another side. A hotbed of fundamentalism, and a centre too for drugs and contraband, the town was swarming with auxiliary forces who carried out frequent identity checks. But at that point, that was something we didn't know.

We walked past two soldiers with their guns resting on their shoulders. They stopped us and asked for our papers. Caught short, I stuttered. We were saved by the cook, who protested in Arabic:

'What? You want tourists to come to Morocco and then you go out of your way to put them off our country! They have just arrived from Rabat, they live in Rome. Why these identity checks?'

The two men continued to scrutinize us but the cook's anger cowed them. They let us through, reluctantly, I thought. Another miracle.

We pretended not to have understood the exchange.

'Morocco isn't Europe,' explained the cook. 'This country is turning into a police state.'

We exclaimed politely. In Italy, things were very different. Then the cook took my hand and I began to panic. While we had been play-acting, it was fine. But reality was much less amusing.

To play for time, we stopped at a grocer's to buy something to nibble. We had forgotten that we were hungry. Abdellatif stared at the shelves in awe, unfamiliar with most of the fruits on display. I prodded him and asked him what he wanted. He chose oranges because he had tasted some in prison. He was afraid to try anything else. But then he left them behind in the shop.

The cook was becoming impatient. He drew me aside and told me he was going to meet some friends to arrange a room. That way I would be able to accommodate my family.

He wanted me to go with him. I refused and asked him to give me the address of a place where I could meet him later. He gave me the name of a café and we said goodbye. I was relieved that I had been able to put off the evil moment.

In the 1970s my mother had bought shares in a hotel in Tangier, the Solazur, which she owned jointly with Mamma Guessous, the friend who had been involved in the business of my father's uniform.

I telephoned her at her home from the grocer's shop.

'Mamma, this is Malika. I'm in Tangier. I need money and a safe hiding place. Could you—?'

'Ah, yes, I see . . . No, no, my husband isn't back yet. I can't, I have to go back to Casablanca tomorrow . . .'

I didn't immediately grasp why she sounded so tense and was giving such evasive answers. I thought it was yet another betrayal by our friends. Disappointed once more, I let it drop.

In fact she had been surrounded by police when I called. Later, when we saw each other again, she told me that one of them was about to grab the handset just as I hung up. They were convinced that I was on the other end of the phone.

All the same, we went to the Solazur, which was nearby. We needed the address of the Hotel Ahlan, which belonged to my friend Salah Balafrèj. Before leaving for Tangier, I had asked Wahid to let him know we were coming.

We had nowhere to go. We felt we had to keep our word and meet the cook at the address he had given us, which was in one of the seediest districts of Tangier. We took the steps that led to the lower part of the city.

The café was in a cellar with such a low ceiling that Raouf had to stoop to get in. I had never seen such a collection of sinister-looking characters. Scarred sailors, junkies with glassy stares, dealers—all the lowlife of Tangier's underworld was clustered around Formica tables. There were no women, and the cook was nowhere to be seen. We waited for him for around ten minutes then we pulled ourselves together. This was no place for us, even in the state we were in. We ran up the stairs and took a deep breath of fresh air.

The only option left was Balafrèj. We were much too exhausted to continue on foot. We hailed a taxi; the driver was a rather grumpy, elderly little fundamentalist. Raouf sat in front and the three of us in the back.

The Hotel Ahlan was about thirty kilometres outside the city. The taxi drove through the outskirts and made its way along a quiet road. After a while, we found ourselves caught in a traffic jam. There was something strange about stopping like that in the middle of the countryside. It boded ill. As we inched forward, we saw a huge roadblock. They'd laid on the full works: the army, the police, the auxiliary forces, the gendarmes and the secret services were all looking for us.

The driver began complaining about the delay. Raouf didn't dare turn round, but we had no need to speak to communicate our terror.

Maria, Abdellatif and I squeezed one another's hands so hard that our nails dug into our flesh. The silence became oppressive.

When our turn came, the car slowly inched forward and pulled up at the roadblock. The policeman approached, flashing a torch. He shone it onto us. I attempted a smile that was more like a grimace. He switched it off and went to talk to a colleague. They came back together and beamed their torches in our faces once again.

We were petrified. I thought I could hear the others' hearts pounding as loudly as mine, and I wondered how it was possible for the policemen not to hear the deafening sound.

'If they stay another minute, I'm going to die of a heart attack,' I thought, almost fainting with fear.

They were looking for four young fugitives. They didn't make any connection with us . . .

In fact our minds didn't work in the same way. According to their thinking, we had no business thirty kilometres outside the city. If we were in Tangier, we would be more likely to make for the port, the beaches, the exit points to get out of the country. The police switched off their torches and waved us on.

It was only after a few kilometres that we were able to breathe again.

THE HOTEL AHLAN

At the Hotel Ahlan—which means 'welcome' in Arabic—I marched up to the reception desk and asked in a peremptory voice to speak to Mr Balafrèj.

'Tell him Mme Albertini's here,' I added.

The male receptionist seemed taken aback that such a strange-looking woman should ask for the manager. But he had gone back to Rabat. I frowned and raised my voice.

'What? That's outrageous, where is my suite? It's reserved in the name of Albertini.'

I was playing for time. I wanted to avoid being asked for our passports. I demanded that he telephone Balafrèj to tell him that

Mme Albertini was waiting for him. The receptionist came back a few minutes later.

'Mr Balafrèj asked us to find you a room.'

But I knew the routine. The man asked for our passports and I feigned anger.

'But I'm a friend of the owner's, this is insulting . . .'

There was nothing doing. No passports, no hotel rooms.

Noisily I turned on my heel, followed by the others. We installed ourselves in a cosy little bar near the reception desk, and after a few coffees we were in better spirits. The receptionist kept walking past us, smiling. Eventually he came over to us and asked me if I wanted to have dinner.

'Don't worry about us. We're leaving the hotel.'

The staff stared at us, intrigued by our shabby appearance which contrasted with our grand airs. Some of them lingered around the bar.

It was nearly 11 p.m. We had decided to hide near the swimming pool and then to spend the night in the hotel nightclub. A few sun loungers were arranged in a circle on the lawn. I sank down on one of them. The canvas was wet and my flimsy tunic was immediately soaked through. Shivering with cold, we huddled together under the trees to wait until the nightclub opened, at midnight.

For fifteen years we had cherished a rose-coloured dream of our return to the world. I, who as a teenager had lived only for dancing, had longed for the time when I would be able to indulge in my nocturnal passion again. But either everything around us had changed or we were no longer like everybody else. In the club, the music was much too loud and the psychedelic lights made our heads spin. This barrage of noise was too much for our poor, hurting brains; it was worse than the cruellest torture. We fled.

This incident underlined the fact that we were fugitives and nothing else. Yet again we were outsiders, and this realization was painful. But, as always, Raouf's sense of humour came to our rescue. He managed to make us laugh with his sarcastic comments on the guests at the club.

Then we went back to the bar and waited until it closed, at 4 a.m.

Earlier, inside the hotel I had spotted the toilets. That's where we spent the rest of the night: Raouf and Abdellatif slept in the Men's and Maria in the Ladies'. I hid behind a cupboard in the corridor and kept watch until daybreak.

In the morning, we tidied ourselves up and then walked back into the lobby, as if we had slept the night elsewhere. We had to drag ourselves along. The noise deafened us, the light hurt our eyes and we were suffering from a whole catalogue of aches and pains.

And yet we had to see our escape through, even though we knew the outcome was uncertain. We had to keep up our act in front of others, when in fact we desperately longed to be looked after, to be listened to, comforted, pitied and loved. It was terribly hard, terribly unjust too, but we had no choice.

The tourists came and went, pouring out of coaches parked in the hotel forecourt and hailing each other in every language. They were tanned, cheerful, smiling, and sometimes irate; they had indigestion problems or the excursion they wanted to go on wasn't included in the package. Life was going on all around us, bustling, joyful, so simple and humdrum, but we were excluded from it. All the time we were being pushed back down towards the dead, when we so desperately wanted to stay among the living.

We left the hotel lobby and found ourselves in the garden, surrounded by magnificent trees. We sat down on some little steps and talked for a long time. It was Wednesday 22 April, nearly three days since we had broken out, and we still hadn't been caught. We were wanted, terrified, and entirely at the mercy of events. But free. We had duped them so far. In this respect our escape had succeeded.

But we missed Mother and the others. We talked about them, laughing and crying. When had the guards discovered we were missing? How were they treating the others? When would we see them again? Some questions were left hanging in the air, and some answers too, so worried were we.

Our problems were not over. Where were we to go? Who should we contact? We decided to call Radio France Internationale. Unfortunately we didn't have the number, and to telephone, we would need to go via the hotel switchboard. At the reception, they were beginning to be suspicious of us.

Our only solution was to find some allies to help us. Earlier that morning we had noticed a sweet-looking elderly French woman, rather ladylike. She was with her son, a maths teacher we discovered later, a dull fellow of around fifty who just seemed to run around after her all the time. We decided to try to win her trust and get her to ask the operator for RFI's phone number for us. For this purpose, we had made up another big lie that we would reel off when the opportunity arose.

The old lady wasn't enough. We needed other friends, who might invite us to dinner or let us sleep in their rooms. We chose the hotel's riding instructor who appeared to be far from indifferent to Maria's charms, a receptionist who had been making eyes at me, and a young Spanish couple in shorts, hippie types who were smiling and friendly.

Maria went off and flirted with the riding instructor, which was quite daring of her. He gave her a light kiss on the lips and she was thrilled. She may have been twenty-five years old legally, but deep down she was still only ten.

Meanwhile I made friends with the receptionist, who asked me to come to his room at around three o'clock. I agreed, telling myself that I would know what to do when the time came.

While waiting for my rendezvous, I went off in search of the old lady to find out where her room was. I followed her, trying to remain as discreet as possible. In front of the lift, she began to complain about the Spanish and their nocturnal habits, and I acquiesced with a smile at everything she said.

She was a nice woman, pleased to meet someone who could understand her.

We exchanged a few platitudes, and parted company with a cheery 'See you later.'

Back in the lobby, I bumped into my receptionist. He seemed harassed and irritated.

'Forget our rendezvous, I haven't got time,' he said. 'The guests are all in a panic. They want to go home. The police are on red alert.'

'But why?'

'They're looking for four criminals, four dangerous escaped convicts.'

He left me standing there and went back to his tourists.

I told the others the news, and they were as anxious as I was. Criminals, us? Dangerous, us? So we were in peril of being shot at in cold blood? It was out of the question: we would not grant them that pleasure, we would rather kill ourselves first. Abdellatif feverishly began to look for power sockets so that we could electrocute ourselves if need be. Madness overtook us again, and despair. Maria and I were sobbing.

We were ensconced in the bar. Then the elderly French lady came in with her son. She greeted us and then, seeing our miserable expressions, came over and asked us why we were crying. We leaped at the opportunity and told her the lie we had prepared for her.

Our sister, a journalist at France Inter, had breast cancer and was going into hospital in Villejuif outside Paris. Our parents didn't know and we had no idea how to get hold of her at the radio station.

'But, children, why don't you call Radio Medi 1? They'll give you the number of RFI in Paris. Then you'll be able to get in touch with your sister.'

We couldn't tell her that the switchboard operators were suspicious of us. We carried on crying, watching her out of the corner of our eye.

'We can't do it ourselves,' I hiccuped. 'We can't talk without crying.'

We must have been convincing. Moved by our tears, she offered to get the number for us.

She went off and then returned with a scrap of paper which she held out to us smiling. She had called Medi 1 and they had given her the number of RFI. We thanked her, then Maria and I slipped off, arranging to meet the boys a little later.

I let Maria deal with the telephone operator and told her to ask for Alain de Chalvron. He was one of the RFI presenters we knew best.

I waited for my sister in the lobby. She came back immediately looking triumphant. Using diplomacy, she had won the operator over. We waited until RFI's number was answered.

Luckily, Alain de Chalvron was there.

'We are the children of General Oufkir,' said Maria. 'We have escaped after fifteen years in gaol. We dug a tunnel out of our prison, and at the moment we are in Tangier. We need help. We want to speak to Robert Badinter and ask him to be our lawyer.'

At first the journalist didn't believe us. He just kept repeating:

'But that's too outrageous, it's terrible . . .'

Then he asked us for proof. He urged us not to panic and asked us to tell him where he could call us back. We gave him the hotel's telephone number and our assumed name, Albertini. We hung up and waited, trembling with excitement. Ten minutes later he called back.

'It's an incredible scoop, do you realize? Do you know that in a few hours François Mitterrand is due to arrive in Morocco on an official visit?'

Alain de Chalvron had called the French Foreign Office, who had passed on the information to the President in his Concorde. The former leading lawyer Robert Badinter couldn't represent us because he was now president of the Constitutional Council. The journalist advised us to appeal to Maître Kiejman for help. He offered to call him for us. He hung up and promised to call us back.

I left Maria standing guard and ran to the car park to inform my brothers. I fell sobbing into Raouf's arms and told him about our conversation. Abdellatif stared at me, trying to understand. Mitterrand, the Foreign Office, Concorde and Badinter were names that meant absolutely nothing to him. We rejoined Maria. Alain de Chalvron had called back, and she was waiting for us before speaking to him again. Over the telephone, we dictated to him our appeal to the King. The gist of this message was that we were only children and that it was unjust to punish us purely because we bore our father's name.

Then the journalist told us that an envoy from the Foreign Office would come and see us that very evening. We arranged to meet him in the car park.

We waited for nightfall, torn between the joy of having made our voice heard, and mistrust. Was Mitterrand's trip a good thing for us? I wasn't sure of anything any more. But I was still impatient to meet this envoy, who turned out to be Hervé Kerrien, RFI's correspondent in Tangier. At first he didn't disclose his identity.

His coldness surprised us. Wasn't he supposed to be our saviour? We'd been expecting warm words, congratulations, a degree of compassion . . . but no, he kept his distance, which disconcerted us. We crossed the car park to avoid prying eyes.

He looked right and left to check that nobody was following us, then he took out a pen and asked us, as dryly as before, if we were indeed the children of General Oufkir.

'Anybody could claim that,' he added. 'Give me proof.'

I began to enumerate my father's political achievements, but he interrupted me.

'No, tell me about his private life.'

I told him that I hadn't known him well, but I did give him one detail, known only to those close to my father. He had a little scar on his upper right arm from a shrapnel wound.

This seemed to satisfy him and he asked lots of other questions. Before leaving, he informed us that the next day we would receive a visit from our lawyer, Maître Dartevelle, Maître Kiejman's partner, who was coming especially from Paris to meet us.

Not knowing what to do next, we returned to the bar, which was filling up with a strange crowd: men in loud clothes and heavily made-up girls who were drinking whisky, smoking cigarettes and openly trying to pick up men. Raouf was not spared their provocative smiles.

My receptionist friend came and sat down beside me.

'I don't understand you. Why don't you take rooms here?'

'Because we have a better hotel in Tangier.'

He offered us a coffee, which we drank unsuspectingly. It was drugged. The staff wanted to find out who we were. They were far from guessing our true identity but thought that Maria and I were prostitutes and that Raouf was our pimp. Or perhaps that we were Italian or Spanish drug dealers engaged in shady business at the hotel. In any case there was definitely something fishy about us.

Under the influence of the drug, we began to talk nonsense. The receptionist suggested we could sleep in the Moroccan lounge.

'You're too out of it. Go in there, it's empty, you'll be safe.'

Our readiness to follow him was the answer he had been waiting for. It was the proof that there was something not right with our situation, although he was not sure what.

Raouf and Abdellatif fell asleep at once. Maria and I remained awake all night, much too agitated to sleep. When they woke up, they were still rambling, and so were we.

We went out to install ourselves at the side of the car park and wait. We couldn't stop laughing, but we tried to calm down so as to appear dignified in front of our lawyer.

We had arranged to meet in the little television lounge of the hotel, which had become our refuge. It was a good hiding place. We sat and watched colour television which still fascinated us. The complexities of satellite television were beyond us. We didn't understand how Spanish channels could be broadcast in Morocco.

Maître Bernard Dartevelle arrived late on the morning of 23 April, accompanied by Hervé Kerrien who was carrying a camera. At the airport, nobody guessed the reason for his visit, and they had been allowed through without difficulty. This was not the case on his return, when he was questioned twice by the police before being released.

Maître Dartevelle delivered a speech all about how outraged France was, France the country of human rights. He swore that his country's economic interests would not take precedence over ours. Then he gave us a message from President Mitterrand:

'You should be very proud of yourselves because while there are millions of children who are persecuted, massacred and imprisoned in the world, you will be remembered as the only ones who did not give up and continued to fight to the end.'

He asked us to sign a document instructing the Kiejman chambers to represent us. Then he told us that he had to take a photo of us. Just as the shutter clicked, the door opened revealing the receptionist who stared at us for a long time before going out.

Maître Dartevelle arranged to meet us again that evening. When he left, we at last began to feel elated. We had climbed Everest. We had succeeded in alerting the press and public opinion. People had listened to us, and taken us seriously. All day that idea comforted us; we talked of nothing but our victory. Soon we would be free. Soon we would all be together again.

When he came back that evening, this time without Kerrien, Maître Dartevelle told us that everything had been arranged for our departure the next morning at ten thirty. We were to flee to Tangier and, once we had reached the French consulate, we would be put on a plane for France.

I pointed out with a certain anxiety that the alarm had been raised, that the receptionist had caught us in the television lounge and that they were increasingly suspicious of us at the hotel. It would be very risky to wait any longer. He could do no more at that point, but he advised us to be very discreet.

When he left, we felt very dispirited.

That night we went and loitered near the guests' rooms. We were hungry. For three days, our only sustenance had been coffee and cigarettes. Outside the rooms were trays with leftovers from room service. We fought over a crust of bread or a little piece of cheese. We found ourselves near the young Spanish couple's room, and knocked on their door.

The man opened it. He was in his underpants. He looked at me, surprised at first.

'Joint?' I asked in French, with my most charming smile.

It was the hippies' magic password the world over.

He smiled back at me and invited us in. His wife lay naked in the bed, and she watched us troop in. She was a little flustered, but he calmed her down with a kiss and motioned to us to sit on the bed. Having spent three days studying this couple carefully, we knew they were the kind who 'share everything'—peace, love and dope.

He rolled a joint, and took a few puffs, passed it to his wife and then offered it to us. We pretended to smoke: the spiked coffee had already taught us a lesson. Raouf did a take-off of Louis de Funès in *Les Gendarmes de Saint Tropez*. Turning to me, he proffered the joint and said in an earnest voice:

'*Amour, amour . . .*'

We creased up laughing and the couple did too. They put our giggling down to the grass.

Stoned, they finally fell asleep and so did we, on the couch.

At daybreak, the birds woke us all up with their irksome twittering. The Spanish couple looked at us oddly. They seemed surprised to find us there. Then they remembered getting stoned. The woman kindly asked me if I wanted to use the bathroom. We all had a proper wash, for the first time in four days. Usually I avoided mirrors; I couldn't stand my ravaged face. To try to conceal it, I put on lots of make-up using the cosmetics I found on the shelf. Maria did likewise.

We thanked them and left. We went straight to the bar to wait for Maître Dartevelle.

Then we heard reception paging:

'Will Mademoiselle Oufkir please go to reception . . .'

I ignored it. It was nothing to do with me, my name was Albertini.

To be completely honest, I didn't think we were going to make it, even so close to our goal. My instinct told me that we would be caught, and even in my greatest moments of elation, I had never underestimated my enemy. But I didn't care. We had played the game, we had gone as far as we possibly could.

I was proud of us, as my father would have been.

'Will Mademoiselle Oufkir . . .'

It was 10.25 a.m. on Friday 24 April 1987. I looked in the direction of the hotel lobby. Instead of Maître Dartevelle's taxi, I saw a police van pulling up in front of the plate glass door.

Ten policemen in khaki carrying Kalashnikovs poured out. A second, then a third, then ten vans drew up.

Clusters of policemen were jumping out all over the place.

I elbowed Raouf and whispered:

'The cops are here. Someone informed on us.'

They lined up at a run. The young Spanish couple, on their way over to join us, caught sight of them and hastily retraced their steps.

Apart from smoking a few joints, what had they done to feel guilty about?

THE ARREST

About half a dozen police officials bore down on us. One of them asked us to state our names.

'Are you Malika Oufkir?'

'Not at all,' I replied haughtily, 'my name is Albertini.'

I was determined to come through with flying colours. Raouf ventured the same lie. The man who seemed to be in charge turned round and signalled to the armed police officers who were now surrounding us. They moved closer. He held up his hand and stopped them. Our arrest was to be discreet. Then he made us walk down the corridor, brutally pushing down our heads to force us to bow them, under the horrified gaze of the tourists. We caught a fleeting glimpse of the old lady and her son as well as the young Spanish couple.

We were bundled into a van, which took us to the police station in Tangier. At the entrance, the police formed a sort of welcoming line. They gazed at us in admiration, and one of them was sobbing noisily. We would not have been surprised if they had started clapping.

The officials came from Rabat. We were treated to the whole works; they called us heroes, which added to our pride. Everywhere we could see the respect in their eyes.

We were measured, they took our fingerprints, and we were put in a cell. Our pride swelled when the public prosecutor telephoned Driss Basri, the Minister of the Interior, in our presence.

'But Your Excellency, I swear it, I have arrested them. I swear it on the head of my children, Your Excellency, they're here before me. Yes, there are four of them, Malika, Raouf, Maria and Abdellatif. Yes, Your Excellency, it was myself in person who captured them. With absolute discretion, yes, Your Excellency.'

He couldn't have been happier if he had caught an arch-criminal like Mesrine or the Baader-Meinhof gang. Raouf and I exchanged glances, smiling covertly. My knees were knocking together, my legs were shaking, and I was overcome with emotion. But now wasn't the time to let myself go. In a corner, the big shots were talking among themselves. They fired rapid orders and Abdellatif was taken away. I was distraught at his departure. I was afraid they would use him to put pressure on us. As if to confirm my fears, they glared menacingly at Raouf and me, to make sure we got the message.

The junior police officers saw my distress and managed to whisper that we had nothing to fear. The others were trying to intimidate us, but we had won. We had defied the authorities and contacted foreign powers . . . now they were tied hand and foot as far as we were concerned.

Gradually the guards grew bolder, coming over to speak to us directly instead of communicating with signs.

Some of them were crying. Others had known us as children. They had been part of my father's escort when we still lived in the Allée des Princesses. And some of them had been at Tamattaght and belonged to the network.

'You can be proud of yourselves,' they said. 'You have restored the Berbers' pride. You have brought your father back to life.'

The officials came over to us, speaking in honeyed, unctuous tones that aroused our suspicion. The prosecutor spoke first.

'Don't panic. Your brother will be treated well. He is the same age as my son, I was at his baptism . . .'

Then he made us leave the room. As we went up the stairs, I once again asked a policeman if it was true that Abdellatif really wasn't in any danger.

'You must be kidding . . . Nobody will dare harm a hair of his head. For four days they've been like cats on hot bricks, they haven't eaten, they haven't drunk. The boss [he meant the King] has been supervising this business in person, and all the time you remained on the loose, they got the brunt of it.'

Rumour had it that during the days following our escape, the King had forbidden his children to leave the palace in Marrakesh, where they happened to be, in fear that we would take revenge.

We were shown into a vast room. To my great relief, Abdellatif was waiting for us there. The officials were standing by the window. I went over to them. Suddenly my legs crumpled, the walls began to spin, and I felt a palpitation in my heart. They rushed over to support me. The emotional turmoil and my fears for Abdellatif had overcome me.

Someone went to fetch me an orange juice. They opened the window and told me to breathe deeply. The police station overlooked a church. I looked out distractedly.

That was when I saw her. Mary. The Virgin. Nestling in an alcove, she was holding the infant Jesus in her arms and gazing at me with a benevolent expression. I nearly collapsed completely, but this time with happiness. She was always there when we needed her, watching over us, protecting us. I signalled discreetly to the others, so they could see her too. The message was clear: she was telling me to be strong, like when we were digging the tunnel. I quickly regained my composure.

They just wouldn't give up. There was no way we could have escaped on our own. It was impossible. We must have had accomplices from Algeria. They interrogated Raouf and me in turn, speaking in the same syrupy tones. They had known my father, they knew our uncle, our grandfather . . . we were a respectable family . . . we had to co-operate with them.

Their questions kept coming.

'Why did you contact a French lawyer? Why don't you trust Moroccan institutions? Why didn't you ask for a royal pardon on the tomb of Muhammad V?'

'You're a daughter of the Palace, you know their ways . . . His Majesty would never have been able to refuse you a pardon and everything would have been fine.'

'And now, be honest, tell us who helped you. Your story about a tunnel? Pull the other one . . . You didn't have anything to dig with . . . You were so well guarded.'

'Nobody escapes from Bir-Jdid.'

I soon grew weary of replying and just sat letting my interrogator talk. He was General Inspector Guessous, a distant relative of Mamma

Guessous. I wondered what he was leading up to, because he obviously had something up his sleeve.

Above his desk was a big clock. He glanced at it frequently, with an anxious air. Finally I realized what it was he was waiting for. It was nearly time for the news. He switched on the radio. After the signature tune, the presenter read the news bulletin:

'Four of General Oufkir's children in spectacular escape bid . . .'

Guessous switched off the radio in fury. I had nothing more to say to him, nor he to me.

I was led out of the room. On joining Raouf, I told him what I'd heard, but he refused to believe me.

'Kika, you're dreaming. You're confusing your wishes with reality.'

'Raouf, I'm not out of my mind. I can repeat what the newscaster said word for word.'

Eventually I did manage to convince him.

Then I felt a surge of inner peace, a sensation of well-being that I hadn't experienced for many years. That newsflash was proof that we had won. At last the whole world knew about us.

Half an hour later, Guessous came back to see us. From his face, I understood that our situation had changed.

They had probably tried to convince the French not to broadcast the news of our escape. Perhaps they had even tried to persuade them that the Oufkir business was an internal Moroccan affair, despite the obvious flagrant violation of human rights. Unfortunately for them, the information had been made public. Now we had to be treated differently.

We were shown into another room, an empty one this time. They had new mattresses brought in which police officers placed on the floor, then we were brought trays laden with food. We ate with pleasure. There were rolls, butter and tea.

For us, this police station was a five-star hotel. We squabbled over where we would sleep. We were exhausted but happy. Our mission was accomplished.

We fell asleep thinking of the others. Mother could be proud of her children. For four days, with our scant means, we had kept the country on tenterhooks.

* * *

Now they treated us with deference. We had become human beings again and that did us good. The next morning, the public prosecutor authorized us to use his personal bathroom in the police station. We had rarely seen such a huge bathroom. There were more than a hundred different bottles and sprays standing on his dressing table—eau de Cologne, perfume, shaving foam, shampoo and conditioner.

After living for ten years with half a packet of Tide per month for soap, this sudden opulence made us laugh until we cried. We had forgotten the consumer society. How could people clutter their lives with so many useless things?

We felt the weight of the bottles, pulled out the stoppers and splashed ourselves with toilet water and aftershave lotion. We were four kids let loose in a funfair. We weren't so thrilled with the mirrors, and avoided dwelling on our reflections. Most of all, it was the look in our eyes that frightened us. Our eyes stared out like those of starving children from the Third World.

We locked ourselves in to wash. Turning on the taps to the full, we caused a flood. We immediately mopped up the carpet with the towels and bathrobes, afraid of leaving a stain. It was that old reflex from building the tunnel . . .

Then the four of us came out laughing. We reeked of perfume. Raouf desperately needed to see a dentist. The abscesses in his mouth were swollen with pus, but the practitioner he was taken to refused to touch them. The infection was so serious that my brother risked cardiac arrest. The operation would have to wait.

Guessous tried to treat us neutrally, as was his duty as an official, but beneath his dry tone was a mixture of admiration for our exploits and compassion for our condition. We really must have been a pathetic sight for him to suggest buying each of us a complete new set of clothes of his own accord.

We were driven to the city centre. Memories came flooding back. I thought of those eleven years at the Palace when I would watch life going on through a window, as I was doing now. All my life, the outside world had been beyond my reach. I wondered how long it would be before I could taste freedom for real. Opening the door would have been so simple, but I no longer had the strength.

In the shops where we were taken, the sales assistants were under police orders. This was their territory, these were their informers, the links in the tightly woven net that kept the country to heel. They spoke to us with deference, wanting to satisfy our every whim, but I didn't want anything and, worst of all, nothing fitted me. Maria, too thin, was lost in the clothes. And I was too bloated. I did, however, choose a skirt and a long tunic. In a shoe shop I selected a pair of clogs for comfort. My feet were still covered with sores and scabs, but I no longer even felt the pain.

We were transferred to the Ben Chérif police station in Casablanca. Notorious among political prisoners, it was run by Yousfi, the divisional superintendent of the city. He had interrogated my mother a few days after my father's death, then he had been sent to Tamattaght when our network had been dismantled.

We went up and down stairs, and down a long corridor at the end of which Yousfi, Allabouch, the head of the secret services, and three other superintendents were waiting for us.

If that moment had been filmed, the director would probably have added a voiceover for extra emotion, or sound effects of clamour rising from the cells or the other prisoners applauding our victory.

But nothing of the sort happened. Our arrival took place in silence.

A silence so heavy that it only intensified the emotion. We experienced something astonishing. These five men, devoted servants of the regime, started congratulating us.

'Bravo,' said Yousfi. 'It really was the Great Escape, that story of yours.'

He continued complimenting us on our courage. While he spoke, I stood staring at the floor.

'Oh, no,' he said to me. 'You've hardly been here two minutes and you're already eyeing the flagstones to plan your escape. Once is enough, don't you think?'

We quickly asked for news of the rest of the family. They were fine, they assured us. Besides, we were going to see them straight away. Yousfi called over an old man dragging his feet, whose job it apparently was to blindfold the prisoners.

He held a stick, and as he passed each door, he cried: 'Banda banda.' That was his nickname too. Banda Banda opened a door and showed us into a cell.

A hunched old lady was eating soup.

It was Mother.

The hunger strike, the suicide attempt and the worry of our escape had prematurely aged her. Before me huddled a shrunken, emaciated, wrinkled woman. She lifted the spoon to her mouth with the slow, deliberate gestures of the elderly. She raised her enormous black eyes towards me. They were filled with infinite sadness. Her gaze was blank. She didn't recognize me. We jostled one another to throw ourselves at her feet. Her hand started to tremble. She put her spoon down on the table and murmured, so low that we could barely hear her:

'My children . . . You are . . . my children.'

We had changed so much that she hadn't recognized us immediately. It wasn't only because we were wearing new clothes. These four days of freedom had rekindled in our eyes the little flame of life that we thought had been extinguished for ever. We were on the other side, outside the walls, while she was still locked up.

Mother was wearing a scarf over her head. The night of our escape, Soukaina and she had sworn they would shave their heads if we weren't caught within twelve hours. They had kept their word. Those two were a right pair when it came to crazy schemes. Mimi was as white as chalk. Achoura and Halima had a wild look in their eyes.

Once we were over our initial shock, we all embraced at length. We laughed, we rolled on the floor, we cried:

'We've won, the nightmare is over, we are no longer in Bir-Jdid.'

The others had been at the Ben Chérif police station since Tuesday 21 April. They had arrived two days after our escape. At first they had been detained in appalling conditions.

They had been lined up against a wall, wearing military jellabahs, the hood pulled down over their blindfolded eyes. They had been made to stand still for hours, listening to the howls of pain as Borro was tortured in the next room. He screamed that he'd had nothing to do with it. They hadn't eaten for a long time, and Soukaina, too weak to stand, had fainted. Their only food had been dog food, a vile runny liquid with rice flour floating in it.

During Mother's interrogation sessions, they had bombarded her with questions to make her give away our destination. She had no idea that our embassy plan had failed. Thinking she was sending them off on a wild-goose chase, she replied that we were heading for Tangier.

That was impossible in their view. They were convinced we hadn't been able to get away from the Bir-Jdid area. At best, we had gone in the other direction, towards the frontier of the Western Sahara. But then we discovered that somebody in Rabat had informed on us. At that point they had to face up to the facts. We could be anywhere in Morocco. They had searched Rabat and then Tangier, concentrating, as we had foreseen, on the places from which we could flee the country.

Two hours before our arrival at the Ben Chérif police station, the prisoners' brutal treatment had stopped. They had finally been brought decent food, breaded escalopes and French beans served on plates and no longer in tin mugs. That was when Mother realized that we must have been caught. The news was confirmed a little later by Allabouch, the director of the secret services.

We told them every detail of our escapades. They stared at us round-eyed, and we were aware how proud they were of us. While we talked, Mother kept getting up, touching us, kissing us, and repeating the same words.

'My children, my little darlings. It's incredible how much you've changed . . .'

It was true. The hardest thing for us was the realization that we were all no longer really part of a whole. We felt a little bit guilty.

So we listened to Mother and Soukaina's accounts very carefully, as if to redeem ourselves for that extra freedom that we had experienced without them.

AFTER THE ESCAPE

At eight thirty that Monday morning, the guards had entered my mother's cell, as they did every morning, bringing her the coffee prepared by Achoura. They had begun their search.

My mother remained very calm. The five women had spent the night trembling with fear for us, especially when they heard the pack of stray dogs howling. But as we hadn't returned, they felt more optimistic.

The guards checked her cell, tapping everywhere. The door to the toilet was ajar.

'My son is unwell,' she told them. 'He's spent all night in the toilet. Do you want to go in and see for yourselves?'

They politely refused, despite her insistence. They left, locking the cell, and went into ours. Soukaina had had enough time to replace and disguise all the floor slabs. The guards were mildly surprised that it was she who greeted them. Usually I was the one who came forward to speak to them.

My little sister was perfectly composed too. Our success had given her the strength to stand up to them.

'Malika and Maria have got their periods,' said Soukaina.

That was the magic phrase to keep the gaolers at bay. Soukaina had arranged our beds in such a way that it looked as though we were still asleep. As usual, Mimi stayed huddled under the blankets and didn't raise her head. But just as they were leaving, she let out a huge sigh to reassure them.

All these details were part of a minutely honed strategy, like everything else. The guards went into the room where the tunnel was, scraped, searched and tapped the walls. Not once did they tread on the hollow slabs.

They went into Achoura and Halima's cell for a cursory routine visit. The two women gave the guards no cause for concern. From their cells, my mother and Soukaina watched them. They heard the guards' footsteps, then the jangle of their keys.

My mother was torn between excitement and pity for those poor wretches who, for ten years, had punctuated the monotony of our days. Our escape spelled danger for them.

Just before they reached Raouf's cell, my mother started hammering on her door. They came back and asked her what she wanted.

'I forgot to tell you something very important. Come back inside.'

They obeyed and opened up her cell again.

'Well, it's this,' she said. 'Malika, Maria, Raouf and Abdellatif have escaped.'

They did not react. She shook them one by one.

'Go and look in the toilet, you'll see for yourselves. Abdellatif isn't there. Go into the girls' and Raouf's cells, pull back the sheets, look everywhere, under the beds . . . They've gone, I tell you.'

It took at least ten minutes for the information to seep into their thick skulls. While my mother became more and more heated, they stared at her pityingly, as if she had suddenly gone mad.

'Pull yourself together, Madame Oufkir. Come on, you're usually a sensible woman . . .'

But Mother wouldn't give up. She darted around the cell, lifted up the straw mattresses and ran into the toilet.

'But what language must I speak? Four of my children have escaped, I tell you.'

They started searching everywhere, following her. Then they stared at one another. There was no trace of Abdellatif. There was a fraught silence. They opened up our cell again. They knew we were capable of the worst. Maybe Abdellatif had managed to slip into our cell and was hiding to give them a fright? Soukaina greeted them with a smile.

'They're here, they're asleep, they've got their periods,' they insisted anxiously. 'So you said, we can see them . . .'

'No,' said Soukaina, 'they're not there. Look for yourselves.'

They looked under our blankets. Soukaina had arranged two heaps of clothing in our beds. Then they looked under the beds and searched everywhere before going into Raouf's cell and turning it upside-down, all in vain.

Then they went berserk. Our escape condemned them to certain death. They came into our cell with picks and prised up the floor slabs. Then they went into the cell with the tunnel and prised out a few more slabs but failed to discover the passage. They couldn't make head or tail of it. They panicked, yelling and rushing about in all directions.

Next they went into Achoura and Halima's cell and beat them brutally to make them confess. They didn't dare touch Mother or my sisters. Then my mother took the initiative and banged on her door to speak to them. They were so distraught that they wouldn't listen to her. She had to scream to make herself heard.

'You must calm down,' she advised them, with great composure. 'And stop wrecking everything. You know Rabat. When they get here, they'll say that you helped them escape.'

The poor wretches were terrified out of their wits.

'You're right, we'll put everything back as it was.'

'No,' said my mother, 'it's too late. It's best to raise the alarm.'

The guards were in serious trouble. Borro wasn't there. As he was off duty on Sundays, he usually went to see his children and came back late the next day. On Monday mornings, the guards carried out their search without him. They weren't used to taking responsibility and were completely at a loss. However, they followed Mother's advice. The news of our escape went straight to headquarters and to the Ministry of the Interior.

Within the hour, the vile Borro arrived. The man who flaunted his tiny bloodshot eyes and gorilla build, who, two months earlier, had threatened my mother with a vine stump, who flattered himself that he had broken us, stood before her, waxen-faced, his eyes lowered. He avoided her gaze.

She was elated, but made every effort not to let it show.

According to him, there was no way we could have escaped. We were hiding somewhere. He gave orders to check the roofs. Of course, the search proved fruitless.

He looked up at my mother and said in a quavering voice:

'They have escaped.'

He had aged twenty years in less than an hour. Gone were his arrogance, viciousness and contempt. He dragged his feet, allowing himself to be led by Mother and Soukaina. He was like a condemned man being led to the gallows.

The guards locked my mother and sisters in our cell. They stayed there waiting for quite a long while. A little later, they heard the sky reverberating; it suddenly darkened as an armada of helicopters landed in the surrounding fields. Officers in full dress uniform poured into the barracks.

The prison gates opened to admit police officers holding ferocious Alsatians on leashes. They gave the dogs our tattered clothes to sniff and then let them loose. At that point, my mother and sisters were very frightened. The *mouhazzin* were replaced by gendarmes, whose methods were cruder.

They blindfolded my mother and led her out into the barracks where they violently forced her to sit down. Their tone was menacing. These were no longer the guards who could be manipulated by us, nor Borro whom we had begun to know well. These officers spoke harshly, without compassion. They were going to make my mother pay for our effrontery.

Mother was shaking with fear, but she didn't allow herself to show it. As soon as he opened his mouth, she interrupted the officer interrogating her.

'General Ben Slimane,' she said, 'don't try and be clever with me, I recognize your voice.'

The man got up abruptly and left, and another took his place. Even though she was blindfolded, Mother could sense their discomfiture. They had all been close to my father and had been guests at our house on numerous occasions. The second officer received the same treatment as Ben Slimane.

'You haven't even got the guts to look me in the eyes,' she said, contemptuously. 'And yet you are a soldier. So you're forced to blindfold me to interrogate me? No matter what you do, I will recognize all of you, even at the ends of the earth,' she added.

She wouldn't tell them anything. Even though she was terrified, she remained dignified and courageous.

'Madame Oufkir, be reasonable. If you don't tell us where they are, they could be in danger. They might be eaten by wolves—the area's swarming with them.'

'I'd rather they were eaten by wolves than by you . . .'

They took her back to her cell. Then it was Soukaina's turn to be interrogated; she was blindfolded too. She had been nine on entering prison and was unable to recognize anybody. But after each interrogation, she described the officers' voices to Mother, who was able to identify them.

They wanted to know where we were, and used every means to find out: threats, intimidation, entreaties and emotional blackmail. But Soukaina stood up to them, remaining impassive despite her fear and anguish.

The first time they returned to the gaol, while she was being taken back to her cell she overheard the generals talking to Borro.

'We'll have your hide. How could you have allowed children to live in such conditions?'

We were no longer even conscious of it, but there was no denying the unspeakable squalor and insalubrity of the place. The walls and gratings were black with soot from the charcoal brazier we used for cooking. Everything was crumbling, grey, dark and oozing with moisture. Conditions were rudimentary: straw mattresses, cardboard boxes for furniture, a beaten earth floor. Caged animals would have been treated better.

The generals had known that the King was wreaking his vengeance on us, but they could never have imagined that we were living in such sordid conditions. They believed we had been receiving books and letters, and that we were relatively pampered. They questioned Soukaina about our diet. She told them that we no longer recalled the taste of foods such as milk, butter or fruit. She described our meals and explained how we made sandwiches with boiled herbs. The generals were all the more appalled because normal food had been supplied to the barracks; the soldiers weren't lacking for anything.

They hadn't yet found the hole by the perimeter fence. After twenty-four hours, they still couldn't understand how we had escaped. It was impossible to dig a tunnel. You needed equipment, manpower. My mother, Soukaina and Mimi were in a deplorably weak state.

Where would we have found the strength to dig?

'We didn't need muscle,' Soukaina finally burst out after several interrogations, during which they asked her the same questions over and over again. 'To escape, all we needed was fifteen years in prison, fifteen years of inhuman suffering, fifteen years of starvation, cold, fear and deprivation. And as for intelligence, you gave us all those years to nurture and develop it.'

They were cracking up. They wanted to know everything. Understand everything. Using force, if necessary.

But Soukaina didn't need to be asked twice. She was unstoppable, taking a malicious pleasure in using our secret language: Chinese lanterns, elephants . . . They stared at her, flabbergasted, torn between bewilderment and anger. Was she making fun of them? They could get really angry . . . Battling against the dread in the pit of her stomach, my sister remained very polite. The interrogations were a terrible ordeal and Soukaina, for all her bravura, was very demoralized. But she was aware of the important part she had to play.

I must say that she managed brilliantly. For the first time, this twenty-three-year-old woman, a prisoner since the age of nine, found herself centre stage. She was like a mute person who suddenly regains the power of speech. She discovered that she was funny, intelligent, cunning, sardonic and impudent. She kept her audience on tenterhooks, even though they were enraged by her audacity.

In spite of their menaces, they were enthralled, intrigued, and sometimes even in stitches.

'But if you didn't have watches, how did you know when it was time to seal up the tunnel again?'

'Cornelius.'

'Who is Cornelius? An accomplice? Don't make fun of us, otherwise . . .'

'But tell us, did you think you were Galileo?'

Soukaina was having a field day. They were really shaken up.

'But it's the escape of the century. It's incredible.' From time to time, they broke in:

'Your father would have been proud of his children.'

They wanted to know who had been responsible for the children's upbringing in prison.

'Malika,' she replied. 'She taught us to read, write and speak, and made us learn table manners. She taught us everything. She was our great support, our mother, father and teacher. Everything that we are, we owe to her.'

They all smoked in front of her. After they had left, she would collect the cigarette butts. An officer who saw her said:

'I could never have coped with what you've been through.'

And he offered her some real cigarettes.

She gave so many precise, verifiable details that eventually they had to believe her. But she wouldn't show them the place where we had dug the tunnel. Before leaving, we had insisted that they had to find it for themselves. She teased them, making it into a game, like 'hunt the thimble'. You're warm, you're cold, you're boiling.

In the end she felt the game had gone on long enough. They were growing increasingly angry, becoming violent and more menacing in their threats.

At that point, she showed them to the cell.

'The tunnel is in there, find it.'

When they removed her blindfold, she saw that all the generals were in full dress uniform. They beamed their torches onto the floor slabs and asked her to wait for the cameraman before opening them. They wanted to film her and photograph her in action, to send the proof of our escape to the King, I suppose.

Soukaina lifted up the stone slabs, cracked the layer of cement and pulled out the elephants and the Chinese lanterns all by herself as they looked on in amazement.

They called the gendarmes to check that there really was a passage. Then they sent the cameraman to film the length of it, as well as our pathetic tools, the spoon, the knife handle and the sardine-can lid.

The dogs retrieved the things we'd dropped on the way—the pepper, iron bar and rags. Meanwhile the helicopters scoured the region in vain; there was no sign of us.

Then my mother and the others were transferred to the police station in Casablanca. They were paralysed with fear and anxiety, more for us, of whom there was no news, than for themselves.

At Ben Chérif, my mother tried to keep a cool head. Judging by the attitude of their gaolers, we hadn't been found yet and that was the only thing that mattered to her.

Halima was slapped and beaten several times. She did not deny herself the pleasure of giving the police a moral lecture, and that infuriated them. She was a very proud woman who revelled in her loyalty and her love for us.

'I followed them to prison because I wanted to, and if I had to do it again I would,' she claimed, 'so don't count on me to betray them.'

Their ill-treatment stopped shortly before our arrival, when it was clear that the whole world knew about our escape. From now on, they couldn't permit themselves to abuse us.

And so, reunited, we spent the night talking, laughing, hugging one another and congratulating ourselves.

We had avenged my father.

From then on we would celebrate 19 April, the date of our escape, as the day our dignity had been restored.

We stayed at Ben Chérif for two and a half months, during which time we never stopped eating. In those first days, there was an endless procession of dishes. French beans, breaded escalopes, rice, desserts . . . the menu wasn't varied, but for us it was luxury.

Out of loyalty to our prison tradition, we nicknamed Raouf 'Bou-Ssena', which means 'one tooth', because the poor thing only had three teeth left. My brother drew a caricature of himself, tall and thin with prominent cheekbones, his neck like a corkscrew and his jaw graced with a single tooth with a diamond shining in it.

We were given a television set. We had known only black and white TV, and now we discovered the world in colour. Morocco unfolded before us, and it was all so unfamiliar. I had to come to terms with the fact that the country had been modernized, and to give the King credit for that. I was torn between pride for my people and resentment against this King who had ruled the country with such success using contemptible means.

His daughter, Princess Meriem, was about to be married and there were endless features on the royal family. I no longer saw the persecutor but the man who had watched over my childhood. My tears flowed: I was powerless to stop them. This attitude amazed the others, who could not understand my loyalty to my past. That's the way it was. I constantly swung between nostalgia and hatred, between love and fear.

Along with the television, we were also given a video recorder. Allabouch owned a huge video library of confiscated films, and he allowed us to borrow as many as we wanted. The cops were always talking about *Rocky*, so we chose a Stallone film. But this one was an X-rated movie: that was how the great Sylvester had begun his career. After the initial shock, we all shrieked with laughter. The next day, Mother thanked Allabouch for the sexual education he had given her children. Deeply embarrassed, the director apologized profusely.

The interrogations started again. They knew all there was to know about the escape now, but they wanted to know what we were planning. They criticized us for having hired French lawyers instead of Moroccan. As if we'd had any choice . . .

Generally, they tried to get us to fall into the most obvious traps. But fifteen years in prison had taught us cunning, and they came off worst. Not that it helped us much: we still didn't know what our fate was to be. We hadn't heard from Dartevelle again.

After a family consultation, we decided to write to the King to ask him for permission to emigrate to Canada. Allabouch was worried: he was afraid we would insult His Majesty, which we had no intention of doing. He read our letter and it made his blood boil.

'Don't say that, don't say that . . .'

We were adamant. We were not prepared to alter a single phrase. We did not want to stay in Morocco. Canada was a good choice, as the King would never allow us to leave for France. We were too much of an embarrassment; he couldn't make us disappear into thin air, now that international public opinion had been alerted. But what on earth was he going to do with us?

While awaiting his reply, we behaved like model prisoners at the police station that seemed the epitome of luxury to us, compared with what we had known. We never complained, even when we were blindfolded to go to the bathroom or the toilets. For once, we were pleased to be heavily guarded, because it elevated us to the same rank as the heroes we admired.

We could read the respect and admiration the policemen had for us in their eyes, and we never tired of basking in it. Each day, we savoured our victory and the scale of our revenge on the King a little more.

'You've screwed them,' they'd say, making a victory 'V' sign.

One day, when we were pacing up and down the corridor, we encountered two Palestinian prisoners. They stood facing us. When the police officers spotted them, they rushed over to lead them away. But they had the time to scream at us in Arabic that we had won, that the victory was ours.

At the end of the corridor, beyond the toilets and showers, there was a locked metal gate that was permanently guarded by an armed policeman in combat gear. We were intrigued. Worn down by our questions, the police finally told us that it was the place where the prisoners were interrogated.

We were determined to go and see it. They found our request odd, but we were so insistent that they eventually gave in. On the other side of this gate, there was a narrow corridor lined with cells.

I implored the policeman who was accompanying me. He shrugged.

'As you wish, but don't say you haven't been warned. It'll finish you off.'

He slid back the cover over a peephole. The cell was so tiny that there was barely room to stand, or even sit down, the ceiling was so low. In the gloom, a man was lying listlessly on a concrete floor slab. He did not react, but stared vacantly through me.

I looked at him, my eyes full of tears, and murmured:

'Courage, courage.'

I was immediately furious with myself. It was as though I had given two drops of water to someone who was dying of thirst in the desert.

The policeman shut the door but I had had time to see the face of the prisoner, who had begun to tremble.

I was sobbing.

'I told you not to go in there,' said the cop.

That man was a political prisoner. One of many.

We awaited the King's reply without much hope.

After two months, Allabouch summoned us and announced that His Majesty had provisionally placed a furnished house with all mod cons at our disposal in Marrakesh. There was even a garden. Everything would be paid for, food, clothing . . . We were going to be looked after.

For us, emerging from hell, this offer was beyond our wildest dreams. We would live there while we waited for His Majesty to come to a decision regarding our request to emigrate.

We were overjoyed at the news. In our excitement, we evaded the real issues. Would we be truly free one day? And when?

But we didn't yet have the strength to ask those questions. We were so tired that the most we could do was eat and sleep.

8

MARRAKESH

1 July 1987–19 February 1991

SIX EUPHORIC MONTHS

The house His Majesty had royally allocated to us was in Targa, a few miles from Marrakesh, the favourite rural holiday spot of the Casablanca bourgeoisie. During my father's lifetime, the Ministry of the Interior used to lend us a farm there, which we used for our winter holidays and for horseriding at the weekend. We had very happy memories of it.

Of all the villas in the area, ours was the most isolated, encircled by high walls that allowed only a glimpse of the treetops beyond. It was surrounded by a neglected garden. The house, which probably dated back to colonial times, was huge and looked, if not attractive, at least comfortable.

After Bir-Jdid, it seemed palatial. We loved the interior with its long corridors, light rooms and the sheer number of them. Most of the bedrooms were on the first floor. I shared mine with Maria. Soukaina, Mimi, Abdellatif and Mother had their own rooms. Raouf, who needed to get away from the overpowering female presence, took the downstairs bedroom that looked out onto the garden. Achoura and Halima had rooms near the kitchen.

The house had two sitting rooms, as did all elegant middle-class homes. The smaller one was furnished in European style, with a sofa and comfortable armchairs arranged around a large fireplace. The other was arranged in the traditional Moroccan way, with mattresses on the floor and a low table. After being deprived of light for so long we were thrilled at the whiteness of the walls, the abundance of windows, the electric switches. There was fresh hot and cold running water—a luxury—and proper toilets and bathtubs.

It wasn't paradise but, for the pariahs of Bir-Jdid, it felt like it.

Excited, the children ran in and out of the rooms, laughing, shouting and bickering over who would have which bedroom. My mood wasn't quite so happy. More walls, more gates, more police, more prohibitions—we still couldn't go out, go for a stroll, live like ordinary people . . .

Another prison, even if it resembled a real house. Where was the freedom we had dreamed of? I didn't want to spoil their happiness so I kept my misgivings to myself and joined in with feigned enthusiasm.

'Yes, it's fantastic, yes, we're going to be happy. Anyway it's not for long, is it?'

To hell with my misgivings, we'd see soon enough.

We had been given carte blanche to buy furniture for the bedrooms, clothes and daily provisions. Books, records, videos, paper, notebooks, pens, women's magazines and Moroccan newspapers were ours for the asking. As for the international press, *Le Monde*, *Libération*, dream on . . . We were also given a hi-fi system, a television, a video recorder and radios. But when we misbehaved, the television programmes were censored.

The Marrakesh *caïd* (a 'chief' or a kind of mayor) and his deputy were responsible for our daily shopping. The first day, they suggested we write a list. We could have anything we wanted.

I didn't immediately understand what they meant by 'anything'. A kilo of meat per week seemed sufficient for nine. Writing the word 'butter', or even thinking of it, was inconceivable. They couldn't understand my hesitation. I kept asking:

'Can we also have fruit? Fresh milk? Chocolate? Sweets? Aren't they forbidden any more?'

They were as good as their word. Our wish was their command.

Gradually we became used to it. Food became our only obsession, our sole reason for living. Every evening we carefully planned the next day's menu in consultation with the police cook who had been placed at our disposal. On his arrival, the poor man hadn't known how to cook. By the time he left, four years later, he had become a real cordon-bleu chef.

We became very demanding. We wanted sweet and savoury pancakes, and *tajines*, couscous, custards and stewed fruit. And let's see, a big birthday cake with lashings of cream every day . . . Why not?

Through food, we rediscovered our appetite for living.

I would often wake up in the night, drenched in sweat, tormented by nightmares or horrendous memories. I no longer knew where I was. Bir-Jdid? Borro? Benaich? I was haunted by ghosts. I would throw on some clothes and tiptoe downstairs to the kitchen where I would often bump into another member of my family, also suffering from insomnia, going back upstairs with a tray laden with food.

'Is that you, Raouf? What are you eating, Abdellatif?'

We'd get a fit of the giggles. Then we'd both head for the fridge and compare our selections. We would sit and gorge ourselves together. The satisfaction provided by these midnight feasts proved to us that we were no longer in gaol.

Our bodies were deficient in everything, and we contracted countless illnesses. Mimi's haemorrhoids required a month in hospital. We suffered mysterious fevers, abscesses and boils, our hair fell out, we had no muscles, spare flesh or teeth; we were nothing but skin and bone, and even that was in a woeful state . . . Even though we ate non-stop and stuffed ourselves with vitamins and medicines, our deficiencies were so serious that it was like pouring a drop of water onto sand.

To get my strength back, I spent every morning exercising like mad: jogging, working out, or playing football with my brothers. I requested books on nutrition for athletes and became a walking encyclopaedia on the subject. I followed this strict regime for two years, but I remained in a dire physical condition for a long time. I pushed myself, rather like a disabled person learning to walk again.

The rest of the day I listened to music and read. I was as hungry for books as I was for food: novels, essays, history books on the Second World War and on Russia—I was interested in everything. At first I wasn't content just to read. I felt so ignorant that I learned lines and whole poems by heart. I looked things up in the dictionary, I read Baudelaire and Chateaubriand, and parsed sentences like a primary school child.

They smuggled in a little typewriter that belonged to my grandfather and, bowing to pressure from the others, I began re-transcribing the Story. I also started making notes for a screenplay and kept a diary.

I was a glutton for films and TV serials, even though most of them left me bewildered. I found *ET* unfathomable. I understood nothing of flying saucers, special effects, the philosophy behind the film. It was hard to make up for a fifteen-year lag.

I think I'm the alien.

Soukaina painted and listened to the songs of her long-time idol Patricia Kaas. Abdellatif played football; Raouf began a law degree by correspondence, and Mother listened to her precious news bulletins and scoured the newspapers they agreed to bring her. We were all coming back to life, each in our own way.

In the evenings, we organized parties when we all put on our glad rags. From seven o'clock, the house hummed with a cheerful bustle. We ironed clothes, tacked hems, plastered down our hair, preened ourselves, put on our make-up, gave ourselves a manicure and painted our toenails. Then we gathered in the sitting room around a magnificent buffet.

As we began to live again, we relearned the emotions that had been repressed for so long. We had hung up our 'battledress' and become more human. Our bodies were starting to reawaken.

I found I became upset when a haunting slow number set my heart fluttering. It was like being a teenager again, spending hours alone in my room sobbing. Despite my thirty-four years, I was still no more than a very young girl with a desperate need for love.

We had a favourite song which we never tired of listening to: the theme music from the film *La Lumière des justes*, sung by Charles Aznavour. It's called '*Etre*'.

One of us would put it on and we'd hug each other, singing the chorus together:

'*Etre, mourir pour mieux renaître* . . . To be, to die better to be reborn . . .'

Was it Aznavour's heartrending voice that brought tears to our eyes, or the words that seemed to have been written especially for us?

Every morning, Superintendent El Haj dropped in to see how we were, and find out if we were satisfied with our lot. Actually, he was instructed to probe our determination to settle in Canada. We weren't fooled.

We were all too familiar with the way the regime worked. Their honeyed words and compliments are calculated to give you a false sense of security, to make you believe they are on your side, then the trick question to trap you comes when you are least expecting it. Luckily, we had become adept at this game of cat-and-mouse, and in our turn we too tried disingenuously to extract as much information as we could.

We were in a state of uncertainty. Our French lawyers, Maître Dartevelle and Maître Kiejman, had given no further sign of life. Their silence worried us. True, we were treated well, but even though the limits had been pushed back—we could now walk, run and breathe, as long as we stayed within the confines of our garden—we were still prisoners.

On 3 July, Georges Kiejman finally paid us a visit. It was our first meeting with him. Visibly moved to see us and very respectful towards us, he made a touching little speech. As someone who had lost members of his family in the concentration camps during the war, he knew what we must have gone through and felt compelled to defend our case to the end. He promised to see us regain our freedom.

I found his words fitting, filled with true compassion for the persecution we had suffered. At last somebody was there to rehabilitate us, recognizing our status as victims. At last someone understood, and that warmed our hearts.

He told us of his audience with the King which had taken place a few days earlier. The King had spoken of us with warmth and passion. He considered me as his daughter and told the lawyer that he had brought me up himself, given me my first thrashing and laughed at my first pranks.

In this unfortunate affair, I was, he claimed, his only sore point, along with little Abdellatif over whom he also tormented himself.

Maître Kiejman seemed moved by my filial relationship with the sovereign. He had been unaware of that chapter of my past.

'You know, Malika, during our three-hour conversation, your name cropped up over and over again. His Majesty is very fond of you.'

We were all much more sceptical than he was regarding His Majesty's concern for us, but we kept our thoughts to ourselves.

The lawyer asked the King to release us. The monarch was not against it, but he refused to allow us to leave for France. His arguments appeared somewhat specious. His Majesty was afraid that a member of the Moroccan community in France might try to kill us. It seemed to us that Maître Kiejman conveyed the King's fears with a certain irony.

Besides, he was able to come out with the rejoinder:

'Your Majesty, the Oufkirs want to emigrate to Canada.'

The King feigned surprise. He thought for a while, then suggested sending us to Israel. His logic was irrefutable. My father's memory was respected there because he enabled thousands of Moroccan Jews to emigrate to Israel after the Six Day War in 1968.

His Majesty simply omitted to add that he would be exiling us to a country at war, where we would be at the mercy of any fundamentalist who could be brainwashed into getting rid of us.

Maître Kiejman sensed this was a trap. He argued against it for all he was worth.

At the end of the audience, he obtained assurances from His Majesty that we would receive our passports and visas for Canada. The King didn't want to hear of us again, but in exchange we were to keep quiet about what we had lived through.

Maître Kiejman gave his promise on our behalf.

Our lawyer had another message for me. Alain Delon had called him and assured him of his friendship for us. He was ready to help us financially and pay the legal costs if necessary. Maître Kiejman added, however, that the actor would not take sides politically. He still had interests in Morocco.

I was greatly comforted by this veiled message. So, Alain hadn't forgotten me. He had no doubt received one of the little pamphlets we had written in prison and sent to political figures and a number of our former acquaintances when we were on the run, in Rabat. Of all of them, he was the only one to have come forward, and that touched me deeply. Yet I declined his offer of help, asking Maître Kiejman to thank him for me.

It was a torrid summer that year, but that didn't matter to us. Our departure for Canada had been arranged for the end of October, so we could easily put up with the discomfort of the heat. We were happy, elated and triumphant. We were going to be able to begin our lives afresh.

We were fascinated by the unknown. We made the wildest plans. We were all going to live together on a huge ranch made up of seven houses, connected by underground passages leading to a games room. None of us was going to get married but we'd all have lots of lovers. We would never leave one another. The younger ones would study and the older ones would work.

We were fantasizing again in our usual fashion.

From time to time, the thought that they might want to do away with us crossed my mind, but I made myself banish it, just as I dismissed the idea that all this was impossible, too good to be true, and that we would never be free.

At last my grandfather was given permission to come and see us. We were told, as always, at the last minute. He arrived on 10 October. At seventy-two he was still as handsome as ever, tall and dignified with barely a wrinkle on his face. Only his brimming eyes betrayed the grief that had ravaged him. Seeing us all together, he burst into tears and could not stop weeping for a long time.

He embraced Mother, then kissed us all in turn and looked at us with great affection mixed with an infinite sadness. He seemed defeated. Doubtless he pitied us. We were still a sorry sight and our young faces had an ancient, hardened look as a result of our ordeal. We had changed so much. We saw that we were ghosts in his eyes. Our return was a miracle. And we understood, on seeing him, all that still divided us from the world of the living.

I had a lump in my throat but I couldn't cry, or even say his name. As a child I had nicknamed him Baba el Hadj, and that name had stuck. But since my father's death, I could no longer bring myself to say *Baba*—daddy. This block created a distance between me and the elderly man.

It was a very emotional moment for everybody.

I had not seen my mother so happy for a long time. She was very fond of her father. He had been battling all these years to release us from our terrible fate. He had contacted Amnesty International, the International League for Human Rights and many other organizations. He had written to all the leading politicians and gone to see Prince Moulay Abdallah, who had authorized him to send us books.

He had received no further news of us after Tamattaght. Several times he had believed we were dead, assassinated by bullets. He had been told that Mimi had died from an epileptic fit and that Raouf and I had been shot while trying to escape. One of his friends had even declared that he had seen my mother's corpse at Avicenne hospital with his own eyes.

He had resigned himself to mourning us. He refused to believe my uncle Wahid even though he swore he had seen the four of us at the Barères'. He told us about Mamma Khadija's death, and his remarriage. We had learned all that from the Barères. But we did not know that he had produced another son, whom he had named Raouf.

The family criticized him for this choice. You don't give a newborn child the name of a living relative.

'But,' he wept, 'I was so certain that you were all dead . . .'

We were touched by this way of paying tribute to our memory.

Our relatives had suffered considerable harassment since our incarceration. In their day-to-day lives they could not escape surveillance, phone tapping, interrogations and all kinds of other nuisance. Moroccan society closed its doors to them. My father's family, packed off into the desert where they had been deprived of everything, suffered even worse. People kept away from the Oufkir family.

He related all this trying to smile through his tears, punctuating almost every sentence with 'God is great.'

In preparation for our departure, on 27 October, the chief had been sent to buy us suitcases and clothes. He also provided us with coats, anoraks and warm boots. We loved making shopping lists. We carefully chose the styles and matched the colours. We were like children around a Christmas tree.

We were given identity cards and passports. Then they were taken away again on the eve of our departure. That made me uneasy. It reinforced the vague sense of anxiety I felt but was unable to articulate. No matter how hard I tried to reason with myself and see the proof I needed in all the preparations for departure and the attitude of the police towards us, I found it increasingly hard to believe that we would be allowed to leave. I was no longer able to share in the general excitement, to show concern about this one's hair or that one's outfit.

During the night, I woke Mother and told her of my suspicions. She refused to believe me, and accused me of having a warped mind. She was more naive than me, and often refused to see the bad side of things. Life at the Palace had taught me mistrust; I knew better than to take everything the King proposed at face value.

I came out of her room despondent, on the verge of tears. Only Raouf could understand. I slipped into his room and he listened to me attentively, sceptical at first, then my arguments convinced him.

He did not sleep a wink, and neither did I.

At seven o'clock in the morning, that 27 October, all nine of us stood ready for action, fully kitted out, perfumed, our hair freshly done and our suitcases and bags packed and ready to go. In fact, we were in travellers' fancy dress, each of us more ridiculous than the next. We had forgotten what it was like simply to board a plane and leave. Words had lost their meaning; we were just clinging to appearances. We had assumed the parts that we needed to play.

We waited anxiously in the sitting room, Raouf and I a little more anxious than the others who did not suspect anything yet. As far as they were concerned, in a few hours we would be far away. But for us . . .

I glanced at him. He flashed me an anxious smile. Mother intercepted our exchange. Clutching her vanity case, she was paler than I had thought. Had listening to my fears shaken her?

Allabouch, Superintendent El Haj, Othman Bouabid, principal private secretary to Driss Basri, the Minister of the Interior, and the chief arrived together. They avoided our eyes, and seemed embarrassed.

Another glance at Raouf. How were they going to set about confessing that this departure was just a farce? It would take some imagination.

They didn't even need that. The words flowed from their lips, even more syrupy than usual. An ocean of honey.

'His Majesty asks you to wait a little longer . . . He has not completely adjusted to the idea of your departure. Hadja, His Majesty wishes to see you before you leave,' they added, addressing my mother.

Once again our dream was shattered, and we embarked on three more long years of prison.

A GILDED CAGE

'But, Mme Oufkir, you can't leave without seeing His Majesty, since it was you who asked to meet him . . .'

The situation had backfired against us. Mother had played the game and written a letter requesting an audience with the King, as she supposedly wanted to see him, but it did not achieve the desired outcome.

There were probably other reasons for our aborted departure. Mother had refused to sign the written pledge that we would not take legal action against the Moroccan state, regardless of the promise Kiejman had earlier given to the King that we would keep quiet.

The sovereign had perhaps not been aware of the full extent of our health problems, nor of the long-term damage. Six months after Bir-

Jdid, we were still in terribly poor shape. Four of us had lung problems that were likely only to get worse.

Was it wise for them to risk showing us to the world, thus providing living proof of this flagrant violation of human rights? The Canadian immigration services would realize the state we were in, and the press would seize on it. The King surely didn't want this adverse publicity. We had to recover our health before being allowed to face the outside world.

But to this day, even with the best health care on earth, our bodies still bear the scars of those terrible years. Mimi continues to have epileptic fits, Maria had bladder cancer, Raouf is forever getting pneumonia and infections, and Soukaina and I have fragile health.

As for our Abdellatif, it is above all his soul that has been damaged.

Our lawyer had nevertheless believed the King's promises right up till the last minute. He was waiting for us in Casablanca where we were to board the plane. Our departure was to be very hush-hush, but the news was leaked, and representatives of the Moroccan Jewish community were waiting to greet us at Montreal airport with welcome banners. The Ministry of Finance had released the sum of four million dirhams for us into a Canadian bank account, and as far as Maître Kiejman was concerned, this money was further proof of the authorities' goodwill.

I'm more inclined to believe that our false departure was a carefully orchestrated charade. The King was not yet even with us, and we still had to pay.

We did not see Maître Kiejman again until a few months later, at the beginning of 1988. He was terribly angry. He declared that he was going to bring an action against Morocco in the international courts and pointed his finger at Allabouch.

'It's your fault and that of the people pulling the strings above you. I'm not used to dealing with people who do not keep their word . . .'

Soukaina took him aside and asked if her suicide could help secure our freedom. Since our aborted departure on 27 October, she had been obsessed with this idea. Maître Kiejman sighed, then carried on railing against a regime that crucified innocent children.

He ranted and raved for a good while. But his anger achieved nothing. Nor did the hunger strike that we began in April 1988, a few weeks after his visit. Our strike lasted twenty days. We had to be put on drips, we were in a very bad state, but we gave up our struggle only when forced to do so by circumstances.

Again, there was no hope for us.

After our aborted departure, we regressed. We went back to being prisoners, as we had been for fifteen years, at the same time resigned and rebellious, passive and combative. By way of consolation, I sometimes reminded myself that my fate had improved after all, and that it was only thanks to my own efforts. I had no illusions: the King was so powerful and we were so weak . . . At least we had the satisfaction of having forced him to bend a little.

We each fell into our own routine. We no longer believed in much. We read, exercised a little and watched television. Abdellatif played football with our cousin Hamza, who was the same age as him and who moved in with us as soon as he was able to come and see us.

Our family were allowed to visit us at weekends, at great personal cost. They were routinely searched. But we no longer organized impromptu parties among ourselves, other than at Christmas and birthdays. No more jolly tea parties or family dinners. We each ate alone, in our rooms.

We lived in our pyjamas, always the same pair that was threadbare from being washed over and over again. We went barefoot, no longer caring about our appearance. When we bumped into one another in the house, we repeated the same questions over and over again:

'When will all this be over? When are they going to free us?'

However, Marrakesh did differ from Bir-Jdid, thanks to the light. We never missed the dawn: it was a moment of rebirth, an extraordinary sensation. All day we stayed outside to make the most of it and, when night fell, we never tired of switching on the lights.

I received letters from my old friends but I couldn't bear their excuses, their guilt. Their letters were just long litanies attempting to justify fifteen years of silence and indifference. I didn't want to revive the past and I had nothing to say to them. Besides, they wouldn't have understood a thing.

We learned of the death of my paternal uncle, Moulay Hashem, my father's brother. We were not permitted to leave the house to attend his funeral, even under a heavy escort. Nnaa, our grandmother, had died shortly before our escape. She'd waited for us as long as she could, but did not have the joy of seeing us again.

We kept dozens of pets, stray cats and dogs that lived, ate and slept with us. Still traumatized by the death of our pigeons, we did not let them out of our bedrooms. Soon we had ten cats and three dogs. Emotionally and sexually frustrated, we transferred our overwhelming craving for love onto our pets, lavishing affection on them.

In prison we had grown accustomed to repressing our slightest impulses and desires. During those first six months in Marrakesh, we had half-opened the door to our emotions and lowered our defences.

After our false departure, we tried to steel ourselves again as we had done during our enforced isolation. We were leading an artificial existence. We felt life pulsating around us, and it would take so little for us to be part of it. But that little was inaccessible. We often tell each other that we would never have survived fifteen years in those conditions. Nothing at all was preferable by far to this 'almost'; struggle was better than resignation.

After being given a whiff of freedom, we were almost back to square one with the awful feeling that it would never be for us. I continually relived our escape. I was haunted by it. I had nightmares about it.

Our treatment became harsher. The police had bugged the sitting room. Raouf discovered the microphones hidden in the fireplace and ripped them out. In retaliation, they scrambled the French foreign service broadcasts on TV 5 when there were programmes that talked about Morocco. Security around us was stepped up. I was not permitted certain books on the Russian Revolution and Nazi Germany that I had requested. Why? I have no idea.

We still had a vestige of humour. We ordered *The Great Escape* on video. Of course our request was refused.

We thought of digging another tunnel for another escape. The earth in the garden was soft, but it would require an energy that we didn't have. We even played with the idea of having a little plane landing in the field on the other side of the wall. We sent one of our aunts to investigate.

The thought of escaping helped us cling to hope, proved to us that we weren't yet completely dead or buried alive.

We were still in Marrakesh at the outbreak of the Gulf War, which suited the King very well. It permitted him to act the role of mediator for the Arab countries, and try to make the world forget the political prisoners, the innumerable disappearances, the prison camps and the violations of human rights—the other facet of a ruthless sovereign.

In nearly twenty years of detention, we had acquired the habit of analysing external events in relation to our own situation. Was this war good for us or not? It didn't make an iota of difference to our fate.

A year later, in 1991, Gilles Perrault's book *Notre ami le roi* (*Our Friend the King*) was published in France. We learned this from Moroccan television and, judging from the outcry up and down the country, His Majesty was not happy with this book. According to the media, the government and the people were behind Hassan II.

We were asked to lend our support to this great cause. We were to write a letter criticizing Perrault and stating loud and clear that His Majesty was not only a great ruler but that he had an exceptional character.

Allabouch and Bouabid claimed that the enemies of the kingdom were behind this book, spearheaded by Danielle Mitterrand and Georges Kiejman. We were expected publicly to disassociate ourselves from a lawyer who dared attack the King. The letter would be published in *Le Figaro*.

Despite countless ploys to avoid writing this letter, we were forced to obey them in the end, but it was published only much later. Was the hour of liberation nigh?

They gave us Perrault's book to read, even though it was banned in Morocco, so that we could see for ourselves. It was so violently anti the King that its effect on me was like a third coup d'état. An outsider, a Frenchman to boot, had the temerity to criticize the King and to accuse and to condemn, without qualms and without compromise.

What's more, the book was full of inaccuracies giving credence to pure hearsay. Our captivity was covered in the chapter entitled 'Iron Masks', and so was our escape. But, in addition to the inaccuracies, implausibilities, omissions and fabrications, Perrault insinuated, as so many others had done, that we could not have escaped on our own. In his view, a corrupt gaoler, or even several, could have helped us from the outside. For us, whose only source of pride in nearly twenty years was this escape, accomplished unaided, those words were like daggers. He mitigated his theory, however, by concluding that if that had indeed been the case, they would not have allowed us to wander around the country without money or support . . .

Even more hurtful still were the personal attacks. According to Perrault, Mother 'exhibited a fondness for young officers' when she was married to my father. On the other hand, he knew nothing of the circumstances of the divorce, got the dates wrong, the causes, the events, and even claimed Mother had had an affair, another one, with Hassan II himself. He added, without proof, on hearsay, that 'the whole of Rabat was whispering that [Soukaina] was the King's daughter'. A 'revelation' that profoundly distressed my little sister for a long time.

Nor was I immune from gossip. According to him, I followed in my mother's footsteps. My father turned a blind eye: 'He was accustomed to it.' The book was peppered with similar insinuations.

From having lived inside the Palace, then, later, amid the hangers-on and flatterers, I was used to gossip. Coming from Moroccans, it did not affect me. On the other hand, what hurt me, what hurt my mother and my brothers and sisters, was that a man like Gilles Perrault could have mistaken gossip for fact. He missed the opportunity to write a properly researched book, and that upset me much more than all his misinformation. There was so much to disclose that he should not have contented himself with reproducing hearsay. The truth would have amply sufficed to bring down the despot.

But he did have the courage to criticize the King.

It was the first time that anybody had attacked the King openly, and that alone was enough for us to refuse to take any action that might harm Perrault.

Besides, he was actually defending us despite his nasty intimations: 'In the name of what strange morality can anyone inflict fifteen years of torture on innocent children? Is there a penal code anywhere in the world that makes the children pay for the crimes of the father?'

Let us render unto Caesar . . . No doubt we are greatly indebted to him.

THE END OF THE TUNNEL

Allabouch, Bouabid and the Walli, the Governor of Marrakesh, came back to see us in the middle of February 1991. Conversations with them were like a game of chess. Each player advanced his pawn according to what their adversary said, and we thought carefully about every word before replying. Subtly, a small dose at a time, they would ladle out a few measures of information, passing judgement.

When we had first arrived in Marrakesh, they'd told us with a certain bitterness and anger that we could be proud of ourselves. Our escape was to have far greater political repercussions than we had imagined.

'Thanks to the stir created by your escape, the international press is going to be increasingly interested in the fate of political prisoners in Morocco,' Bouabid had stated.

That day, our guardian angels settled themselves down on a divan and began to chat about this and that, dwelling at length on minor things.

The Governor teased me about feminism to wind me up. He enjoyed provoking me. It was all very good-natured, but we couldn't understand what they were leading up to. For nearly three hours we had been talking about nothing.

Then Bouabid looked at me and said point-blank, in a conversational tone:

'YOU ARE FREE.'

The bomb exploded at our feet.

But it had no effect on us.

We couldn't, or wouldn't, understand.

We carried on talking as if we hadn't heard.

Allabouch, Bouabid and the Governor looked at each other, dumbfounded. We were on another planet, light years away from grasping the meaning of their words. We felt a little ill at ease, however, for we did sense that something bizarre was happening.

'For God's sake,' yelled Allabouch, 'you've been waiting for this moment for eighteen and a half years, and that's your reaction? You are free, I tell you! Free . . . !'

Free? What did that word mean? One second earlier we had been prisoners, and now we were being told that our ordeal was at an end? Our liberty had been granted in an instant, just as it had been taken from us so many years earlier. The King's goodwill . . .

Were they telling the truth? Were we being taken for a ride again? Before we had properly digested them, those three little words 'you are free' sent us plunging back into our old state of hunted convicts. We did not react. We didn't dare speak or look at one another.

It took us a good while to grasp that the King had pardoned us. Public opinion had put pressure on him, and the Americans and the French had intervened on our behalf.

When I recovered the power of speech, I asked them why they had taken so long to tell us the news.

'For some time now we've been having meeting after meeting to find the best way of breaking it to you. We couldn't just tell you out of the blue, it was very difficult, we didn't want to kill you.'

Free . . . so, we were free . . . But where were we to go? We no longer had a home, and we had very few friends left. What were they going to do with us once we got to Rabat? Were they going to dump us like unwanted baggage?

'Take your time,' they said, 'and first get used to the idea that you are free, thanks to His Majesty's generosity. We will come back to fetch you in a week.'

Only after their departure did we kiss one another and boisterously express our joy. But at the same time our delight was strangely detached. We were wildly happy on the outside and empty inside. Free . . .

A week was not too long for us to become acclimatized to the idea. Already the hours of the day were no longer the same. The sun no longer shone in the same way, and it set differently from before: it no longer rose on the prospect of another day even bleaker than the last.

The sky was bluer, nature came back to life, our appetites returned. Our senses sharpened. I now saw life in Cinemascope, and no longer on a tiny screen.

We were like blind people whose sight had suddenly been restored, with all the anxieties and fears that can bring.

'I'm going to make up for lost time with women,' said Raouf.

'I'm going to study music,' mused Soukaina, 'and meet Patricia Kaas.'

'Become a professional footballer,' shouted Abdellatif.

'Get married, and have a child,' murmured Mimi blushing.

And what about me? I wanted to love, travel, go for walks, eat, talk, laugh, sing, make films, study, sit on the terrace of a café, work in advertising . . . not necessarily in that order.

And why not all at the same time?

Then immediately we went into a panic. Would we be able to cope? Wasn't it too late? As each day passed, the more afraid we felt, and the more we were afraid of feeling afraid.

To comfort ourselves, we concentrated on packing our suitcases and belongings.

Our family came to see us as usual at the weekend. We hadn't yet told them anything about our impending release.

My aunt Mawakit, who is a medium, regularly used to read our cards. She had always seen that we would be released one day, but she had not been able to give the date. That Saturday, she took the tarot cards and asked me to cut the pack with my left hand. She then announced without any preliminaries that our release was imminent.

'You're useless as a medium, Mawakit,' I said with a shrug. 'We've been prisoners for four and a half years, and I don't see why that should change now.'

The more adamant she became the more I argued against it. She assured me that the cards were never wrong, begged me to tell her the truth, implored Mother and the others. We all remained poker-faced.

We kept up this little game for nearly two hours, and then I finally admitted what I still found it difficult to express:

'We're free, Mawakit. Free.'

9

A STRANGE KIND OF FREEDOM

OUR FIRST STEPS

So, we were free.

After saying the word over and over again in our minds, after dreaming about it for twenty years, day and night, we were no longer certain that we knew what it meant.

Free means going out in the street without having the police at your heels.

For the next five years we would be followed, watched, kept under close surveillance and our phones tapped.

Free means being allowed to work.

I was the only one who managed to find a proper job in Morocco, thanks to a brave employer who defied the taboos.

Free means associating with whoever you please, loving whoever you please, going wherever you please.

Our friends were all interrogated by the secret services; our love affairs with foreigners were forbidden.

Our passports were not returned to us.

But all the same we were free . . .

And we took our first steps back into the world on 26 February 1991.

* * *

I put a great deal of thought into choosing my outfit for re-entering the world: a pair of jeans, a man's shirt, a cravat and a navy-blue silk blazer. I was anxious to please, charm and seduce freedom. The suitcases stood ready, the pets waited patiently and calmly in their cages. They sensed that it was an important moment. A historic moment.

For once we eagerly awaited the arrival of the police and the secret services. A convoy of cars and vans drew up outside our house. There was a crowd of people, noise, comings and goings, commotion. No doubt that is what it is to be free: seeing more people in one hour than we had seen in twenty years. The garden gates opened, and so did my heart.

It was an unforgettable feeling.

They would never close on us again.

We clambered into the cars and the convoy set off. Everything was jumbled in my mind, the noises, the smells, the colours and the excitement of the moment. At last I could look out without sadness or dread, quite the opposite. I was fascinated by every detail of life on the streets: two lovers holding hands, a mother accompanied by her daughter, a dog frisking about, a bird alighting on a branch.

All this would soon belong to me.

We stopped in a small town and were asked if we wanted to stretch our legs. Full of misgivings, we refused to budge: what dirty trick were they going to play on us now? It took endless persuasion before we accepted their offer.

As I walked into the café, I felt giddy. I tripped on a step and stumbled. I didn't know how to walk any more. In fact I didn't know anything any more. Excuse me, how do you walk? Put one foot in front of the other and repeat it over and over again? How do you stand at a bar, casually order a Coca-Cola, pour it into a glass and drink it with little murmurs of satisfaction?

Excuse me, how do you live?

In this bar where we lined up like docile prisoners, the lights seemed too bright, the music too aggressive. We felt hunted. We wanted to get back into the cars.

The journey from Marrakesh to Rabat took three hours, which I spent looking eagerly out of the window. I had noticed the transformations Morocco had undergone with my own eyes, first when I escaped, then from watching films and TV broadcasts, but now I could observe all these changes with an enthusiastic eye. I was amazed at this surge of affection I felt inside me. I couldn't wait to arrive. I urged the driver to go faster.

At last the convoy reached Rabat, and drew up outside my uncle Wahid's house. The whole family dressed in full Moroccan costume was standing on the doorstep. According to custom, they had set out milk and dates to welcome us. It ought to have been a moment of joy, but their expressions, like ours, were filled with great sadness. Twenty years cannot be erased in five minutes.

They can never be erased.

As I alighted from the car, my legs buckled under me. I have forgotten what happened next. I know that people were hugging me, kissing me, that I went from embrace to embrace. No doubt I was moved. But I was strangely passive, unable to express any emotion.

In the following days the house was constantly full of people. People came flocking to see us. Like at a market or an exhibition, we were offered to the crowds of people who loved us and who had not forgotten us. And who all the same had waited for two or three days for permission from the Palace before coming to see us.

My friend Houria was among the first visitors. Loyal to the hilt, she had wanted to come with us into exile. The minute she caught sight of me at the top of the stairs, she rushed towards me, while I took a step backwards. Fearful of reconnecting with my youth, I wanted to run away. Later she told me that the expression on my face had terrified her. In twenty years I had become a stranger. As all these people had become strangers to me.

Sitting in a chair, I watched them file past, and I could not understand why nearly everyone started crying at the sight of us. Had we changed so much? Aged so much? Were we in such a bad state? I felt as though I had been drugged. I wanted to be alone, shut up in a dark room. That wasn't possible. My uncle's apartment was tiny and we were all crowded into the living room downstairs to sleep. For the first few nights, I wasn't able to close my eyes.

Wahid insisted that I go out. Go out? There were crowds of journalists milling around outside the house demanding interviews, but we refused to speak to them. How could I confront this horde? It took me three days to muster the courage to go to the door. I asked my uncle to open it for me.

'Kika, why don't you do it yourself? You're free now.'

I gently opened it a fraction and ventured a glance outside. Everything was fuzzy, the pavements, the cars, the passers-by, it was all a grey blur and I couldn't make out a thing. It frightened me even more than prison. I came over dizzy and nearly passed out. I needed to wait a little longer before facing the outside world. My brothers, on the other hand, went out immediately.

Allabouch and Bouabid, our 'guardian angels', dropped in every day in the late afternoon. They sat in the living room like old friends and asked Wahid to pour them an apéritif. They attempted to coax us out of our state of shock, chatting about this and that, joking and trying to make us laugh.

How could our former torturers change so radically? Were they our persecutors or our benefactors? I was torn. They seemed to have the solution to all our problems, to hold the key to our lives in their hands. They wanted to answer in our stead. They advised us on every detail. They were very nervous that we were being hounded by the press, and didn't want us to give interviews. His Majesty would not tolerate it.

We obeyed them, but we were wrong. We should have spoken to the journalists and used the media as a means of bringing pressure to bear. But we couldn't rid ourselves of our prisoners' reflexes just like that. We were afraid. We would feel that irrational, uncontrollable terror, and the shame that goes with it, as long as we stayed in Morocco.

The police kept us company day and night. We weren't sure whether the guards who never left our side were there to protect us or keep us under surveillance. A chauffeur was placed at our disposal, all the better to keep track of our movements. We were followed wherever we went, our telephone conversations were tapped, and they interrogated anyone who came into contact with us. Free, us?

Maître Kiejman phoned us soon after our arrival. Was he advised not to come and see us? There was no further sign of him. Immediately after his call, we were told that His Majesty had ordered our property and belongings to be returned to us and that two leading Moroccan lawyers, Maître Naciri and Maître El Andalouss, would be acting for us.

The two big names came to see us separately. If they were to be believed, everything was going to be resolved very quickly; all we needed to do was make an inventory and everything would be returned to us. We drew up that inventory, first with one, then with the other, and we waited as they suggested. We are still waiting.

My aunt offered us her apartment. I moved in with my sister Maria and all our pets. We seldom went out, and when we did we hugged the walls, afraid to walk in the centre of the pavement. We were scared of the light, the noise and the cars. Our footsteps were hesitant. We were convinced that the whole world was staring at us, which is what happened in the end because we looked so weird. But we made it a point of honour to get dressed up and put on make-up, even just to cross the street. It was our way of celebrating freedom.

Later, when I was able to go further than the little patch I had marked out for myself and visit other districts of the city, take a taxi or a train on my own and walk in unfamiliar areas, I continued to suffer panic attacks for a long time. I would break out into a sudden sweat and have difficulty getting my bearings.

Even in Paris, eight years after my release from prison, I still sometimes panic in a crowd or lose my way on a journey I know by heart. I no longer have any spatial awareness.

I have had to learn everything anew. To walk, sleep, eat and express myself. For years time had just flowed by, it had no meaning for me, and I no longer knew how to organize it. I have no morning or afternoon, no boundaries. An hour can last for days or for minutes. I have difficulty understanding other people's time, their hurry or their slowness, their time constraints. I still can't manage it.

Rebirth is a strange feeling. At first I sometimes felt overloaded. I marvelled at the sky, the sun, the light, noise, movement—it all thrilled and exhausted me. I could not go out for a whole day without feeling giddy. Then I became bolder. I would stop in a café and order a drink, go into a restaurant or a shop, go to the market, drive . . . these activities cost me a great effort but gave me immense pleasure. I savoured every second of freedom.

Each day is a miracle that intoxicates me. I want more. I greet every morning like a new pleasure. And yet I am keenly aware of all life's artifices. Getting dressed, wearing make-up, laughing, having fun—isn't all that just playing a role? Am I not more profound, carrying the burden of those twenty years when I 'wasn't alive', than all those who rushed around in vain during that time?

I often compare myself to somebody who has spent their entire life listening to the sound of a fairground without being able to join in. I wasn't part of the action, certainly, but does that mean that nothing was going on in my life during all those years? In prison, my inner life was a thousand times richer than that of others, and my thinking a thousand times more intense. I was a lot more aware than people who are free. I learned to reflect on the meaning of life and death.

Today everything seems artificial to me. I can't take anything seriously.

Abdellatif became very close to his beloved cousin Hamza, who cut short his studies in Canada to be with him. They sowed their wild oats together. My little brother was learning to live: going out at night, women, music, dancing, cafés . . . He seemed happy. Hamza was his best friend.

Soukaina painted and wrote; Mimi struggled to improve her health, and Raouf tried to make up for lost time with women. We had different views on this subject. For me, this relentless search was a blind refusal to come to terms with things. I believed only in true love and I was waiting for it.

Mother could count her old friends on the fingers of one hand. In society circles people avoided us; our name aroused fear. For twenty years, nobody had dared utter it at the risk of incurring the most terrible sanctions. People had put it so far from their minds that it was as if we were dead. Our resurrection perturbed them.

Most of them reduced our ordeal to something negligible. Twenty years of 'house arrest', in a 'castle', come on, that wasn't so bad . . . After all, we were still alive, and physically still in one piece.

Our father, the executioner, the traitor, the regicide, had only got his just deserts. Besides, weren't we his heirs? Nobody said it to our faces, but they insinuated as much. They said so to our close friends. We were accused, guilty, enemies of the monarchy. We were an embarrassment.

For my thirty-eighth birthday, which I celebrated a month and a half after leaving Marrakesh, I received four hundred postcards from all over the world. People had learned of our release through Amnesty International, and this was their way of demonstrating their solidarity.

I was touched and angered at the same time. It was when we were in prison that we needed these tokens of friendship. Now we were free we didn't need it any more, especially not wishes for a rosy future. All this came too late.

Too late, that was our overriding feeling. Too late for love, for friendship and for family. Too late for life. Our elation gave way to moments of profound despondency. Wouldn't it have been better if we had died?

A few weeks after our release, Raouf and I were taken to the latest trendy nightclub in Rabat, Amnésia. That evening Hassan II's eldest son, Crown Prince Sidi Muhammad, and his sisters were sitting in a private booth with some of their entourage. On seeing us, they invited us to join them.

I had known the Prince from birth. He was nine when we were imprisoned. I was grateful to him for sparing me the humiliation of having to bow down to kiss his hand. He might have changed and become an adult, but I could still picture the child I had known and, through him, the King whom he resembled closely.

I was moved and so was he. His sincere words touched us. He told us that his house would always be open to us, and he would always be there to help us. We could knock on his door at any hour.

Then he called over his private secretary, and repeated those same words in his presence.

'But the past is the past,' he added. 'You must look forward, not back on what you have been through.'

He made no allusion to his father. Princess Lalla Meriem stood behind him, as pale and shaken as we were, but she did not say anything.

News of our meeting was all over Rabat.

A little later there was an article about it in *Le Monde*. The author seemed convinced that this was a new strategy of the King's to settle the Oufkir affair. According to the journalist, the King had sent his children as scouts to attempt a reconciliation. It was not hard to guess Sidi Muhammad and his circle's reaction. From now on they avoided us when we met.

My encounter with Lalla Mina took place soon afterwards. She invited me to lunch and I willingly accepted. I felt no animosity towards her. Seeing her again was to reclaim my childhood, rekindle feelings that I had repressed deep down inside me, but which were perhaps not quite dead. I also wanted to prove to the King that, unlike him, I was able to make a distinction between him, the man who remained my enemy, and the other members of his family.

Lalla Mina still lived at the Villa Yasmina. She had also built a stables on a huge estate on the outskirts of Rabat, not far from the Dar-es-Salem Palace. Riding was still her great passion. She had revived racing in Morocco, and had built riding schools.

To join her, I had to cross half the estate on foot. I recognized many familiar faces who stopped and greeted me. I was pleasantly surprised: so I hadn't been altogether forgotten.

I caught my first glimpse of her through a plate-glass door. Although she had changed a lot, I immediately saw the shadow of the little girl I had known. This large woman in jodhpurs had the same smile, the same facial expressions and the same mischievous eyes. I felt very emotional.

When the Princess caught sight of me, she came out of her office, stood there for a few seconds without speaking, and walked slowly towards me. Then she quickened her step and finally broke into a run and flung herself into my arms. She hugged me very tight and took my hand. She said nothing for a few minutes and then she managed to blurt out:

'Kika, are you well?'

I followed her into her office, more shaken up than I wanted to admit to myself. That voice, that walk . . . The past came back in waves. Our laughter, our games, Zazate, the parties, Mamaya and even the dreadful Rieffel . . .

She gave orders that we were not to be disturbed, and closed the door. We stood there, looking at each other, unable to speak. She stared at me for a long time and I held her gaze. My eyes were brimming. She held back her tears but I could see her lip was trembling. Then she turned round and banged the table with her fist:

'What a disgrace to our family.'

She questioned me closely, wanting to know everything.

Despite my affection for her, which I now knew unchanged, I remained cautious.

I was too well acquainted with her milieu not to be aware that anything I said would be repeated, commented on and dissected.

'Answer me,' she said, 'is it true they killed your pigeons? True that each day they killed two or three?'

So she knew everything about our life, day to day . . .

We talked for a long time. She gave me news of various people. For years, she told me, Latifa, the King's wife, had pleaded on our behalf, which did not surprise me. She was a very brave woman. On each religious holiday she had slipped in a word in our favour. She arranged to do it when he went to see his granddaughter, whom he had named Soukaina.

The King was so besotted with the child that when somebody was sentenced to death, it was enough to utter her name in his presence to obtain a pardon. On these occasions, Latifa would speak to him above all about my brother Abdellatif. She hoped to tug at his heartstrings, but he remained obdurate.

I was happy to see my childhood friend again, but felt uneasy as I left her house. Carried away by my joy at seeing her, had I said too much? Had I thrown caution to the winds?

Lalla Mina often invited me over. She wanted to reintroduce me into the circles which were no longer mine. I decided to visit less often, and then I stopped going altogether.

Life has driven a wedge between us, but I continue to feel enormous affection for her. I still see her as the child and teenager she used to be, my half-sister and my companion in loneliness. I bear no more resentment towards her than I do towards any of those whom I once loved at the Palace.

ERIC

Clearly, Morocco didn't want us.

It was impossible for us to work. I am indebted to the obstinacy and courage of Nureddin Ayouche, head of Shem's advertising agency, for giving me a proper job. He was not deterred by the pressure, the nuisance or the police. I spent three years working with him and learning the profession of production manager. My first pay packet was for Mother.

Mimi achieved her dream. She married a cameraman. Their daughter, Nawel, was born in November 1994. Raouf became a father: Tania came into the world in September 1993. The child was born in Geneva, but my brother was unable to obtain permission to go to Switzerland to see her first smile.

Not without difficulty, Maria managed to adopt an adorable little boy, Michaël, who bears the Oufkir name. Achoura lives with her and is helping her raise the child. Halima returned to her own family but complained that nobody understood her. She is wasting away from cancer. Of us all, she is the most deeply scarred. She has now come back to live with Mother.

Soukaina composes songs, writes and paints. Her talents have blossomed. She applied for a passport, but it was refused.

A few female friends helped us survive ostracism, loneliness and the lack of freedom. Soundous, Neïla, Nawel and Sabah, whom I finally tracked down, surrounded us with their love, without worrying about being tailed, interrogated and, above all, incurring public disapproval.

One certainty helped me to keep going: I would not be spending the rest of my life in Morocco.

* * *

In spring 1995 I was invited to the wedding of a friend, Mia. She was marrying Kamil, whom we had seen again, and who was still as I remembered him: kind and loyal. She asked me to take charge of the decorations. I accepted without really knowing why. I usually avoided these society receptions. They made me feel ill at ease. I hated those dolled-up women dripping with jewellery, their hypocrisy, artificial values—money, power, success—and their contempt for ordinary people.

Three young men, friends of the bride, arrived from Paris. That same evening they would be at the wedding. The unmarried female guests were all very excited, whispering that the young men were handsome, intelligent and . . . eligible. They paid a visit to the bride-to-be that afternoon.

While the girls lavished attention on them, I got on with my work, discussing details with the photographer and the decorator, adding a layer of paint, dealing with the tablecloths, the flowers and the hangings . . . I had my hands full, which didn't prevent me from glancing at the newcomers out of the corner of my eye.

I noticed one of them in particular. He was tall and smiling, with small round spectacles framing his kind, mischievous eyes. But I couldn't even dream of it. That man was not and never would be for me. I didn't want a relationship with a Frenchman when I wasn't allowed out of the country. Besides, one of the guests had already made a beeline for him. I didn't stand a chance.

Around eight o'clock I went home to change into my ceremonial kaftan. The phone rang. On the other end of the line was one of my girlfriends, a clairvoyant when the fancy took her. She didn't seem to be herself. I found her strangely excited.

'Kika, you've met him, you've met him . . .'

'Met who?'

'You know very well who I'm talking about . . . I've seen him hundreds of times in my cards . . . the man from across the sea. The man of your life. He's here, you've seen him but you didn't notice him. You're going to see him again this evening.'

No matter how hard I reasoned with myself, saying it was all nonsense, I arrived at the party intrigued, my heart racing, ready to believe her. This wedding was my first real outing. Next to all these sumptuously attired and bejewelled girls, I was very plainly dressed and made up. But it didn't matter to me. I had long preferred simplicity.

My friends were already sitting with the Parisians. They signalled frantically to me to join them. There was a lot of noise, music and laughter. People were staring at me. I felt slightly uncomfortable and already regretted accepting the invitation. I planned to have a drink or two and then go home. I suddenly needed the peace and quiet of my own little room. I still couldn't get used to crowds.

The man I had noticed that afternoon rose as soon as he saw me. In a flash, he was sitting beside me. He told me he was an architect and that he had grown up in Lebanon. He spoke Arabic fluently, and understood our 'untranslatable' jokes. That was a plus.

He took my hand in his quite naturally. At once he realized, from my skin, the pressure of my fingers, my voice, the way I spoke to him, looked at him, that I was just a frightened child dressed up as a woman.

I couldn't stop my mind from racing, wondering where all this would lead me. An irrepressible little voice whispered to me not to ask too many questions. He was handsome, young and full of life. Besides, he was so gentle, so normal, that suddenly I no longer felt afraid. With him, I have never been frightened. It was as though I had known him for centuries. This was the first time that a man had made me feel so strong, so safe. My intuition told me that he would never bow under pressure, he would never allow anyone to influence him.

I knew he would love me for what I was, without any questions.

I was not mistaken. Eric has never let me down. He has always been there in a crisis, inspiring me with his energy, courage and confidence, and his *joie de vivre*. He saved me from death, turning my darkness into light.

He succeeded in taming me.

I'm not so easy to love. Nobody, not even he, can understand what binds us together. He shares my nightmares, he is prepared to live with my craziness; he allows me to escape from time to time and dive back into my refuge, my cell. He has acknowledged the difference between us: I will never be like everybody else.

All that I thought was lost, is lost no longer because of him. He freed me from Hell.

My life will not be in Morocco.

And yet I deeply love my country, its history, its language and its customs. I love the ordinary people who are poor and oppressed, but proud, funny and generous. There are no barriers between them and me. People often tell me that I'm *chahbia*—of the people. It is the best compliment anybody could pay me.

In prison, hatred helped me to survive. The hatred I felt for the King became mixed up with what I thought I felt for my country. On my release, I rejected both.

Now I swing between the deepest resentment and the sincere wish to feel no more hatred. Hatred eats you up, hatred paralyses you and stops you living. Hatred will never enable me to make up for the lost years. Not me, not my mother, not my brothers and sisters. But I've still got some way to go.

I rediscovered my peace of mind and my love for Morocco in the desert. I have travelled back and forth across it, my favourite destination being the Tafilalet desert, the cradle of my paternal ancestors. The desert soothed me. It reconciled me with my past, and helped me understand that I am just passing through. In the desert, there is no need for pretence, I am truly myself. Nothing matters except the eternal.

I feel I come from this land, I belong to it body and soul.

In the midst of the ochre dunes, among these vast expanses of golden sand, in the palm groves inhabited by the Blue Men, I realized where my roots lay. I am Moroccan through and through, to the core of my being.

But I also feel very French, through the language, my culture, mentality and intellect.

The two are no longer incompatible. In me, East and West at last cohabit in peace.

POSTSCRIPT

For a year, Eric Bordreuil regularly shuttled between Paris and Casablanca to be reunited with Malika Oufkir, the woman he loved.

On 25 June 1996, Maria Oufkir, Malika's younger sister, escaped from Morocco by sea, with her adopted son Michaël and her cousin Achoura Chenna. She reached Spain and then made her way to France.

This escape marked the end of the Oufkir family's nightmare. Under international pressure, the government issued them all with passports and visas.

On 16 July 1996, Malika Oufkir arrived in Paris with her brother Raouf and her sister Soukaina. She was forty-three years old.

She had spent twenty years of her life in Moroccan gaols, incarcerated since the age of eighteen, and then another five years under close surveillance in Morocco.

On 10 October 1998, Eric Bordreuil and Malika Oufkir were married at the town hall of the 13th arrondissement in Paris.

AUTHORS' NOTE

On 29 October 1987, the European Parliament invited Morocco to release the 400 'disappeared' and other political prisoners.

In 1991, Amnesty International welcomed the release of 270 'disappeared', including some who had been imprisoned for nineteen years. Abraham Serfaty (see p. 71) was deported to France and banned from returning to Morocco. The Bourequat brothers, accused of espionage, arrived in Paris in 1992.

Amnesty International states that there are still hundreds of political prisoners, especially among the Western Saharans, many of whom died in Tazmamart, a prison camp in the High Atlas which was evacuated and demolished in 1991.

In 1998, through the Committee on Human Rights, Morocco admitted to the deaths of 56 political prisoners in Moroccan gaols between 1960 and 1980, out of a list of 112 names of people who had 'disappeared'.

ACKNOWLEDGEMENTS

A warm thank you to all those who helped us see this project through.

Thank you to Jean-Claude and Nicky Fasquelle.

Thank you to Manuel Carcassonne (and his Turkish slippers).

Thank you to Susan Chirazi (without whom . . .) and Soraya Khatami.

Thank you to Isabelle Josse, Aurélie Filipetti, Martine Dib, Stephen Smith, Paulo Perrier, Marion Bordreuil, Françoise and Pierre Bordreuil; thank you to Hugo for his little cakes, to Léa for her smile, to Nanou for her kisses; thank you to Roger Dahan, Sabah Ziadi and Soundous Elkassri.

And lastly, thank you to Eric Bordreuil and Guy Princ for their unconditional support from the first moment, and for their endless patience.

READING GROUP GUIDE

"The days dragged on interminably. Our main enemy was time. We saw it, we felt it, it was tangible, monstrous, threatening. The hardest thing was to master it. During the day, all it took was a gentle breeze wafting in through the window to remind us that we were prisoners.

In the summer, dusk brought back memories of the sweetness of the old days, the end of a day at the beach, time for an apéritif, the laughter of friends, the smell of the sea, the tang of salt on my bronzed skin. I relived the little I had experienced."

AN INTRODUCTION TO *STOLEN LIVES*

The eldest daughter of General Oufkir, the King of Morocco's closest aide, Malika Oufkir was adopted by the king at age of five as a companion for his daughter. She spent most of her childhood and adolescence within the gilded walls of the palace, living an extraordinarily privileged yet secluded life.

Her world was shattered on August 16, 1972, when her father was executed for his part in an attempt to assassinate the King. Along with her mother and five siblings, Malika was imprisoned in a penal colony. The Oufkir family spent the next fifteen years in prison, the last ten in solitary confinement, until they managed to dig a tunnel and escape. Their freedom ended five days later, however, when they were captured and returned to prison. In 1996, after twenty-four years of incarceration, the Oufkir family was finally granted permission to leave Morocco.

In *Stolen Lives*, Malika recounts her family's story with unflinching and heartrending honesty. She recalls their day-to-day struggle for survival in harsh conditions, being watched around the clock by prison guards, and communicating with her family solely through prison walls for more than a decade. She tells of raising her brothers and sisters, teaching them good manners and attempting to provide them with some semblance of a normal life. They celebrated Christmas and birthdays, saving up rations to make cakes and fashioning toys out of cardboard. Through it all, Malika managed to draw upon her sense of humor, which, she says, "allowed us to survive even—and most of all—at the worst moments."

In the Preface to *Stolen Lives*, co-author Michèle Fitoussi recalls that, upon first meeting Malika, she asked herself, "How can anyone appear normal after such suffering? How can they live, laugh, love, how can they go on when they lost the best years of their life as a result of injustice?" The answers are found in this poignant and inspiring account of a family who endured with courage, determination, and dignity the cruel and unjust circumstances fate had in store for them.

DISCUSSION QUESTIONS

1. Malika, whose name means "Queen," considered herself a princess, although she wasn't one by birth. The world view she has in the beginning of the book obviously changes drastically as the story progresses. At what moment does her romantic vision of her life begin to break down?

2. Adopted at the age of five by the King of Morocco, Malika came to regard him as a father figure. How does she reconcile the fact that this man who had taken her into his home is eventually responsible for the death of her father and the imprisonment of her family? What are her feelings towards her father? Does she blame him for her family's ordeal?

3. The Oufkir family is forced to suffer many indignities and hardships in prison. Did these details give you a specific sense of what it is like to be in prison or did you, as the reader, still feel separated from their experiences?

4. Malika and her family strive to keep some normalcy in their lives by celebrating birthdays and other special holidays while imprisoned. It is as though they were opting to create the best possible world for themselves instead of just opting for survival. What do we learn about them from these actions? What heroine from world literature does Malika most remind you of?

5. Malika created The Story to entertain her family and to occupy their minds, fabricating the tale of a Russian prince to which she added new chapters each night for ten years. What did The Story come to mean to the family? Why was it so important to them?

6. Malika wanted to grow up to be a film actress. What elements of her story seem the most cinematic, the ones that would translate the best to the big screen? Do you think that her desire to be an actress actually helped her through this ordeal?

7. What part of the Oufkir family's story did you find the most harrowing? The most uplifting?

8. Do you consider this book to be a memoir, an autobiography or a political story? Discuss what you learned about Morocco and the politics of the country.

9. How does the relationship between Malika and her family change as their years in prison progress? How do they manage to help one another even when, for more than a decade, they are confined to solitary cells?

10. What thoughts and feelings did you come away with after reading this book?

Malika Oufkir is now forty-seven years old and lives in Paris. She recently married a French architect. When *La Prisonnière* was published in France it sold over 100,000 copies, rose to No. 1 in the best-seller lists, and was awarded the Maisons de Presse Document prize. Rights to the book have been sold to twelve countries.

Michèle Fitoussi is of Tunisian descent, and is the author of two novels and a collection of short stories as well as being the literary editor of French *Elle*.